1/09

EISENHOWER PUBLIC LIBRARY

3 1134 00319 2499

917 40 Bai /

S0-BOI-625

Eastern Pennsylvania

Eastern Pennsylvania

Includes Philadelphia, Gettysburg, Amish Country & the Pocono Mountains

Laura Randall

with photographs by the author

The Countryman Press ✳ Woodstock, Vermont

Dedication
This book is for my parents, who introduced me to soft pretzels, Tastykakes, and other wondrous Pennsylvania inventions, and passed on their enthusiasm for exploring new places to me a long time ago.

Copyright © 2008 by Laura Randall

First Edition

All rights reserved. No part of this book may be reproduced in any way by electronic or mechanical means, including information storage and retrieval systems, without permission in writing from the publisher, except by a reviewer, who may quote brief passages.

ISBN 978-0-88150-747-8

Cover photo © Carl Christensen
Interior photos by the author unless otherwise specified
Book design by Bodenweber Design
Page composition by PerfecType, Nashville, TN
Maps by Mapping Specialists Ltd., © 2008 The Countryman Press

Published by The Countryman Press, P.O. Box 748, Woodstock, Vermont 05091

Distributed by W.W. Norton & Company, Inc., 500 Fifth Avenue, New York, NY 10110

Printed in the United States of America

10 9 8 7 6 5 4 3 2 1

EXPLORE WITH US!

Welcome to the first edition of *Eastern Pennsylvania: An Explorer's Guide*, the definitive guide to Philadelphia and the large and diverse regions that surround it. It's the ideal companion for exploring the Brandywine Valley, Bucks County, Amish Country, Gettysburg, and the Pocono Mountains. Here you'll find thorough coverage of big cities and small towns, plus everything in between, with detailed listings on the best sightseeing, outdoor activities, restaurants, shopping, and B&Bs. Like all other Explorer's Guides, this book is an old-fashioned, classic traveler's guide, where an experienced and knowledgeable expert helps you find your way around a new area or explore some fascinating corners of a familiar one.

WHAT'S WHERE

In the beginning of this book, you'll find an alphabetical listing of special highlights and important information that you may want to reference quickly. You'll find advice on everything from navigating the state liquor laws to ordering cheesesteaks.

LODGING

We've selected lodging places for inclusion in this book based on merit alone; we do not charge innkeepers for their inclusion. Prices: please don't hold us or the respective innkeepers responsible for rates listed as of press time in late 2007. Changes are inevitable. At the time of this writing, the state room tax was 6 percent (plus an additional 1 percent in Philadelphia) and city and county room tax was 6 percent.

RESTAURANTS

In most chapters, please note the distinction between Eating Out and Dining Out. By their nature, restaurants included in the Eating Out group are generally inexpensive. A range of prices is included for each entry.

KEY TO SYMBOLS

- ✍ Child-friendly. The crayon denotes a family-friendly place or event that welcomes young children. Most B&Bs prohibit children under 12.
- ♿ Handicapped access. The wheelchair icon denotes a place with full ADA—Americans with Disabilities Act—standard access, still distressingly rare in these remote areas.
- ☂ Rainy day. The umbrella icon points out places where you can entertain yourself but still stay dry in bad weather.
- 🐾 Pets. The dog's paw icon identifies lodgings that allow pets—still the exception to the rule. Accommodations that accept pets may still charge an extra fee or restrict pets to certain areas, as well as require advance notice.
- 🎖 Special value. The blue-ribbon symbol appears next to selected lodging and restaurants that combine quality and moderate prices.
- 🍸 Good bars. The "martini glass" icon appears next to restaurants and entertainment venues that have them.
- ▼ Gay-friendly. The inverted triangle denotes establishments that cater to gay clientele.

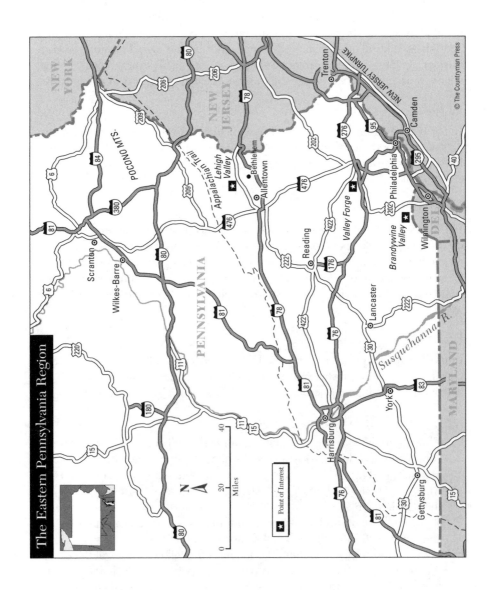

The Eastern Pennsylvania Region

★ Point of Interest

© The Countryman Press

CONTENTS

ACKNOWLEDGMENTS

F irst, I want to send heartfelt appreciation to each business, chamber of commerce, and convention bureau staff member, and historian and park ranger who contributed information, offered assistance, and patiently answered my many, many questions about their towns and attractions.

This book also wouldn't have been possible without my network of friends and family throughout the state who were always on hand to recommend, opine on, and describe their favorite places to eat, stroll, shop, and sightsee. While it is impossible to list every name, a few stand out. Thanks and appreciation must go to my parents, Bill and Rosemarie Randall, for their tireless reconnaissance work, which involved everything from sampling milk shakes to visiting a pot-bellied pig farm; to Sherri Schmidt, for her last-minute help and willingness to share secrets only a true Philadelphian knows; and to Ayleen Stellhorn, for passing along her knowledge of all things Hershey and her tips and opinions on the entire Lower Susquehanna. The folks at Countryman Press also deserve a shout for their guidance and infectious enthusiasm for travel.

And, as always, thanks to my husband, John Kimble, for his ever-calming presence and willingness to visit nature preserves, mom-and-pop stores, quirky museums, and cheesesteak stands with me at all hours of the day and night.

INTRODUCTION

With its abundant natural resources and central role in early American history, eastern Pennsylvania attracts a wide swath of travelers to its cities and rural towns. It is home to the Liberty Bell and Independence Hall, the country's second-largest Amish community and one of its biggest shopping malls, and more than a hundred lakes, rivers, and state parks. Philadelphia may be the area's anchor and urban soul, but it is surrounded by miles of rolling green farmlands, forested mountains, and villages that haven't changed much since the king of England bequeathed the state to William Penn. Within an hour or two's drive from the city's center, you can tour a dozen historic battlefields, shop for antiques, go tubing along a pristine stretch of the Delaware River, visit a chocolate factory straight out of Willie Wonka, and eat chicken corn soup and chow-chow in an 18th-century farmhouse. The area really does offer something for everyone.

I am a native Pennsylvanian who grew up near Valley Forge National Historical Park and went to college within cannon-firing distance of the battlefields of Gettysburg. I spent summers cycling the Schuylkill River, devouring lemon water ice at Rita's, cheering on the Phillies (during those halcyon Mike Schmidt days), and hiking and swimming in the Pocono Mountains. As an adult, I lived in a corner of a converted sugar mill in Old City, Philadelphia, just as the area was beginning to explode into the vibrant neighborhood it is today, and got married amid the B&Bs and quirky shops of New Hope, Bucks County. My husband and I chose to marry there because it represented to us an idyllic (yet accessible) place where our friends and family could kick back, explore at their leisure, and leave with a happy memory or two. In putting together a guide to the area for out-of-town guests, we coaxed local acquaintances into divulging their favorite haunts, walked the river towpath to check out the trails and views ourselves, and banged on doors of small colonial inns that had neither a Web site nor e-mail address.

That's also the way I will treat this guide—by relying on word of mouth and my own research and instincts rather than on websites or paid media advertisements. There's the Bucks County innkeeper who steered me to the wonderful strip-mall trattoria where she goes anytime she wants a good inexpensive meal, and the York B&B owner who told me about the small no-name bakery down the road where you can buy bread and pies straight out of the oven on certain days of the week.

If a hotel or restaurant isn't included in this book, it's more likely that it didn't have what it takes to make the cut than because I didn't know about it. There is much to see and do in eastern Pennsylvania, but I like to think that only the very best places made it into this book. We don't bestow superior titles lightly here. Just ask the countless restaurant owners who have lost out to a tiny corner stand in the never-ending debate over who makes the area's best cheesesteak.

I also bring to this guide 20 years of experience as a travel writer and globe-trotter who appreciates a four-star dining experience as much as the discovery of a bargain hotel room that's as clean and attractive as the significantly more expensive chain place around the corner. I have traveled extensively in the Caribbean, Latin America, and Europe, writing dispatches for the *Washington Post*, the *Los Angeles Times*, the *Christian Science Monitor*, and National Geographic News Service. I have lived and worked in Washington, D.C., Puerto Rico, New Jersey, and Los Angeles, yet I still consider Pennsylvania home and return several times a year to see family and friends and get my fix of cobblestones, 18th-century architecture, and, yes, cheesesteaks. No matter what they tell you, they just aren't as good west of the Susquehanna.

Another significant way this guide stands out from the pack is that it devotes as many pages to the areas surrounding Philadelphia as it does to the city itself. The covered bridges of Bucks County and hex signs of northern Burks County will get as much attention as Constitution Hall and the Mummers Parade. I understand that visitors to the area are as interested in hiking a forest trail, hearing the Gettysburg Address at its original site, and shopping for Amish-made farm tables as much as they are in seeing the Liberty Bell, and I have applied that knowledge accordingly. This book is written for Pennsylvania residents who enjoy taking short excursions in their home state throughout the year, and it is written for those who own or rent vacation homes in places like the Pocono Mountains and want to gain a better understanding of their adopted neighborhoods. It's also written for American history lovers and for parents who want to introduce their children to names like Hershey, Crayola, and Daniel Boone.

Most of all, however, this book aims to introduce eastern Pennsylvania's beauty and diversity to the many people who assume that the region is defined only by the nation's fifth-largest city. As much as I love Philadelphia and take great pleasure in profiling it for this book, there is much more to the region than the city and its immediate surroundings. There is a whole "idyllic and accessible" side of eastern Pennsylvania that's also well worth a visit.

WHAT'S WHERE IN EASTERN PENNSYLVANIA

AMISH COUNTRY Lancaster County is home to one of the country's largest Amish populations. They don't drive, but you will undoubtedly see them out and about in horse and buggies or walking to and from shops. Please respect their wishes and don't snap photos. The best ways to learn more about their culture and lifestyle are via buggy rides that wind through backcountry roads and farms or by joining an Amish family for dinner in their home, which can often be arranged by B&B owners.

ANTIQUES Quaint shopping districts abound in this part of the state. Serious antiques buyers flock to **Adamstown** near Reading, **Hawley** and **Honesdale** in the Pocono Mountains, and **Chadds Ford** and other small towns in the Brandywine Valley. You'll also find a good concentration of antiques shops in the Bucks County villages of New Hope, Riegelsville, and Kintnersville.

CAVES There is nothing like a cave to make you feel your mortality, and eastern Pennsylvania has at least three that are open to tourists. **Indian Echo Caverns** near Hershey is a favorite, and **Crystal Cave** and **Lost River Caverns** are the ones to hit if you're in the Reading/Kutztown area or the Lehigh Valley.

CHEESESTEAKS It's one word in Philadelphia. And the favorite way to order it is with Cheez Whiz and fried onions. **John's Roast Pork** near the waterfront has been the king of the steak sandwich in recent years, garnering rave reviews of food critics, though many Philadelphians remain loyal to the two South Philadelphia

institutions, **Pat's** (215-468-1546; 1237 E. Passyunk Ave.) and **Geno's** (215-389-0659; 1219 S. Ninth St.).

CIVIL WAR The Battle of Gettysburg yielded the largest number of casualties of any battle of the American Civil War and is often cited as the war's turning point. Today, thousands of Civil War buffs come to south-central Pennsylvania to visit the solemn battlefield site and the countless other attractions that have sprung up around it. No Civil War–themed trip to the state should neglect to include the **National Civil War Museum** in Harrisburg, which takes pains to tell the story of the Civil War without taking sides. Numerous other smaller battles were also fought here in towns like Hanover, Fairfield, and Carlisle.

CONVENIENCE STORES Once you get past the funny name, you'll realize that Wawa is the Toyota Prius of convenience stores. If you're driving around the state and looking for a pick-me-up Tastykake or hoagie, this is the place to go. Everything here is fresh, the prices are reasonable, and the clerks are usually polite, if not downright friendly. Many branches sell gas at a discount, too. There are more than five hundred Wawa stores in Pennsylvania, New Jersey, Delaware, and New York.

COVERED BRIDGES Forget the Bridges of Madison County. More than two hundred covered bridges dot the Pennsylvania landscape between Philadelphia and Pittsburgh. Entire Web sites are devoted to their beauty and preservation. The places to find them in the eastern part of the state are Bucks County, especially the central and upper parts, Lancaster County (Pinetown is a favorite), and the back roads of the Brandywine Valley.

FESTIVALS Eastern Pennsylvania loves a good party, especially if it involves Ben Franklin, fireworks, or green beer. Some of the state's best annual events can be found in small towns like Kutztown (the **Kutztown Folk Festival**), Kennett Square (**Mushroom Festival**), and Shawnee (**Pocono Garlic Festival**). In Philadelphia, the feather-and-sequins **Mummers Parade** on New Year's Day is like no other costume parade you'll ever experience.

FISHING A license is required to fish in Pennsylvania's rivers, lakes, and streams. For more information, go to www.www.pgc.state.pa.us.

FLEA MARKETS They are rampant around here, and offer terrific people-watching opportunities, not to mention the chance to buy things like handmade quilts and sticky buns. Two of the biggest and oldest are **Zern's** near Reading and **Rice's** in New Hope.

GARDENS Philadelphia and its outlying areas are home to dozens of world-class gardens. For a comprehensive list, pick up *A Guide to the Great Gardens of the Philadelphia Region* by Adam Levine (2007, Temple University Press).

HUNTING Hunters are expected to follow the rules and regulations of the state game commission. For more information, go to www.www.pgc.state.pa.us.

ITALIAN ICE If you visit eastern Pennsylvania in the late spring or summer, chances are you'll see lines of people gathered at small stands selling Italian ices. Also called water ice, it's a dessert made from shaved ice and flavored with concentrated syrup (lemon is a favorite). Rita's Water Ice is a homegrown chain with stands throughout the state.

LIQUOR LAWS As anyone who has spent any time here knows, Pennsylvania has some of the most restrictive laws in the country concerning the purchase of alcohol. Ironically, it also has more BYO restaurants than just about any other city. You can buy wine and spirits only in stores that are run by the state-run Liquor Control Board. This book includes a BYO section at the end of each **Where to Eat** section to help you find Wine & Spirits stores in the area. For a complete

list of stores in the state, go to www.lcb.state.pa.us.

MUSEUMS You'll find all kinds represented here, from the diverse offerings of the free **State Museum** in Harrisburg to niche facilities devoted to woodcarving, 19th-century quilts, and human anatomy. Don't miss the **Barnes Foundation**, the **National Liberty Museum**, or the **Rodin Museum** if you're in Philadelphia. Elsewhere, the **Brandywine River Museum** in Chadds Ford, **Dorflinger Glass Museum** in Honesdale, and **Wharton Esherick Museum** in Malvern are all worth a special trip. Children will love the **Please Touch Museum** in Philadelphia and the **National Canal Museum** and **Crayola Factory** in Easton.

PENNSYLVANIA DUTCH FOOD If you see chow-chow, chicken corn soup, or shoofly pie on a menu, chances are you're within spitting distance of Lancaster County. **Chow-chow** is a sweet and sour relish made up from end-of-summer garden leftovers. **Shoofly pie** is a crumb-topped pie with a sticky

molasses bottom. Other not-to-be-missed Pennsylvania Dutch delicacies: **whoopie pie**, an oversized cakelike Oreo, and **funnel cake**, fried dough topped with powdered sugar sold often at carnivals and festivals. The strong-of-stomach may also want to try **scrapple**, a pan-fried slab of cornmeal mush and pork byproducts, and "**church spread**," an Amish invention of corn syrup or molasses, marshmallow cream, and peanut butter.

RAILROAD Eastern Pennsylvania was a leader in rail travel during the 1800s, and today you will find many, many places here that celebrate that heritage. You can still view the rolling hills and farmland from restored passenger cars on the **Strasburg Railroad**, the **Stourbridge Lion** in Honesdale, and **M&H Railroad** in Hummelstown. Train lovers also shouldn't miss the **Railroad Museum of Pennsylvania** in Strasburg.

SMOKING Smoking is prohibited in all bars, restaurants, and other indoor establishments in the city of Philadelphia. At press time, a bill to ban smoking in most public places throughout the state was making its way through the legislature, and was expected to pass.

STATE PARKS You'll find dozens of state parks in this part of the state; many offer camping, swimming, boating, and hiking, and horseback riding options. **Promised Land** in the Pocono Mountains, **French Creek** between Reading and Valley Forge, and **Nockamixon** in upper Bucks County are a few favorites.

THEME PARKS With its wide appeal, reputation for cleanliness, and choco-

late connection, **Hershey Park** dominates in this department. The state also has some smaller amusement parks that are worth a look: **Dutch Wonderland** in Lancaster is great for preschoolers, and **Knoebels** way up in Elysburg is known for its free admission, friendliness, and good food.

WATERFALLS The Pocono Mountains have some of the best cascades this side of Niagara. **Bushkill Falls** is probably the most famous, but there are also many free ones that are well worth a look, including **Raymondskill Falls**, **Dingmans Falls**, and **Shohola Falls**.

WINERIES The state's wineries may be light years away from matching the Rhone or Napa valleys in terms of quality, but its boutique wineries have expanded and upgraded in recent years and many are producing drinkable wines, much to the pleased surprise of everyone involved. Bucks County, the Lehigh Valley, Gettysburg, and York County all have several wineries and often combine events and fun activities with tastings.

Philadelphia

INTRODUCTION

E ver since William Penn landed on its shores in 1682 and dubbed it the City of Brotherly Love, Philadelphia has been a place of contrasts. It gave the world Grace Kelly and Rocky Balboa. Its cheesesteak stands garner as much attention as Le Bec Fin, one of the country's finest French restaurants. In Center City, sleek skyscrapers coexist next to neighborhoods of neat brick rowhouses, where residents still throw block parties.

First and foremost, Philadelphia is the nation's birthplace, home to countless historic sites, pioneering architectural styles, and American firsts. It was here that the U.S. Constitution and Declaration of Independence were signed, the first stock exchange opened, and the first urban planning experiment was set in motion. History is evident on just about every block, whether it's a plaque commemorating the Founding Fathers, an 18th-century Federal townhome, or a gravestone with the name Franklin etched on it. It's here that you'll find the country's oldest mint, art museum, post office, lending library, zoo, and continuously occupied public street.

Yet you don't have to be a history buff to visit Philadelphia. You will find things to enjoy if you like good food, soulful jazz, high-end shopping, and top-tier art museums. Philly, as it's often called, is home to top-notch restaurants, dozens of colleges, a terrific urban park that's many times larger than New York City's Central Park, and scores of restaurants, shops, hotels, and theaters. Reading Terminal Market, a massive indoor marketplace directly across from the Pennsylvania Convention Center and a few blocks from City Hall, unites locals and tourists alike with its fresh-cut flowers, vibrant produce, Amish-made breads and apple butter, and two-fisted pork sandwiches.

Observers and tourism officials like to say the city truly came into its own as a standalone travel destination in the late 1990s and early 2000s, with the openings of a one-million-square-foot convention center, the $250-million Kimmel Center for the Performing Arts, two new sports stadiums, and the National Constitution Center. They have a point, but as someone who has spent time here since the 1970s, I like to think many of the right elements were in place long before that. The city, despite a host of urban problems like crime and graffiti that continue to this day, has always had good food, loud and loyal locals, and a walkable, easy-to-navigate downtown. It has always had Independence Hall, the Liberty Bell, and Ben Franklin's spirit.

First-time visitors should also expect experiences that they might not have elsewhere in the country, for better or for worse. You will hear "Yo!" more often than you can imagine. You will probably be called "hon," whatever your gender, by everyone from the curbside hot dog vendor to the stylish clerk at your boutique hotel. You may get snarled at, or at least a raised eyebrow, if you ask for anything but fried onions and Cheez Whiz on your cheesesteak. And anyone who spends time at a sporting event here in which the home town is losing will question why it deserves its City of Brotherly Love title.

The easiest and most satisfying way to see Philadelphia is to walk. It is laid out in a grid pattern of wide, straight streets that cross at right angles (thank you, Mr. Penn). Those in moderately good shape can walk or jog from the University of Pennsylvania campus all the way to the Delaware River, via Walnut or Spruce streets, passing by Independence Hall, Washington Square Park, and many cobblestoned alleys along the way. Detour over a few blocks to the north and you'll find yourself climbing the steps of the Philadelphia Art Museum, where Rocky took his famous victory lap.

Philly is home to more than one hundred neighborhoods. Center City is its core, anchored by City Hall and split to the east and west by Broad Street. South Philadelphia is home to multigenerational families, the bustling Italian market, and some of the best trattorias around. The University of Pennsylvania's influence is strong amid West Philadelphia's corner stores and brownstones, while the Philadelphia Art Museum and other first-class museums dominate the Benjamin Franklin Parkway Area to the north. Much of the historic district, including Independence Hall and the Liberty Bell, lies in or around Old City, a once-industrial area that has been transformed in recent years to a hip neighborhood with some of the city's best restaurants, nightlife, and art galleries. On the outskirts, Chestnut Hill, Germantown, and Manayunk have some of the city's best boutique shopping and examples of preserved 18th-century architecture.

Whatever your reason for visiting, Philadelphia is an important part of travel within the eastern Pennsylvania region, a place that can serve as a base for day or overnight trips to Gettysburg or Pennsylvania Dutch Country or spark your interest in visiting them independently.

CENTER CITY EAST & SOUTH PHILADELPHIA

AREA CODE The area code for Philadelphia is 215.

GUIDANCE Independence Visitor Center (800-537-7676 or 215-965-7676; www.independencevisitorcenter.com), Sixth and Market streets, is a must for anyone visiting the historic district. It's the place to pick up free timed tickets to Independence Hall, as well as paid tickets to other attractions, plus it offers a cafe, gift shop, and a huge selection of publications and maps of the city and its surrounding counties. Volunteers and National Park Service employees are on hand to answer questions.

GETTING THERE *By car:* Several major interstate highways lead through Philadelphia. From the north or south, take I-95 to I-676 (Vine Street Expressway), which cuts right through Center City. From the west, I-76 (the Schuylkill Expressway) branches off the Pennsylvania Turnpike and follows the river to South Philadelphia.

By air: **Philadelphia International Airport** (215-937-6800) is about a 20-minute drive from Center City, and served by all major airlines. The Southeastern Pennsylvania Transportation Authority (SEPTA) R1 line offers direct service to the airport.

By bus: **Greyhound** (800-231-2222) and **Peter Pan** (800-343-9999) offer service between Philadelphia and dozens of major cities, operating out of the Greyhound terminal next to Reading Terminal Market.

By train: Amtrak stops at 30th Street Station on its Northeast Corridor route between Richmond, Virginia, and Boston. SEPTA's R7 suburban train runs to Trenton, New Jersey, where New Jersey Transit trains run to New York's Penn Station. The R7 stops at the Market Street East station, about four blocks from Independence Hall.

GETTING AROUND SEPTA municipal buses run all over the city, though they can be daunting for first-time visitors. The Market–Frankford Line is a rapid-

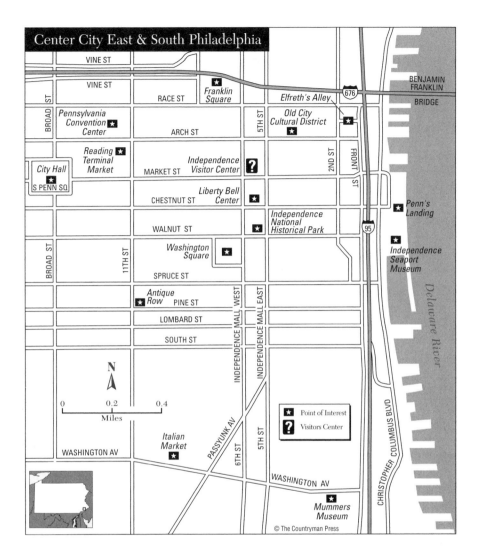

Center City East & South Philadelphia

VINE ST

VINE ST

BROAD ST

RACE ST

Franklin Square

Elfreth's Alley

676

BENJAMIN FRANKLIN BRIDGE

Pennsylvania Convention Center

ARCH ST

5TH ST

Old City Cultural District

City Hall

S PENN SQ

Reading Terminal Market

MARKET ST

Independence Visitor Center

2ND ST

FRONT ST

Liberty Bell Center

CHESTNUT ST

Independence National Historical Park

Penn's Landing

95

WALNUT ST

Washington Square

Independence Seaport Museum

BROAD ST

11TH ST

SPRUCE ST

Delaware River

Antique Row

PINE ST

LOMBARD ST

SOUTH ST

INDEPENDENCE MALL WEST

INDEPENDENCE MALL EAST

N

0   0.2   0.4
Miles

Italian Market

PASSYUNK AV

6TH ST

5TH ST

Point of Interest

Visitors Center

WASHINGTON AV

CHRISTOPHER COLUMBUS BLVD

WASHINGTON AV

Mummers Museum

© The Countryman Press

transit line that stops in Old City (Second and Market) and near the University of Pennsylvania's campus, ending in the city's far northwest corner. If you're staying in Center City, the most rewarding way to get from one destination to another is by walking. If it's late or you're tired, it's fairly easy to flag down a taxi in Center City, especially on main thoroughfares like Market and Walnut streets.

The purple **Phlash** bus (215-599-0776; www.phillyphlash.com) runs a continuous loop between the city's major attractions, including the historic district and Penn's Landing. Buses stop every 12 minutes at designated purple lampposts and operate daily May through Sept. Cost is $1 a ride, or $4 for an all-day pass.

PARKING There is restricted metered parking available on the street throughout Center City. If you're spending the day, your best bet is to park in one of the many parking garages in the city's historic area and near City Hall. Central Parking Auto Park at Independence Mall (Sixth St. between Market and Arch), lets you enter Independence Visitor Center without having to go outside. Convenient to both the historic district and the convention center is the **Philadelphia Parking Authority's Auto Parking Plaza** (215-925-4305), 801 Filbert St., which offers early-bird specials to cars entering before 10 AM.

MEDICAL EMERGENCY Pennsylvania Hospital (215-829-3000) 800 Spruce St., Philadelphia.

WHEN TO GO Philadelphia's many museums, theaters, and shops make it a good place to visit year-round. The lines at many of its historic sites, like Independence Hall and the Liberty Bell, tend to be shortest in Jan. and Feb. If you prefer warmer weather and lots of activities, try to plan your visit in the summer, when Penn's Landing and the city's squares are alive with all kinds of entertainment and festivities.

✳ Neighborhoods

Old City. At the edge of Independence National Historical Park, Old City has its share of worthy historic sites including Ben Franklin's grave and Elfreth's

JOHN'S ROAST PORK

Alley. It's best known, however, for its lively nightlife and gallery scene, the result of a gentrification in the 1990s that transformed its dilapidated warehouses and factories into loft apartments and art studios.

Society Hill. This neighborhood between Old City and South Street is known for its preserved Federaland Georgian row homes and cobblestone streets. The only high-rises are three apartment towers designed by I. M. Pei in the 1970s to help revitalize the area.

South Street/Queen Village. South Street between 10th and Front streets is a commercial strip of nightclubs, cheesesteak stands, and shops that sell everything from leather pants and goth hair dye to antique armoires and Reeboks. To the south is Queen Village, a quieter neighborhood of narrow streets, antiques shops, and neighborhood BYO cafés that always seem to be buzzing.

Washington Square West. The sprawling neighborhood between Independence Hall and Broad Street contains the shopping districts of Jeweler's Row and Pine Street Antiques, several hospitals, and a mix of high-end restaurants, cheap electronics stores, and old taverns. It's also home to Gayborhood, the city's small but thriving gay community and a handful of bars and B&Bs.

Waterfront/Columbus Avenue. Once a thriving port area, it is now known for its warm-weather festivals and wide-open views of the Benjamin Franklin Bridge. Penn's Landing, several big-box stores, and a couple of huge river-view bars like Dave and Buster's are the main anchors, but it's also home to only-in-Philly treasures like John's Roast Pork, a family-owned cheesesteak stand that has been around for decades. I-95 divides the waterfront from Old City and South Philadelphia, but there are two pedestrian bridges that lead to Penn's Landing.

✳ To See

MUSEUMS National Liberty Museum (215-925-2800, www.libertymuseum .org), 321 Chestnut St., Old City. Open daily in summer, Tues.–Sun. the rest of the year. $7 adults, $2 ages 5–17. This eclectic museum is dedicated to promoting the ideals of freedom and diversity. Exhibits include a showcase of oh-so-fragile glass sculptures by Dale Chihuly, memorials to America's Nobel Peace Prize winners, and a gallery featuring frank images and statistics on youth violence. Tucked away in a corner on the upper levels is a framed picture of John Lennon's handwritten lyrics to "Beautiful Boy."

Mummers Museum (215-336-3050; www.mummersmuseum.org), 1100 S. Second St. (at Washington Ave.), South Philly. Closed Mon.; $3.50 adults. Philadelphia's version of Madame Tussaud's, featuring wax figurines dressed in the feathered and spangled costumes that characterize the city's raucous New Year's Day parade. There's also an exhibit explaining the parade's history and live string-band concerts in the summer (call for dates and times). This is the way to experience the Mummers Parade without having to endure the cold weather or the smell of hops.

HISTORIC SITES Carpenter's Hall (215-925-0167), 320 Chestnut St. Open 10–4 daily; closed Mon. and Tues. Jan. and Feb.; free. This red-brick Georgian building was the original home of a guild of carpenters and architects and served as the site of the First Continental Congress in 1774. It was also, surprisingly, the site of the nation's first bank robbery. On display are some of the original Windsor chairs on which the representatives sat, as well as displays of carpenters' tools, and a parade float built to celebrate the ratification of the U.S. Constitution.

Franklin Court (215-965-2305), 314-322 Market St., Old City. Fans of Ben Franklin won't want to miss this fascinating (and slightly hokey) complex of buildings and exhibits that pay homage to the city's wittiest and most influential inhabitant. Enter through a brick archway on Market Street to a courtyard where Franklin's original house once stood, now outlined by a steel frame "ghost sculpture" designed by architect Robert Venturi. Nearby is an underground

Independence Hall (215-497-8974), Chestnut St., between Fifth and Sixth. Open 9–5 daily. If you have time to visit only one historic attraction in Philly, this should be it. Free guided tours of the restored Georgian building include a stop in the regal blue Assembly Room, where the Declaration of Independence was adopted in 1776 and the U.S. Constitution was drafted in 1787. Artifacts on display include the "rising sun" chair used by George Washington during the Constitutional Convention and the silver inkstand used in the formal signing of the Declaration of Independence and the Constitution. Between Mar. and Dec., all visitors must pick up free timed tickets at the Independence Visitor Center. The 30-minute tours run every 15 minutes, but they do fill up, especially during the summer months. Outside the hall, you can take a guided horse and buggy ride through the historic district or grab a bench under a tree in Independence Square, site of the Declaration's first public reading. Across the street sits the **Liberty Bell Center** (215-597-8974) Sixth and Market streets, home to the 2,080-pound bronze bell that heralded the country's most significant achievements before cracking and becoming unusable in 1846. It's worth a brief stop, though it can be challenging to get a clear photo of the bell. Expect shoulder-to-shoulder crowds on weekends during the summer. It's free, but all visitors must pass a security screening.

From April to October, the park hosts the **Lights of Liberty Show,** an audio-visual spectacular that takes visitors into the heart of the American Revolution through hand-painted images projected onto the buildings around the Independence National Historical Park, while a musical score composed for the show and performed by musicians of the Philadelphia Orchestra is played through special headphones. Get tickets at the visitor center.

LIBERTY BELL, INDEPENDENCE HALL, SKYSCRAPERS

museum that displays Franklin's many inventions, plus a couple of oddities like a motorized diorama depicting Franklin's career as a diplomat and a hall of mirrors featuring his most famous phrases. On the way out, stop by Franklin's small printing office and bindery, 320 Market St., and take a postcard to get hand-stamped at the B Free Franklin Post Office two doors down.

Elfreth's Alley (215-574-0560; www.elfrethsalley.org), Second St., between Race and Arch, Old City. This narrow block of 32 row homes built between 1728 and 1836 is believed to be America's oldest continually occupied residential street. It is named for a blacksmith who once lived here, alongside carpenters, pewter makers, and other craftspeople of the period. Today, all but two of the homes are privately owned and occupied. No. 126 is a small museum that offers daily 15-minute tours, perhaps to dissuade visitors from peeking into the windows of the other homes as residents try to cook supper. It's open year-round, but be sure to call ahead first. Many residents also throw open their doors to the public every June (see *Special Events*).

Christ Church Burial Ground (215-922-1695), Fifth and Arch streets. $2 adults. Throw a good-luck penny on Benjamin Franklin's gravestone, located within the brick walls of this small cemetery that also holds the remains of Franklin's wife Deborah and several other signers of the Declaration of Independence.

Masonic Temple (215-988-1910) 1 N. Broad St. $8 tours; $3 exhibit only. This stunning Norman-style structure near City Hall was a meeting place for 28 Philadelphia-based Masonic organizations in the 18th century. Guided tours of the seven extravagantly decorated lodge halls are given daily; call for exact times. A small first-floor exhibit includes George Washington's Masonic apron, a fragment of mahogany taken from his coffin, a collection of historic walking sticks, and many, many portraits of solemn white men.

✹ To Do

FOR FAMILIES ✐ **National Constitution Center**, open daily, except Thanksgiving, Christmas, and New Year's Day; $12 adults, $8 ages 4–8. It's easy to spend several hours in this shiny new building, which opened in 2003 and quickly became one of the city's top attractions. Begin your visit in the theater, where a live costumed actor tells the "We the People" story with the help of 360-degree multimedia images, then head to the high-tech exhibit hall where interactive, in-depth displays will appeal to both novice history students and serious historians. Older kids will have fun reciting the presidential oath of office from a podium and donning the robes of Supreme Court justices before rendering their opinions of key cases. Don't miss Signers' Hall, featuring life-size bronze statues of all 42 Constitution signers as they may have been seated or standing during the convention.

✐ **Franklin Square**, 215-629-4026, www.onceuponanation.org), Sixth and Race streets. When the kids are about to wig out from history-lesson overload, this 7.5-acre park is where you want to go. An easy walk from Independence Hall and Old City, it was completely overhauled in 2006 and features a carousel, Philly-themed mini-golf (the *Rocky* theme plays at the 12th hole), two playgrounds, a vintage marble fountain, and benches where costumed storytellers hold forth late May through Sept. Don't miss the stand selling waffle ice-cream sandwiches.

🐾 **Penn's Landing** stretches along the Delaware River between Vine and South streets and includes the spot where William Penn first arrived from England in 1682 aboard the ship *Welcome*. Once the center of Philly's maritime activities and a thriving commercial district, it's now a waterfront park with a promenade, outdoor events plaza, and nice views of the Benjamin Franklin Bridge. It's also home to **Independence Seaport Museum**, (215-413-8655, www.phillyseaport .org), a drab concrete building that belies the interesting exhibits on local and national shipping history inside. The museum also manages the USS *Olympia*, the oldest steel warship and only U.S. vessel remaining from the Spanish-American War and the USS *Becuna*, a submarine that patrolled the South Pacific during World War II. Admission to the museum is $9 and includes tours of both ships. The area hosts outdoor concerts, fireworks, and movies throughout the summer; go to www.pennslandingcorp.com for more information. It can be accessed by walking across the pedestrian bridge at Walnut and Front streets or by car via I-95 at the Columbus Boulevard exit.

✴ Green Space

🐾 🐾 **John Heinz National Wildlife Refuge at Tinicum** (215-365-3118, www.fws.gov/northeast/heinz/), 8601 Lindbergh Blvd. Open daily; free. This 1,200-acre refuge is just a mile from Philadelphia International Airport and home to the largest remaining freshwater tidal wetland in the state. Once threatened by plans to reroute I-95, it was saved by local environmentalists and the late senator for whom it's named. Today, you can hike, bike, canoe, and fish here. Wildlife include muskrats, fox, deer, turtles, and 280 species of birds. The hiking trails are wide and flat and great for families and leashed dogs. Pick up a map at the Cusano Environmental Education Center near the entrance.

✴ Outdoor Activities

BOAT EXCURSIONS **Ride the Ducks** (215-351-9989, www.phillyducks.com) offers 80-minute tours of the historic district and Penn's Landing using World War II–era amphibious vehicles from May to Dec.

RiverLink Ferry (215-925-5465), Penn's Landing. Open May–Sept.; $6 adults,

♿ 🐾 **Macy's,** in the fabled Wanamaker's building at Market and South 13th streets, is home to the first and only pipe organ ever to be designated a National Historic Landmark. Its 28,000 pipes debuted in 1911 and still rattle the rafters of the grand old building several times a day, Mon. through Sat. The annual Christmas Light Show is a treat for kids and adults alike. For a concert schedule, visit www.wanamakerorgan.com.

$5 kids. Ferries depart from Penn's Landing every hour 9–6 and head across the river to the Camden, New Jersey waterfront. The trip takes 15 minutes and offers terrific views of the Philly skyline.

Horse-drawn carriages, led by guides in colonial garb, wind their way through the historic district on most days and evenings. Many local couples have become engaged during a romantic moonlit ride. Tours last anywhere from 15 minutes to an hour and cost from $25 to 70 for up to four people. Carriages line up on Chestnut and Sixth streets near Independence Hall most days and at South and Second streets most evenings.

ICE SKATING **Blue Cross RiverRink** (215-925-7465), Columbus Blvd. at Market St., is open for public skating late Nov. through early Mar. A two-hour session is $6, skate rental $3.

✳ Lodging

HOTELS & INNS ♿ **Penn's View Hotel** (215-922-7600; 800-331-7634; www.pennsviewhotel.com), Front St. This small family-owned hotel has a prime Old City location, elegant rooms, and dignified Old World vibe. The 27 rooms and suites are large and decorated in colonial style; many have jacuzzi tubs, fireplaces, or balconies. Try to snag one on the top floor facing the Benjamin Franklin Bridge (though that also means you'll have a distant view of I-95). It's an easy walk to Independence Hall, Penn's Landing, and Old City's nightlife. Another bonus: one of the city's best wine bars is downstairs (see *Dining Out*). Rooms and suites $145–230, including continental breakfast.

Morris House Hotel (215-922-2446; www.morrishousehotel.com), 225 S. Eighth St., between Walnut and Locust streets. This attractive 1787 Federal mansion was once home to Philadelphia mayor Anthony Morris. The 15 opulent rooms have modern amenities like DVD players and wireless Internet access; extended suites with kitchens, living areas, and jacuzzi tubs were added in 2005 in a separate wing. Afternoon tea is served daily by a roaring fireplace or in the peaceful back garden. Children are welcome. Rooms $179–239, including continental breakfast.

🐾 ♿ 🏠 **Loew's Philadelphia** (215-627-1200; www.loewshotels.com), 1200 Market St. Yes, it's a chain that caters to convention crowds, but this 581-room hotel is housed in a beautiful art deco building that was renovated in 2000 and has many charms, including a large gym, friendly staff, and over-the-top pet services. Pets are allowed for an extra $25 per stay. The downside is it's on a busy, characterless section of Market Street. Rooms $159–300.

BED & BREAKFASTS The **Bed and Breakfast Connection** (800-448-3619; www.bnbphiladelphia.com), acts as a liaison for many private homes and small B&Bs in Center City, Valley Forge, and outlying areas including Bucks County and Lancaster. Rates usually range $80–200 a night and include breakfast. Some allow pets. Photos and descriptions of many of the homes are posted on the Web site.

Thomas Bond House (215-923-8523; www.winston-salem-inn.com/

philadelphia), 129 South Second street. Ben Franklin probably didn't sleep in this 1769 townhouse, but he surely knocked back a few within its walls with Mr. Bond, his friend and a prominent local physician. Now owned by the National Park Service, it sits next to a parking garage and is surrounded by many of Old City's top bars and restaurants. The 10 rooms are decorated in colonial style with four-poster beds and reproduction furniture. Don't expect superior service or gourmet breakfasts, but it's a unique lodging option in a central location. Rooms $105–190.

✱ Where to Eat

DINING OUT ← ⍦ **Fork** (215-625-9425), 306 Market St. Lunch and dinner daily; brunch Sun. This stylish bistro was one of the first upscale restaurants to open in Old City in the late 1990s and has outlasted many places that followed it. Owner Ellen Yin is a fixture in the handsome dining room, which has a visible kitchen and large *Cheers*-like bar. Look for innovative dishes like penne with chervil hazelnut pesto and garlic-crusted rib-eye with guajillo pepper coulis. For Old City club-goers, there's a late-night menu served Thurs.–Sat. Reservations recommended. Lunch $9–14, dinner entrees $19–33.

← ⍦ **Ristorante Panorama** (215-922-7800), Front and Market streets. Dinner daily. This Old World Italian restaurant in the Penn's View Hotel is known for its legendary wine bar, which offers more than 150 wines by the glass, flight, or bottle. The food is traditional and reliably good: try the pappardelle with duck ragout or the fig-stuffed veal chop in a gorgonzola reduction. Don't miss the triple-cream tiramisu for dessert. Entrees $18–28.

⍦ **Vetri** (215-732-3478), 1312 Spruce St. Open for dinner Mon.–Sat. Sept. through May; Mon.–Fri. June and July. Closed for 3 weeks in Aug. A very intimate Italian restaurant that has been showered with praise by experts from Mario Batali to *Gourmet*. The bold a la carte menu might include roasted goat, a whole salt-crusted branzino with truffle sauce, and sweetbread ravioli. The appetizer of spinach gnocchi with shaved ricotta and brown butter is divine. Reservations required. Entrees: $19–36; tasting menu: $90–110.

South Philly

Tre Scalini (215-551-3870), 1533 S. 11th St. Dinner Tues.–Sun. This three-room restaurant is a tad more sophisticated than other South Philly mom-and-pop joints: menu highlights include figs and prosciutto appetizer, homemade gnocchi, and black squid-ink pappardelle with crab and shrimp. Leave room for the tiramisu. BYO. Dishes $16–25.

Villa di Roma (215-592-1295), 936 S. Ninth St. Lunch Fri.–Sun; dinner daily. For a true South Philly experience, head to this family-run "gravy" trattoria in the center of the Italian market area. You'll forget about the no-frills ambiance and wagon-wheel chandeliers as soon as you get a whiff of the oregano-spiked marinara sauce simmering in the kitchen or take a look at the reasonably priced menu. Regulars get misty-eyed over the fried asparagus in scampi butter; there's also steamed mussels marinara, spaghetti and meatballs, and sausage cacciatore. No credit cards. Dishes $9–27.

EATING OUT 🐾 **Dimitri's** (215-625-0556) 795 S. Third St. Dinner daily. This popular bistro two blocks off South Street is known for its fresh Greek-style seafood. It doesn't take reservations, and you might wait up to 90 minutes for a table, but the food is worth it. To kill time, you can hang out at the bar at the New Wave Café across the street, where the staff will fetch you when a table is ready. BYO. Cash only. Entrees $15–25.

🦞 ☿ **Vietnam** (215-592-1163), 221 N. 11th St., Chinatown. Lunch and dinner daily. Good food, reasonable prices, and a relaxing wood-paneling and bamboo ambiance. Try the crispy duck or anything that comes with a dipping sauce. Dishes $8–20.

Sabrina's Café (215-574-1599, 910 Christian St. Breakfast and lunch daily, dinner Mon.–Sat. Tucked into three cozy rooms in a South Philadelphia row house, Sabrina's serves lunch and dinner, but is best known for its good and hearty breakfasts. The weekend brunch menu might include challah French toast stuffed with cream cheese or a three-egg frittata. No reservations; expect a wait on weekends. BYO. Breakfast and brunch $4–12; lunch and dinner $10–18.

Carman's Country Kitchen (215-339-9613), 1301 S. 11th St. Breakfast and lunch Fri.–Mon. Kentucky-born Carman Luntzel cooks according to season and whim in her tiny and colorful eatery in South Philly. The small menu might include cornflake-crusted French toast with Georgia peaches or wild game chili with fried eggs. Breakfast is usually terrific, if pricey

for the neighborhood. Expect a wait on weekends. Dishes $12–15.

♿ **John's Roast Pork** (215-463-1951), 14 Snyder Ave. (near Columbus). Open for breakfast and lunch Mon.–Sat. Outdoor seating only. Philadelphia restaurant critic Craig LaBan conducted a citywide project to determine the best cheesesteaks in the area. This family-owned shack near the waterfront won hands down. They also make egg sandwiches, hoagies, and hot pork sandwiches. Dishes $4–7.

Ishkabibble's (215-923-4337), 337 South St. A popular spot for late-night chicken cheesesteaks, gravy fries, and water ice. Seating is limited to a few bar stools or the curb out front. Dishes $3–8.

COFFEE & PRETZELS **Federal Pretzel** (215-467-0505), 636 Federal St., South Philly. Many locals think these are the best soft pretzels in the city. They even sell chocolate-covered ones.

Old City Coffee (215-629-9292), 221 Church St. Tucked off a cobblestone alley about three blocks from Independence Hall, this small shop serves the best coffee east of Broad Street.

BYO **Where to buy wine in Center City and South Philadelphia:**

Wine & Spirits Shoppe (215-560-6900; 724 South St.) offers a wide selection of wines and liquors in the heart of the South Street scene. In Old City, just south of Market, is **State Liquor** (215-625-0906; 32 S. Second St.). Closer to City Hall and the convention center is **State Liquor Super Store** (215-560-4381; 1218 Chestnut St.).

SCRAPPLE

Along with soft pretzels, cheesesteaks, pork roll, and Italian water ice, scrapple will go down in history as a beloved local food that sets the Philadelphia area apart from the rest of the planet. You will find it on the menus and breakfast platters of most diners around here: a pan-fried gray slice of cornmeal mush and pork byproduct that has been made fun of by outsiders more often than Johnny Carson dissed the city of Burbank. In reality, it's no worse, and arguably tastier, than a hot dog when made properly—a crisp exterior and soft creamy inside that tastes more like seasoned mashed potatoes than pig parts. Perhaps the best way to experience scrapple is at Reading Terminal's annual **Scrapplefest** (215-922-2317; www.readingterminalmarket.org). Held in Apr. (usually the third Sat.), it features scrapple-making demonstrations (not for the weak of stomach), tastings, a towering gray wedding cake fashioned out of scrapple, and an Iron Chef–like scrapple competition.

✳ Entertainment

MUSIC ♼ **Tin Angel** (215-928-0770), 20 S. Second St., attracts top acoustic and singer-songwriter acts who perform in an intimate cafe-style setting. Seating is unreserved, unless you dine at Serrano restaurant downstairs before the show.

♼ **Ortlieb's Jazzhaus** (215-922-1035), 847 N. Third St. This narrow no-frills bar north of Old City hosts some of the city's best jazz and blues acts. Cover starts at $5.

Painted Bride Art Center (215-925-9914, www.paintedbride.org), 230 Vine St. A multifaceted Old City gallery with changing art exhibits and a variety of cutting-edge dance, jazz, and spoken-word performances.

MOVIES/FILMS **Ritz 5** (215-925-7900, www.ritztheatres.com), 214 Walnut St., shows first-run art and independent films on five screens. **Ritz at the Bourse,** a couple of

blocks away at 400 Ranstead St., has an additional five screens.

THEATER ♿ **Arden Theatre** (215-922-1122; www.ardentheatre.org), 40 N. Second St., stages classic and cutting-edge dramas, comedies, and children's shows. It has a slew of awards to show for its work and has been named "Theatre Company of the Year" four times by the *Philadelphia Inquirer.*

♿ **Walnut Street Theatre** (215-574-3550, www.walnutstreettheatre.org), 825 Walnut St., is the city's oldest theater, serving as the debut stage for Ethel Barrymore and Edwin Forrest. It often features big Broadway musicals on its main stage.

NIGHTLIFE Old City and South Street area are packed with nightspots that appeal to a variety of crowds.

♼ **Lucy's Hat Shop** (215-413-1433), 247 Market St. There's never a cover charge at this laid-back Old City joint.

Pool tables, pinball machines, rock and roll DJs, and 25-cent wings keep the crowds coming.

Ⴘ **The Continental** (215-923-6069), 134 Market St. Beautiful people sip espresso martinis and snack on tapas under olive-shaped halogen lamps in this diner-turned-cutting-edge nightspot.

Ⴘ **The Dark Horse** (215-928-9307), 421 S. Second St. Formerly the Dickens Inn, this dark-walled English tavern just off South Street has four bars, a hearty pub menu, and TVs tuned to rugby and soccer matches.

Center City

Ⴘ **McGillin's Old Ale House** (215-735-5562), 1310 Drury St. Philly's oldest (and hardest to locate) pub is tucked in an alley between 13th and Juniper streets. The brick-walled downstairs room is decorated with American flags, black-and-white cityscape photos, and framed liquor licenses that date back to the 1800s. The crowd tends to be young and festive; there's karaoke on Wed. nights.

Ⴘ ▼ **Woody's** (215-545-1893), 202 S. 13th St. Popular nightclub in the heart of Philly's small gay community.

✳ Selective Shopping

Philly has several quaint districts featuring a dozen or more stores that specialize in similar items. **Antique Row** runs on Pine Street where you'll find shops selling grandfather clocks, estate jewelry, hand-carved cabinets, and more. **Jewelers' Row** is the place to go for discounted diamonds; its shops line a red-bricked block of Sansom Street between Seventh and Eighth Streets. In Old City, many art galleries stay open late on the first Friday of the month, when the area is

a packed with art lovers and partyers.

Clay Studio (215-925-3453, (www.theclaystudio.org), 139 N. Second St., Old City. An innovative selection of ceramic cups, bowls, vases, and tiles.

Scarlett Alley (215-592-7898), 241 Race St., Old City. Stylish gifts for the person who has everything: designer cutting boards, ceramic bowls, cashmere robes, creative baby mobiles, and much more.

Viv Pickle (215-922-5904), 21 N. Third St. A unique and colorful assortment of handbags, wallets, backpacks, and diaper bags. Or design your own with the help of a consultant.

Book Trader (215-925-0511), 7 N. Second St., Old City. A reader's haven of used books, comfy old chairs, and friendly cats, just up the street from Elfreth's Alley.

Robin's Books (215-735-9600), 110 S. 13th St., Center City. A huge African-American studies section, plus a decent assortment of general interest books. Author readings and other events are held upstairs.

MARKETS ♿ **Reading Terminal Market** (215-922-2317; www.reading terminalmarket.org), 12th and Arch sts. Open 8–6 daily, though some stalls are closed on Sun. and the Amish-owned stalls are closed Sun. through Tues. This fabulous indoor collection of food, flower, and produce stalls has been operating since 1893 on the lower level of the Reading Terminal, home to the largest single-arch train shed in the world. It's a great introduction to Philadelphia's flavors and people, and an excellent place to get a quick lunch if you're in the area. In the northwest corner, Amish women serve up

READING TERMINAL MARKET

scrapple, home fries, and eggs at the counter of the **Dutch Eating Place**. Across the way, you can take home Lancaster County baked goods like whoopee pies, sticky buns, and shoofly pies, and sample soft pretzels still warm from the oven at **Fisher's**. Ice cream lovers won't want to miss **Basset's**, a venerable local ice cream company that serves the richest vanilla double dip around, and hungry omnivores should check out **DiNic's** (smack in the center) for juicy roast pork sandwiches. Tucked in between the food stalls are vendors selling everything from used cookbooks to dried flower arrangements. Saturday morning is the best time for people-watching and for finding all the stalls open, though expect shoulder-to-shoulder crowds if a convention is in town (the convention center and several large hotels are nearby).

Italian Market, Ninth St. between Washington and Christian, South Philadelphia. Closed Mon. Anyone who has seen *Rocky* will remember the boxer's famous training run through this indoor-outdoor street market on his way to the steps of the art museum. It's loud, rude, chaotic, and fascinating—a mix of outdoor stalls offering fresh produce, live seafood, bootleg CDs and T-shirts, and brick-and-mortar stores selling spices, cheeses, homemade ravioli, and pastries. Several Mexican taco stands and Vietnamese grocers have opened in recent years and added to the area's vibrancy.

✳ Special Events

January: **Mummers Parade** (New Year's Day), Broad and Market streets—raucous string-band parade that began in the 1700s and features thousands of men (and a few women) strutting and strumming their way up Broad Street in outrageous sequined and feathered costumes.

March: **Philadelphia Flower Show** (first and second week), Pennsylvania Convention Center—the world's largest indoor flower show with elaborate exhibits, expert lectures, and culinary demos, all of which are centered around an annual theme like the Legends of Ireland or America the Beautiful.

May: **Jam on the River** (Memorial Day), Penn's Landing—three-day waterfront festival featuring a diverse group of headliners that might include a Grateful Dead tribute band, reggae singers, progressive electronic bands, and rap groups, plus crafts displays and food vendors selling everything from cheesesteaks to crawfish pasta.

June: **Fete Day** (second Sat.), Elfreth's Alley—residents of America's oldest continually occupied street throw a block party and invite the public to partake of house and garden tours, live music, and crafts demon-

strations (see also *Historic Sites*).

July: **Independence Day Celebration** (July 4th), Historic District—series of events that begins with the awarding of the prestigious Liberty Medal in front of Independence Hall and capped by an evening concert and fireworks across town on the Benjamin Franklin Parkway.

October: **Outfest** (first weekend), Spruce and Pine streets, between 11th and 13th streets—Philly's four-day National Coming Out Day festival has grown to be the largest in the world, according to its organizers.

SOUTH PHILLY'S ITALIAN MARKET

CENTER CITY WEST & UNIVERSITY CITY

GUIDANCE An information center in the east portal of **City Hall** (215-686-2840; Broad St.) has local guides and brochures, a retail store, and a video monitor showing continuous footage of local attractions. Purchase tickets for City Hall tours here (see also *To See*). There is also a visitor center for Fairmount Park at 16th St. and JFK Blvd., in the spaceshiplike building on the northeast corner, that has park maps and other info. Both are open 9–5 weekdays.

GETTING THERE *By car:* Several major interstate highways lead through Philadelphia. From the north or south, take I-95 to I-676 (Vine Street Expressway), which cuts right through the Center City area. From the west, I-76 (the Schuylkill Expressway) branches off the Pennsylvania Turnpike and heads to South Philadelphia, with exits for the Benjamin Franklin Parkway and 30th Street Station.

By air: **Philadelphia International Airport** (215-937-6800) is about a 20-minute drive from Center City Philadelphia, and served by all major airlines. SEPTA's R1 line offers direct service between Center City, University City, and the airport.

By bus: **Greyhound** (800-231-2222) and **Peter Pan** (800-343-9999) offer frequent service between Philadelphia and dozens of major cities.

By train: **Amtrak** (800-USA-RAIL) stops at 30th Street Station on its Northeast Corridor route between Richmond, Virginia, and Boston. SEPTA's R7 suburban train runs to Trenton, New Jersey, where New Jersey Transit trains run to New York's Penn Station. The R7 stops at Suburban station, about four blocks from Rittenhouse Square, and 30th Street Station.

GETTING AROUND SEPTA municipal buses run all over the city, though they can be daunting for first-time visitors. The **Market–Frankford Line** is a rapid-transit line that stops outside City Hall (Broad and Market) and near the University of Pennsylvania's campus, ending in the city's far northwest corner. The purple **Phlash** bus (215-599-0776; www.phillyphlash.com) runs a continuous loop between the city's major attractions, from Penn's Landing to the Parkway

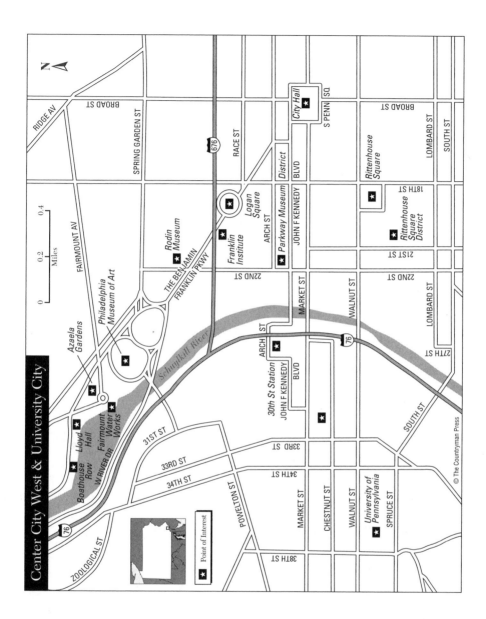

Center City West & University City

museums. Buses stop every 12 minutes at designated purple lampposts and operate daily May through Sept. Cost is $1 a ride, or $4 for an all-day pass.

MEDICAL EMERGENCY Hospital of the University of Pennsylvania (215-662-4000) 3400 Spruce St., University City.

✳ Neighborhoods

Logan Square anchors the northeast end of the Benjamin Franklin Parkway and is one of five original planned squares laid out on the city grid. Originally called Northwest Square, the park has a somewhat macabre history of being a site of public executions and burial plots until the early 19th century. In 1825, it was renamed Logan Square after Philadelphia statesman James Logan. Among the sites you'll find nearby are the Academy of Natural Sciences, the Franklin Institute, the Free Library of Philadelphia, and the Roman Catholic Cathedral-Basilica of Saints Peter and Paul. It's also close to the art museum area, a pretty and walkable neighborhood of urban row homes, high-rise apartment buildings, and good local watering holes.

Rittenhouse Square. This affluent pedestrian-friendly neighborhood takes its name from the tree-filled square that anchors it. It is named after David Rittenhouse, the astronomer and descendent of Philadelphia's first papermaker William Rittenhouse, and home to many of the city's top restaurants, hotels, and shops. Walnut Street between Broad and 21st streets is its commercial pulse, but don't be afraid to wander; the historic architecture along residential streets like Spruce and Delancey are delightful. Residents vary widely, from silver-haired doyennes to young families and Penn graduate students.

University City. This West Philly neighborhood got its start in the late 1880s when the University of Pennsylvania moved across the Schuylkill River from Center City, though no one really referred to it by its current name until the 1960s. Life here still revolves around the Ivy League school (as well as nearby Drexel University). Though the area has struggled with blight and crime problems, you will find streets lined with beautiful old Victorian row homes here, and

RITTENHOUSE SQUARE

in recent years the area near campus has added a luxury movie theater, national retailers, and many hip restaurants.

✳ To See

HISTORIC SITES Eastern State Penitentiary (215-236-3300), 2124 Fairmount Ave. Open daily Apr. through Nov. $9 adults, $4 ages 7–12. Willie Sutton and Al Capone were among the inmates who slept in the vaulted, skylit cells of this 1829 prison, whose wagon-wheel design (and belief in reform through isolation) served as a model for dozens of other 19th-century prisons. Admission includes a 30-minute guided tour of the decrepit cellblocks (including Capone's), plus interesting details on life as an inmate. The prison's popular "Terror Behind the Walls" event, held evenings in Oct., features five separate haunted houses, complete with howling prisoners and sadistic guards, and a DJ-hosted Monster Mash.

⚑ **Edgar Allen Poe National Historic Site** (215-597-8780, www.nps.gov/edal), 532 N. Seventh St. Open 9–5 Wed.–Sun.; free. The 19th-century horror author penned "The Tell-Tale Heart," "The Fall of the House of Usher," and more in this small brick house north of Old City. Visitors may view a short film about Poe, walk through the mostly empty building, and check out the basement that's said to be the inspiration for "The Black Cat." It's a little off the beaten path, but worth a side trip for any literary buffs.

CITY HALL

Laurel Hill Cemetery (215-228-8200; www.thelaurelhillcemetery.org), a national historic landmark whose tenants include astronomer David Rittenhouse, 40 Civil War–era generals, and six victims of the *Titanic* sinking. It's a peaceful place for a stroll or jog, with a bluffside setting overlooking the Schuylkill River. The office sells a map and guide for $5, or you can take a guided theme tour, such as "Dead White Republicans" or "Sinners, Scandals, and Suicides" for $15. Call for days and times.

City Hall (215-686-2840), Broad St. ($10 adults; $8 ages 3–18). Tours Mon.–Fri. at 12:30. This granite monolith in the center of town, capped by a 37-foot statue of William Penn, has the distinction of being the country's largest and most costly municipal building. It's also a beautiful example of Victorian architecture, when it's not hidden by scaffolding.

BENJAMIN FRANKLIN AT PENN

University of Pennsylvania, at 30th and Walnut streets in West Philadelphia, is the city's oldest and most prestigious university. Founded by Benjamin Franklin and others in 1740, it boasts the nation's first medical, law, and business schools. While the neighborhood surrounding Penn has undergone a revitalization, the campus itself is worth a visit, whether you have a connection to it or not. Anyone may stroll across its attractive quadrangle and admire the Gothic-style buildings and centuries-old trees. Don't miss the three statues of Franklin on campus—one depicts the school's founder as a carefree teenager newly arrived from Boston, another as portly statesman, and a third seated on a bench engrossed in the *Pennsylvania Gazette.* Also worth checking out while here is the **University Museum of Archaeology and Anthropology** (215-898-4000, 3260 South St.; $8 adults; $5 children), home to a 12-ton sphinx, Egyptian mummies, and other artifacts the university has acquired through 350 years of sponsored archaeological expeditions. Finally, art lovers should check out the latest exhibit at the bold **Institute for Contemporary Art** (215-898-5911; 118 S. 36th St.), which hosted the first-ever museum shows of Andy Warhol and Laurie Anderson. Closed Mon. and Tues.; $6 adults; free on Sun. from 11 to 1.

PENN'S GOTHIC ARCHITECTURE

The one and a half hour tour details the building's history, architecture, and sculpture, and includes a visit to the tower observation deck. Tours of only the observation deck, which affords one of the best panoramic views in the city, run every 15 minutes 9:30–4 for $5. All tours leave from the information center near the east entrance.

MUSEUMS ♿ **Philadelphia Museum of Art** (215-763-8100), 2600 Benjamin Franklin Pkwy. Closed Mon.; $12 adults, $8 ages 13–18. This grandiose Greco-Roman temple is America's third-largest art museum and home to more than 225,000 works of art, including important collections of Pennsylvania German and French impressionist paintings, 18th- and 19th-century furniture, and a stunning reconstructed Hindu stone temple that dates back to 1550. Allow for at least several hours to tour the two hundred galleries and adjacent azalea garden. If you don't have time to go inside, you can jog, Rocky-style, up the steps of the grand old building, or just settle for posing next to a bronze statue of the Italian Stallion at the foot of the steps. The museum throws a big "Art after 5" cocktail party every Fri. evening with live music, movie screenings, and mingling events. In 2007, the museum opened the Ruth and Raymond G. Perelman Building across the street at 2501 Benjamin Franklin Pkwy. It features special exhibits, as well as the museum's photography and textiles collections.

Rodin Museum (215-763-8100, www.rodinmuseum.org), Benjamin Franklin Pkwy. at 22nd St. Open Tues.–Sat.; $3 adults. Home to the largest collection of Auguste Rodin sculpture outside of France, including his most notable work, "The Thinker." Free guided tours are held every Sun.

Rosenbach Museum & Library (215-732-1600; www.rosenbach.org), 2010 Delancey Pl. $8 adults, free Tues. Bibliophiles will love the intriguing literary

PHILADELPHIA MUSEUM OF ART AND WATER WORKS

treasures found in this 1863 double townhouse off Rittenhouse Square: James Joyce's handwritten manuscript for *Ulysses*, a lock of Charles Dickens's hair, and Bram Stoker's notes and outlines for *Dracula*, to name a few. The owners and brothers, A. S. W. and Philip Rosenbach, were 19th-century art and book dealers; there are also personal letters penned by George Washington, the reassembled Greenwich Village living room of poet Marianne Moore, and more than 10,000 illustrations and manuscripts by Maurice Sendak. Tours are given several times a day.

&. Pennsylvania Academy of Fine Arts (215-972-7600), 118 N. Broad St. Open Tues.–Sun.; $7 adults, $5 ages 5–18. An impressive collection of American paintings and sculpture by Benjamin West, Mary Cassatt, Thomas Eakins, Winslow Homer, and others housed in an exquisite Victorian Gothic building that served as the nation's first art museum and school. Next door, the contemporary Samuel M. V. Hamilton building displays works by Georgia O'Keefe, Roy Lichtenstein, and Mark Rothko.

Mutter Museum (215-563-3737, www.collphyphil.org), 19 S. 22nd St. In 1858, Thomas Dent Mutter, a retired professor of surgery, donated his collection of cancerous tumors, skeletons, and other anatomic specimens and medical artifacts to the College of Physicians of Philadelphia. Today, they're on display in all their gruesome glory in a room off the school's lobby.

✳ To Do

FOR FAMILIES &. ✍ **Franklin Institute Science Museum** (215-448-1200; www.2.fi.edu), 222 N. 20th St. Open 9:30–5 daily. Adults $14, seniors and children 4–11 $11. Kids and grown-ups alike will find many things to enjoy at this favorite Parkway attraction. Founded in 1824, it has a planetarium, an IMAX theater, and many hands-on exhibits that celebrate and teach the wonders of science, from sports to trains to Isaac Newton. A walk through the giant *papiermache* replica of a beating heart is a must—so is a stop in the Franklin Gallery, where you'll find many of Ben's own inventions and models, including his lightning rod and a reproduction of his bifocals.

✍ &. **Academy of Natural Sciences** (215-299-1000), 1900 Benjamin Franklin Pkwy. Open daily. Another Philly attraction that was the first of its kind (it's the nation's oldest natural history museum), this neighbor to the Franklin Institute is the place to go for dinosaurs and enormous mounted-animal dioramas. Future paleontologists can dig for fossils in Dinosaur Hall (weekends only) and mingle with live butterflies (for an additional $2) in a re-created rain forest.

✍ &. **Please Touch Museum** (215-963-0667; www.pleasetouchmuseum.org), 210 N. 21st St. (behind the Franklin Institute). Open 9–4:30 daily. This is a fun stop for the under-seven set; there's a Maurice Sendak area that lets kids interact with props from *Where the Wild Things Are* and an Alice in Wonderland room complete with a rabbit hole. Avoid going here on weekday mornings during the school year. It's scheduled to move to bigger quarters in Fairmount Park's Memorial Hall in late 2008. Check the Web site for updates.

✍ **Smith Memorial Playground** (215-765-4325), 33rd and Oxford streets.

Open 10–4 Tues.–Sun. Kids will love the giant wooden slide and three-story "play mansion" at this venerable playground in east Fairmount Park.

SCENIC DRIVES A pleasant urban drive begins at the Museum of Art and follows Kelly Drive north past Boathouse Row. Turn right at Hunting Park Avenue and look for Laurel Hill Cemetery on the bluff to your left, cross Ridge Avenue, and then turn left onto Henry Avenue and follow it about a mile to 3901 Henry Avenue, site of the childhood home of Grace Kelly. Continue north on Henry Avenue about 3 miles past neighborhoods of brick and stone row houses and make a right onto Wise's Mill Road, which will bring you back into Fairmount Park. Follow the narrow tree-lined road as it winds next to the Wissahickon River to the **Valley Green Inn** (215-247-1730), where you can have a leisurely lunch or brunch on its front porch overlooking the creek and bicycle path.

✳ Outdoor Activities

BICYCLING/RENTALS The Schuylkill River Trail is a paved bicycle and jogging trail that follows the Schuylkill River 23 miles from Center City to Norristown. A popular 9-mile loop for walkers, joggers, and cyclists begins at the art museum, runs north past Boathouse Row and up the east bank of the Schuylkill, crosses the river at Falls Bridge, and works its way back to the museum along the west side of the river.

Bike rentals are available near the path's Center City portion from **Trophy Bikes** (215-222-2020), 3131 Walnut St. (in the Left Bank apartment building). Bikes are $20 for 4 hours, $25 for 24 hours. Over near the art museum, you can rent bikes and rollerblades on weekends from **Drive Sports 2** (215-232-7900), 1 Boathouse Row, next to Lloyd Hall.

The city closes the 4-mile stretch of Martin Luther King Drive west of the Schuylkill River to vehicular traffic on weekends between Apr. and Oct.; it fills up fast with cyclists, runners, and in-line skaters.

BOATING Rowing along the Schuylkill near Boathouse Row is reserved for trained athletes, but anyone can play spectator on the river's banks. Apr. through Sept., you can watch regattas on the Schuylkill River, which have been held for more than a century. Contact the **National Association of Amateur Oarsmen** (215-769-2068) or the **Boathouse Association** (215-686-0052) for a complete schedule of races.

FISHING You can fish for bass and catfish behind the Philadelphia Museum of Art at the Water Works pier, and along the river north of Boathouse Row. A required license of $17 for Pennsylvania residents, or $15 for 3 days, $30 for 7 days, and $35 for a season for out-of-staters, is available weekdays at the Municipal Services Building, 1401 John F. Kennedy Blvd., near the visitor center.

GOLF **Cobbs Creek Golf Club** (215-877-8707), 7200 Lansdowne Ave., a well-maintained course on the northwest edge of the city, offers a challenging par-71 course.

Chamounix Dr., Fairmount Park. Riding lessons are available Wed. and Fri. through Sun. Apr. through Nov. It's $125 for four one-hour lessons. Nearby bridle trails.

✳ Green Space

Bartram's Gardens (215-729-5281, www.bartramsgarden.org), 54th St. and Lindbergh Blvd. Open daily 10–5, except holidays. John Bartram planted what would become the nation's oldest living botanical garden here in 1728. It's a beautiful property, despite its location in the middle of an industrialized neighborhood near the airport. Guided tours of the house are available for $5 a person four times a day; admission to the grounds is free.

✳ Lodging

HOTELS & INNS ⓗ **Rittenhouse Hotel** (215-546-9000; www.ritten househotel.com), 210 W. Rittenhouse Sq. If you're looking to splurge, this is the place to go. Overlooking one the city's best public squares, it has 98 elegant and spacious rooms, luxurious marble bathrooms, and attentive service. The amenities are endless: plush bathrobes, twice-daily maid service, an indoor pool and fitness center, TVs in the bathrooms. It's also home to LaCroix, a well-regarded French restaurant, and the Boathouse Row Bar (see *Nightlife*). Rooms $299–480, suites $640–2,500.

ⓗ ♨ **Sofitel** (215-569-8300), 120 S. 17th St. Hip and businesslike at once, this 306-room hotel was once home to the Philadelphia Stock Exchange and is in a prime location near Rittenhouse Square's best bars and restaurants. The handsome rooms were renovated in 2000 and have cloudlike king beds and modern cherry-wood furniture. Rooms $295–420.

ⓗ **Club Quarters** (215-282-5000; www.clubquarters.info), 1628 Chestnut St. This private hotel for business travelers opens its doors to nonmembers on weekends (and occasional

weekdays) through Internet booking services like Orbitz and Hotels.com. The rooms are on the small side, but spotless and attractively decorated with mahogany furniture and colorful linens. There is free high-speed Internet access throughout the hotel, a small fitness center, and 24-hour room service. The inviting lobby is stocked with magazines, comfy couches, and brewed coffee. Rooms $149–199.

BED & BREAKFASTS **La Reserve** (215-735-1137; www.lareservebnb .com), 1804 Pine St. Centrally located in a residential neighborhood a few blocks from Rittenhouse Square, this 19th-century townhome has six comfortable rooms with shared baths and one efficiency apartment. Guests are encouraged to play the baby grand piano in the lobby or read in the high-ceilinged library. Parking is challenging around here, but guests do receive a small discount at a nearby parking lot. Rates $89–159 (includes breakfast).

University City

ⓗ **Inn at Penn** (215-222-0200; www .theinnatpenn.com), 3600 Sansom St. Just as the name implies, this 238-room

ALONG BOATHOUSE ROW

Covering 9,200 acres that resemble the shape of an elephant's head, **Fairmount Park** (215-683-0200; www.fairmountpark.org) is one of the nation's oldest and largest urban parks. It lines either side of the Schuylkill River from the Philadelphia Museum of Art north to Manayunk, then snakes west and north through the leafy Wissahickon Valley. You could spend days here and not cover all of its diverse attractions. Maps are usually available at Lloyd Hall, the modern two-story community center that has a cafe with limited hours and a bike rental outfit. The lower section (from Falls Bridge south to the art museum) is the part that's easiest accessible from Center City. It includes **Boathouse Row**, a line of Victorian boathouses along Kelly Drive that make up a group called the Schuylkill Navy. (East River Drive was renamed Kelly Drive in 1985 after local oarsman Jack, who also happened to be Grace Kelly's brother.) Each boathouse is decorated with strings of lights, creating a festive gingerbread-house-style display at night; I've passed Boathouse Row at night hundreds of times and never fail to be awed by the sight. Below is a collection of the lower park's best attractions. For information on the upper section of Fairmount Park, see *Chestnut Hill, Germantown & Manayunk*.

✦ **Philadelphia Zoo** (215-243-1100; www.philadelphiazoo.org) 3400 W. Girard Ave. Open year-round. $16.95 adults, $13.95, ages 3–11. The country's oldest zoo is a compact 42 acres that is home to 1,800 species of animals, including polar bears, red pandas, camels, and two rare white African lions. Kids will love the $5 camel rides and swan boats (also $5). Its newest attraction is the Zooballoon, a hot-air balloon ride that gives you a bird's eye view of the animals. Parking will set you back another $10.

Nearby is the **Smith Civil War Memorial Arch**, 4231 N. Concourse Dr., which honors the state's Civil War heroes. At its base are the whispering benches, developed in a way that a whisper into the wall at one end will carry all the way to the other end of the side. It's also a popular local spot to get engaged or steal a first kiss.

After the yellow fever epidemic in 1793, many city dwellers built country homes along the Schuylkill River to escape the heat and disease. Today, many of these **Fairmount Park Mansions** remain intact and about a dozen are open several days a week for tours. The neo-classical **Lemon Hill** (215-235-1776; 7201 N. Randolph Dr.) in the park's eastern section was meticulously restored in 2005 and has three stacked oval rooms with curved doors and floor-to-ceiling Palladian windows. **Strawberry Mansion** (215-228-8364; 2450 Strawberry Mansion Dr.) so named because it once served as a restaurant with a signature dessert of strawberries and cream, is known for its antique toy and doll collection and array of Federal and Empire furniture.

SWAN RIDES AT THE PHILADELPHIA ZOO

The park's most interesting and unsung mansion has got to be the **Ryerss Museum and Library** (215-685-0544; 7370 Central Ave.), about a 20-minute drive from Center City in the city's Fox Chase section. Robert Ryerss, president of the Tioga Railroad and an avid collector of Asian art and artifacts, scandalized society when he married his housekeeper eight months before he died and willed her his family's Italianate summer home with the stipulation that she eventually leave it to the city to run as a public museum. She did, but not before traveling around the world and adding to her husband's 25,000-piece collection with such treasures as an 11th-century Buddha from Japan and a Chinese *papier-mache* puppet theater. Don't miss the family's beloved pet cemetery. Tours are free (Fri. through Sun.), also at the behest of Mr. Ryerss.

FAIRMOUNT PARK'S RYERSS MUSEUM AND LIBRARY

inn caters to those with connections to the University of Pennsylvania, which sits just across the street. It is run by the Hilton chain, but maintains an independent and polished academic air. Rooms are large and elegant and include coffeemakers, plush robes, and high-end bath amenities. There's also a fitness center, a restaurant, and a clubby lounge called the Living Room, where coffee, tea, and cocktails are served. Rooms start at $219.

▼ **Gables** (215-662-1918; www .gablesbb.com), 4520 Chester Ave. Built in 1889, this beautiful Victorian building with its wraparound porch and gardens is a less expensive and homier alternative to the big hotels surrounding Penn. It's near Spruce Street, about six blocks from Penn's campus. Owners Don Caskey and Warren Cederholm bought and restored the place in the early 1990s; many of the 10 rooms feature antique brass beds and fireplaces; two have shared baths. Breakfast might include baked almond French toast or sausage and veggie strata. Rooms $105–165.

HOSTELS Chamounix Mansion (215-878-3676; www.philahostel.org), 3250 Chamounix Dr., Philadelphia. This 1802 country estate in Fairmount Park attracts a wide mix of frugal travelers for its leafy setting and close proximity to Center City. Each dormitory-style room has between 4 and 16 beds and little else. The elegant parlor in the main house, however, will make you feel like a privileged guest of the original owners. There's also laundry and kitchen facilities, and Internet access. Beds $20–23.

✳ Where to Eat

DINING OUT

Rittenhouse Square
Audrey Claire (215-731-1222), 20th and Spruce streets. Dinner Tues.–Sun. This terrific corner bistro near Rittenhouse Square serves Mediterranean-influenced dishes like roasted chicken with lemon and feta- and garlic-crusted rack of lamb. Don't miss the amazing selection of appetizers, especially the grilled flatbreads and spicy hummus. No reservations; be prepared for a long wait on weekends. BYO. Entrees: $14–20.

& 𝖸 **Nineteen** (215-790-1919), 200 S. Broad St. Open daily for lunch and dinner, Sun. brunch. This nineteenth-floor restaurant in the Park Hyatt at the Bellevue has panoramic views of the city, fabulous cuisine, and an elegant dining room featuring a raw bar and a huge pearl chandelier. The menu emphasizes seafood, with dishes like tarragon crab cakes and a fabulous halibut with Lancaster County ham and fiddlehead ferns. Don't miss the signature dessert: lemon-foam carrot cake served with cream cheese sorbet. Dinner entrees: $10–20.

𝖸 **Rouge** (215-732-6622), 205 S. 18th St. Open daily for lunch and dinner. This trendy late-night bar and restaurant has stellar views of the square and attracts a stylish clientele with prices to match. The food tends to be American with a French influence. Extensive wine list. Entrees: $15–33.

University City
𝖸 **White Dog Café** (215-386-9224), 3420 Sansom St. Open for lunch and dinner daily, Sun. brunch. This gourmet hub for social activists is Philadelphia's version of Berkeley's Chez

Panisse. Its menu pushes locally grown and raised produce; you might find Kung Pao tofu with toasted peanuts and free-range Lancaster County chicken for dinner, and smoked salmon sandwiches with caper cream cheese for lunch. The piano parlor features live music on Fri. and Sat. nights, and there are regular lectures and film events. Lunch and brunch $10–15, dinner entrees $16–29.

Marigold Kitchen (215-222-3699), 501 S. 45th St. Serves a small, appealing Mediterranean-influenced menu in a cozy Victorian brownstone on a residential street. Dinner highlights include leg of lamb with Egyptian artichokes and eggplant cannelloni with Bulgarian feta. Service can be underwhelming when the place is busy. Reservations recommended. BYO. Entrees $21–30.

EATING OUT ♈ **Monk's Café** (215-545-7005) 264 S. 16th St. Lunch and dinner daily. This narrow neighborhood tavern regularly wins "Best of Philly" awards for its huge Belgian beer selection. It also has swell burgers (beef and veggie), beer-braised mussels, and pomme frites served with bourbon mayonnaise. Dishes $7–25.

♈ ✿ ♿ **Pietro's Coal Oven Pizzeria** (215-735-8090), 1714 Walnut St. Lunch and dinner daily. This casual trattoria serves thin-crust pizza with gourmet toppings like goat cheese and prosciutto and a wide selection of pastas and salads. It's good for families looking for a reasonable meal in Rittenhouse Square that doesn't involve yellow arches. Full bar. Dishes $9–16.

♈ **Tria** (215-972-8742), 123 S. 18th St. Sleek and stylish, it's perfect for an after-dinner drink and light meal. The excellent wine list is longer then the menu, and the cheese list (ranked by stinky, approachable, stoic, and racy) is longer than an average grocery list. A fine selection of local and imported beers, too. Dishes $7–10.

CAFES & BAKERIES **Abner's** (215-662-0100), 3813 Chestnut St., University City. If you need a cheesesteak fix west of Broad, this is the place to go; it's usually packed with Penn students. Sandwiches $4–8.

Rittenhouse Square
Darling's (215-545-5745), 404 S. 20th St. Locals flock to this cute cafe for breakfast, lunch, and cheesecake. Besides an assortment of omelettes, salads, and sandwiches on home-baked bread, the place serves 10 different kinds of cheesecake daily, from classic to Bananas Foster—all divine. Look for Bailey's Irish Cream cheesecake around St. Patrick's Day. There's also a branch at 2100 Spring St., near the Franklin Institute. Lunch $5–7.

♿ **Di Bruno Brothers** (215-665-9220), 1730 Chestnut St. Lunch daily. This outpost of the Italian Market cheese shop has an upstairs cafe that's perfect for a quick gourmet lunch (try the Mamma Mia panini with prosciutto, fresh mozzarella, and roasted peppers). Afterward, browse the selections of imported olives, pates, and specialty cheeses. BYO. Sandwiches $8.

La Colombe Torrefaction (215-563-0860), 130 S. 19th St. Open daily. No lattes, teas, or attitude—just fabulous house-blend coffee served in an art-filled room with large windows.

BYO Where to buy wine west of City Hall:

Around Rittenhouse Square, there is a **Wine & Spirits store** at 1913 Chestnut St. (215-560-4215). In University City, there's a **state store** at 4049 Walnut St. (215-823-4709).

✳ Entertainment

MUSIC & THEATER Curtis Institute of Music (215-893-5261), 1726 Locust St., Rittenhouse Square. This prestigious conservatory holds free student recitals every Mon., Wed., and Fri. Oct. through May. Arrive early; seating is on a first-come basis.

&. **Kimmel Center** (215-790-5800; www.kimmelcenter.org), 260 S. Broad St. The city's newest performing arts center is home to the 2,500-seat Verizon Hall, where you can catch the Philadelphia Orchestra and other musical performances.

𝖸 **Natalie's Lounge** (215-222-5162; 4003 Market St.). This narrow, smoky jazz club in West Philly has hosted John Coltrane, Grover Washington Jr., and other jazz and blues legends. It's still going strong after 60 years.

𝖸 **World Café Live** (215-222-1400), 3025 Walnut St. This smoke-free club and restaurant near Penn is the best place in town to catch cutting-edge indie artists. A smaller upstairs stage features new and local talent.

MOVIES &. 𝖸 **The Bridge: Cinema de Lux** (215-386-3300), 40th and Walnut sts. The city's newest (and most expensive) cinema offers six screens with stadium seating, wireless Internet access, and a hip cocktail lounge.

&. **International House** (215-387-5125), 3701 Chestnut St. The place for spaghetti westerns, John Carpenter triple features, and avant-garde cinema.

NIGHTLIFE 𝖸 **Alma de Cuba** (215-988-1799), 1623 Walnut St., Rittenhouse Square. Comfy chairs, dim lighting, and splendid pomegranate martinis make this a worthy after-dinner stop if you're in Rittenhouse Square. There's live Cuban jazz on Wed. nights.

𝖸 **The Bards** (215-569-9585), 2013 Walnut St., Rittenhouse Square. An agreeable mix of barflies, professionals, and Wharton MBA students share Guinness on tap and shepherd's pie at the long bar of this friendly Irish pub. Its weeknight happy hour is very popular, and there's live Irish music on Sun. evenings.

𝖸 **Pod** (215-387-1803), 3636 Sansom St., University City. A college bar for students with trust funds (or at least some extra cash) and a taste for sake martinis and conveyor-belt sushi. Its futuristic all-white decor and hip sound system make this a fun alternative to the city's 19th-century beer taverns.

✳ Selective Shopping

Rittenhouse Square has many upscale designer clothing and gift boutiques along Walnut Street, plus several hidden gems like **Joseph Fox Bookshop** (215-563-4184; 1724 Sansom St.), an independent bookseller with a great architecture selection, and **Petulia's Folly** (215-569-1344; 1710 Sansom St.), a clothing and housewares boutique known for its wide selection of stylish women's fashions and subtle service. Chestnut Street (between 16th and 17th) is home to the **Shops at Liberty Place**, where you'll find Nine West, J. Crew, and other upscale chains; there's also a large food court. In University City, **Sansom Commons** (215-573-5290) at 36th and Sansom has dozens of specialty, fashion, music, book, and gift shops, including Urban Outfitters and Barnes & Noble, all catering to collegiate tastes. Nearby, the **Black Cat** (215-386-6664); 3424 Sansom St., features an eclectic collection of handmade jewelry, books, folk art, and lovely handicrafts from Asia, Latin America, and Africa. Owned by the adjacent White Dog Cafe, it stays open late most nights.

✳ Special Events

April: **Penn Relays** (last weekend), University of Pennsylvania—America's first intercollegiate and amateur track event takes over Franklin Field. Besides the races, you'll find food stands, live music, and other activities around campus.

June: **Bloomsday** (June 16), Rosenbach Library, Rittenhouse Square—the home of James Joyce's original *Ulysses* manuscript celebrates the famed literary holiday with Irish music, food provided by nearby pubs, and a series of readings by local celebrities on Delancey Place. Inside, there's a special exhibit of Joyce materials.

CHESTNUT HILL, GERMANTOWN & MANAYUNK

Chestnut Hill, Germantown, and Manayunk all lie outside Philadelphia's original boundaries and have a slightly suburban feel, each in its own separate way. Because they are outside Center City, they often aren't included in maps or travel stories on Philadelphia, but they are well worth a visit, especially if you like boutique shopping, cobblestoned streets, and preserved Victorian houses. Germantown sits the closest to Center City and was once one of Philadelphia's most affluent communities. Today, it has a grittier feel and is less pedestrian-friendly than its neighbors to the north, but its historical monuments are well preserved and among the finest and least crowded in the city, most notably the elegant and bullet-riddled Cliveden, site of the Battle of Germantown in 1777. Chestnut Hill is just a 10-minute drive north up Germantown Avenue, with its thriving main drag of boutique shops, sidewalk cafés, and attractive architecture. Once a farming community, it is now a sought-after address for many young Philadelphia families who like its easy access to Center City, wide tree-lined

CHESTNUT HILL STREET SCENE

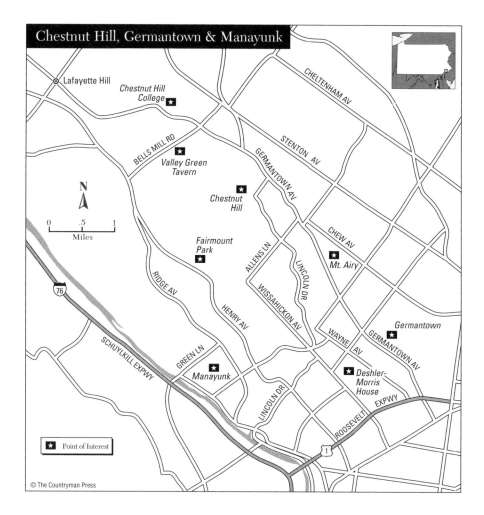

Lafayette Hill

Chestnut Hill College

CHELTENHAM AV

BELLS MILL RD

STENTON AV

GERMANTOWN AV

Valley Green Tavern

N

0   .5   1
Miles

Chestnut Hill

CHEW AV

Fairmount Park

ALLENS LN

LINCOLN DR

Mt. Airy

RIDGE AV

HENRY AV

WISSAHICKON AV

WAYNE AV

GERMANTOWN AV

Germantown

76

SCHUYLKILL EXPWY

GREEN LN

Manayunk

LINCOLN DR

Deshler-Morris House

ROOSEVELT EXPWY

1

★ Point of Interest

© The Countryman Press

streets, and Queen Anne–style homes. You're bound to spot plenty of Bugaboo strollers and four-figure pocketbooks as you stroll along Germantown Avenue in Chestnut Hill, but the snobbish attitude you might find in other well-to-do areas isn't as evident here. Manayunk, a former textile-manufacturing center perched above the Manayunk canal a bit farther north, has transformed its main street into a happening string of restaurants, loft apartments, boutiques, and tattoo parlors, though the hilly streets above it still have the feel of a tight working-class community. Its name is, fittingly, a Native American expression for "where we go to drink." If you like a lively night out that is sure to include young Yuengling-guzzling crowds and parking challenges, then this is the place for you. Others might want to stick with a daytime visit, when shopping and strolling are easiest, or make an early dinner reservation and leave before the late-night gridlock takes over Main Street.

GUIDANCE The **Germantown Historical Society and Visitor Center** (215-844-1683), 5501 Germantown Ave., serves as a local museum as much as a venue for maps and brochures. On display are cannonballs from the Battle of Germantown, paintings by Charles Wilson Peale, and old photographs and etchings of the town. In Chestnut Hill, stop by the small **visitor center** (215-247-6696), at 8426 Germantown Ave., for a walking map of town and information on surrounding attractions.

GETTING THERE *By car:* For Chestnut Hill and Germantown, take I-76 to Lincoln Drive and follow it east to Germantown Avenue in Mount Airy; head right (south) for Germantown or left for Chestnut Hill. Manayunk is also off I-76; exit at Manayunk (No. 338), turn right and follow Greene Lane Bridge to Main Street. Turn right and follow it into the heart of town.

By bus: **SEPTA** bus route 61 runs along Ridge Avenue between Manayunk and Center City.

By train: **SEPTA** regional R7 and R8 lines (215-580-7800, www.septa.org) run regularly between 30th Street Station and Chestnut Hill, with stops in Germantown and Mount Airy. The Chestnut Hill West station is within walking distance of the town's main drag.

Manayunk is on the R6 line, which runs from Center City out to Norristown.

GETTING AROUND Ridge Avenue and Germantown Avenue are the main north-south thoroughfares between Center City and its northern neighborhoods.

Manayunk and Chestnut Hill are terrific walking towns with thriving main streets. In Manayunk, pick up the canal towpath behind Restoration Hardware on Main Street and follow the route that was originally used by mules pulling boats loaded with coal to the textile mills that lined the river.

The **Chestnut Hill Historical Society** (215-247-0417; 8708 Germantown Ave.) sells detailed maps and offers walking tours of Chestnut Hill in spring and fall.

MEDICAL EMERGENCY **Chestnut Hill Hospital** (215-753-2000) 8835 Germantown Ave., is at the north end of Chestnut Hill.

✷ To See

MUSEUMS ♿ ⸸ **Woodmere Art Museum** (215-247-0476; www.woodmereartmuseum.org), 9201 Germantown Ave., Chestnut Hill. This fine small art museum is located in a stately stone mansion just north of Chestnut Hill's main drag. It features the work of Philadelphia-area artists such as N. C. Wyeth, Benjamin West, Daniel Garber, and Violet Oakley.

HISTORIC SITES **Cliveden** (215-848-1777; www.cliveden.org), 6401 Germantown Ave., Germantown. Open 12–4 Thurs.–Sun. $8 adults, $6 ages 6–12. More than a hundred British troops holed up in the home of Pennsylvania's first chief justice in 1777 as General Washington army's attacked the home unsuccessfully before retreating. As legend has it, the Brits didn't surrender because they feared the bluecoats, still fuming over their failure at the Battle of Paoli, would

CLIVEDEN, GERMANTOWN

kill them anyway. So while the Battle of Germantown was unquestionably a defeat for the Americans, it served to boost morale and was a significant turning point in the Revolutionary War. Today, docents give regular tours of the bullet-riddled mansion, which contains many of original 18th-century furnishings of the Benjamin Chew family. A free reenactment of the battle is held on the grounds every October (see also *Special Events*).

🏛 **Deshler-Morris House** (215-842-1798; www.nps.org/demo), 5442 Germantown Ave. Open 1–4 Fri.–Sun.; free. George Washington really did sleep, eat, and drink here. They have his personal silver tankard to prove it. The first president and his family stayed here in 1793, to escape the yellow fever epidemic that ravaged the city, then they returned for vacation during the summer of 1794. Now run by the National Park Service, it is the oldest presidential residence still in existence in the U.S. At press time, the place was closed through 2008 for renovations and the installation of new exhibits. Check the Web site for updates.

🏛 **Johnson House** (215-438-1768; www.johnsonhouse.org), 6306 Germantown Ave., Germantown. Open Thurs. and Fri. by appointment, Sat. for tours at 1:15, 2:15, and 3:15; $5 adults, $2 ages 2–11. Built in 1768, this two-story home that belonged to a local family of abolitionists was a stop on the Underground Railroad and is believed to have sheltered and fed Harriet Tubman and William Still as they guided hundreds of slaves to freedom. The 40-minute tour includes a visit to the third-floor hiding place and exhibits on American slavery and abolitionism.

Wyck (215-848-1690, www.wyck.org), 6026 Germantown Ave. Tours 1–4 Tues., Thurs. and Sat. and by appointment; $5 adults. The formal garden, featuring more than 30 varieties of old roses (in bloom May and June), is the star of this 2-acre Germantown property, but the house, which doubled as a field hospital during the Battle of Germantown and was home to nine generations of one Quaker family, is also worth exploring. It contains an extensive collection of early horticultural books.

✳ To Do

✎ ♿ **Morris Arboretum** (215-247-5777; www.upenn.edu/arboretum), 100 Northwestern Ave., Chestnut Hill. Open daily year-round; $10 adults, $5 ages 3–18. The official state arboretum bills itself as "a tree place" and is indeed known for its collection of old and rare specimens, including one of the largest Japanese katsura trees in the United States. John and Lydia Morris, wealthy Quaker siblings who never married, deeded their 92-acre summer property to the University of Pennsylvania in 1932. In May and June, the walled rose garden is a popular spot, and the property is covered with brilliant foliage in the fall. For kids, there's a miniature Garden Railway that runs past naturally made bridges, buildings, and trestles May through Oct. I like to combine a visit here with a stop at the nearby Woodmere Art Museum or an afternoon of shopping in downtown Chestnut Hill. The grounds stay open late and host outdoor concerts in the summer.

MORRIS ARBORETUM

SCENIC DRIVES Germantown Avenue is one of the oldest streets in America, and home to dozens of historic buildings and churches, upscale shops, and vibrant pedestrian-friendly communities. Begin your drive near **Vernon Park** in Germantown and follow the cobblestones north past the **Johnson House**, **Cliveden**, and other historic sites that played a role in the Battle of Germantown during the Revolutionary War. Continue through Mount Airy, a neighborhood of beautiful old row homes where you can stop for lunch at **Cresheim Cottage** (7402 Germantown Ave.). Then head into Chestnut Hill for some window-shopping and perhaps an ice cream cone at **Bredenbeck's** (7402 Germantown Ave.). The drive is less than 8 miles, but could take you a full afternoon if you stop at all the interesting sites and shops along the way. Cap the day with a home-brewed raspberry mead-ale at the **General Lafayette Inn** (646 Germantown Pike).

✳ Outdoor Activities

BICYCLING/RENTALS The Manayunk Towpath connects with the 22-mile Schuylkill River Bicycle Trail. It can be accessed from several spots along Main Street. **Human Zoom** (215-487-7433), 4151 Main St., in Manayunk rents standard adult hybrids and road bikes. Prices start at $8 an hour, or $25 for 24 hours.

FISHING The Pennsylvania Fish and Boat Commission stocks the Wissahickon Creek with rainbow and brown trout in the spring, summer, and early fall. Small- and largemouth bass can also be caught in the creek.

ICE SKATING **Wissahickon Skating Club** (215-247-1759), 550 W. Willow Grove Ave., Chestnut Hill. Open skate sessions on Fri. evenings and some Sat.

KAYAKING Kayak tours of the Manayunk Canal and Schuylkill River are offered in the summer by **Hidden River Outfitters** and the **Schuylkill Project**. Call 215-482-9565 for a schedule. They usually include paddling instruction and lunch.

✳ Lodging

Lodging options are limited in Germantown and Manayunk, but Chestnut Hill has a few small and friendly inns.

Anam Cara (215-242-4327; www .anamcarabandb.com), 52 Wooddale Ave. Anam Cara means "soul friend" in the Celtic language. Indeed, you'll feel like you're staying at the very clean and hospitable home of a good friend here. Located in a quiet neighborhood and an easy walk to downtown Chestnut Hill, it has two small comfortable rooms and five adjacent apartments available for weekly or monthly rental. Rooms are $115–125, apartments start at $650 a week.

Chestnut Hill Hotel (215-242-5905; www.chestnuthillhotel.com), 8229 Germantown Ave. This rambling 19th-century inn in the middle of downtown has been a hotel since before the town of Chestnut Hill existed (it was rebuilt in the 1800s). Today, it attracts more business travelers than vacationers. Its 36 smoke-free rooms and suites have pencil-post double beds, plasma TVs, wireless access, and showers or baths. The adjacent Chestnut Hill Grill has outdoor seating and is always hopping with lively crowds. Rooms $109–149; suites $179, includes a continental breakfast. Rates are a little higher on weekdays.

Silverstone (215-242-3333, www .silverstonestay.com), 8840 Stenton Ave., Chestnut Hill. This imposing Victorian Gothic home has six spacious rooms that look like a grandmother (with good taste and meticulous housekeeping habits) might have decorated them. Guests can make their own breakfast (eggs, bacon, bread, and all cookware provided) in the kitchen; there's also a luggage elevator, laundry facilities, and a back garden. It's a short walk on a curb-less road from the Chestnut Hill East train station. Ask for a room that doesn't face busy Stenton Avenue. Kids are welcome. Rooms $85–125.

GREEN SPACE Wissahickon Valley Park (215-685-9285) is part of the Fairmount Park system and stretches northwest along the Wissahickon Creek past Chestnut Hill. It's home to breathtaking natural settings and some of the best hiking and biking trails in the city. Maps and free trail permits are available at the **Wissahickon Environmental Center** (215-685-9285, 300 Northwestern Ave.), located at the north corner of the park and a short drive from the Morris Arboretum. On the site of a former nursery, it's worth a stop alone for its huge wildlife mural, aquarium, and helpful staff.

Other top attractions include **Rittenhouse Town** (215-438-5711, 206 Lincoln Dr.), the site of the first paper mill in North America, built in 1690 by William Rittenhouse (great grandfather of David, the scientist for whom Rittenhouse Square is named). By the late 18th century, the area grew into a small self-sufficient community with more than 40 buildings. Today, seven buildings remain, including a barn which houses a papermaking studio and the original Rittenhouse family homestead and bakehouse. Pick up a self-guided walking map at the

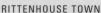
RITTENHOUSE TOWN

✴ Where to Eat

DINING OUT Jake's (215-483-0444) 4365 Main St., Manayunk. Lunch and dinner Mon.–Sat., brunch and dinner Sun. If you want a special-occasion meal in Manayunk, this is the place to go. The small dining room and tiny front bar may not win any awards, but it's the consistently good food and service that keeps locals coming back. The contemporary American menu changes seasonally and might include apple cider–barbecued salmon or ancho-espresso grilled filet of beef. Reservations recommended. Lunch $11–17; dinner entrees $24–32.

Cresheim Cottage (215-248-4365, www.cresheimcottage.com), 7402

WISSAHICKON'S FORBIDDEN DRIVE TRAIL

visitor center, or try to visit on a weekend in the summer, when guided tours are given. Call for specific hours. Even when the buildings aren't open, its creekside setting just off Lincoln Drive is a pleasant place to read or let the kids run around.

Forbidden Drive is the park's top hiking, biking, and equestrian trail, a wide gravel road that parallels the Wissahickon Creek. It has been closed to car traffic since the 1920s (hence the name) and begins off Lincoln Drive near RittenhouseTown, winding 5 miles one way past WPA shelters from the 1930s, a covered bridge, and dense woodland to Northwestern Avenue at the city's limits. A local rite of passage is brunch at the **Valley Green Inn** (see also *Eating Out*), a full-service restaurant with a front porch that over-looks the trail. There's even a place to hitch your horses while you eat.

Germantown Ave., Mount Airy. Closed Mon. This colonial stone cottage is good for a bite to eat before or after visiting Germantown's historic sites, though it usually closes between 2 and 5. The American-eclectic menu features organic and locally grown ingredients and changes seasonally. Highlights include a chicken meatloaf muffin stuffed with blue cheese, a crab BLT with horseradish-tomato sauce, and an upscale cheesesteak with mushrooms and carmelized onions. Desserts are sensational; try the coconut rice pudding. There's also an extensive wine list. Service can be a little spotty when it gets busy, which is often. Reservations recommended. Lunch $8–16. Dinner $12–24.

EATING OUT Al' Dana (215-247-3336), 8630 Germantown Ave., Chestnut Hill. Closed Mon. This unpretentious bistro at the south end of downtown serves delicious Middle Eastern cuisine. Try the garlic-fried cauliflower or any of the lamb dishes. There are several good vegetarian entrees, like broccoli topped with tahini, fried onions, and toasted almonds. Dishes $10–18.

Geechee Girl Rice Café (215-843-8113), 5496 Germantown Ave., Germantown. Dinner Tues.–Sat.; brunch Sun. except in summer. Delicious Southern comfort food makes up for slow service at this funky tangerine-walled cafe. Try the creamy shrimp and grits or the tomato-based gumbo served with California Gold rice. Cash only. BYO ($2 corkage fee). Dishes $11–17.

McNally's Tavern (215-247-9736), 8634 Germantown Ave., Chestnut Hill. Lunch and dinner daily. The specialty of this hole-in-the-wall bar is the Schmitter, a pumped-up version of the Philly cheesesteak that includes fried onions, tomato, salami, and Russian dressing. They also serve chicken Caesar salad and ham, turkey, and roast beef sandwiches. Daily specials might include crab cakes or prime rib. Dishes $6–15.

Tommy Gunn's (215-508-1030), 4901 Ridge Ave., Manayunk. Lunch and dinner daily. Philly isn't known as a barbecue town, but this mustard-yellow shack at the edge of Fairmount Park does its 'cue up right. On the menu are a variety of classics like Kansas City baby backs, Carolina-style pulled pork, Texas beef brisket, and Philly-style spare ribs. Vegetarians will love the portobello mushroom sandwich with fresh mozzarella. Sides include sweet and smoky baked beans, deep-fried mac 'n' cheese, and Carolina coleslaw. Eat in the small dining room or outside on the deck, or get it to go like most locals do. Sandwiches $5–8; platters $8–22.

Valley Green Inn (215-247-1730), Valley Green at Wissahickon. Lunch and dinner Mon.-Sat., brunch and dinner Sun. Known for its elaborate Sun. brunches, this former 19th-

VALLEY GREEN INN

century hotel sits in the middle of Wissahickon Valley Park overlooking a lovely creek. The brunch menu borders on the obscene, with offerings that include Brie-stuffed French toast, smoked salmon Benedict, and lobster, shrimp, and scallop hash. Lunch is a typical assortment of salads, burgers, and sandwiches. For dinner, there's pretzel-crusted pork chops, Alaskan king crab legs, and filet mignon. Try to get a table on the front porch for a front-row seat to the bikers, hikers, and nature lovers who meander by. Lunch $7–12, dinner $20–28, brunch $18–23.

BYO Where to buy wine in Chestnut Hill:

There's a premium **Wine & Spirits store** (215-753-4520), 8705 Germantown Ave. in the Top of the Hill Shopping Center behind Borders.

Chestnut Hill
Bredenbeck's Bakery and Ice Cream Parlor (215-247-7374), 7402 Germantown Ave. Delicious butter cookies and hand-dipped ice cream and milkshakes.

Chestnut Hill Farmers Market (215-254-4900), 8829 Germantown Ave. Open Thurs.–Sat. The area's first farmers market features more than a dozen vendors selling fresh flowers, produce, free-range chicken, and several tasty lunch options inside an old warehouse behind the Chestnut Hill Hotel. Free parking is available off Southampton Avenue.

Night Kitchen Bakery (215-248-9235), 7725 Germantown Ave. This small white cottage serves lemon-curd cake, sticky buns, and other baked goods.

MUSIC North by Northwest (215-248-1000), 7165 Germantown Ave., Germantown. *Philadelphia Magazine* calls this former Woolworth's store "a restaurant and nightspot with good food and even better music." It attracts a wide range of talent that includes everything from local rock and blues bands to national zydeco acts.

Grape Street Philadelphia (215-483-7084), 4100 Grape St., Manayunk. This two-story nightspot dropped "pub" from its name and underwent a renovation in 2001, but it hasn't lost its mellow, neighborhood-bar vibe. The small downstairs stage attracts folk and rock bands. Upstairs, there's hip-hop music and spinning DJs.

THEATER Sedgwick Cultural Center (215-248-9229), 7137 Germantown Ave., Mount Airy. A beautiful 1,600-seat art deco movie theater that is now a showplace for dance, music, and other performing arts.

Stagecrafters (215-247-8881; www.thestagecrafters.org), 8130 Germantown Ave. is an all-volunteer community theater in Chestnut Hill that stages five shows a season.

NIGHTLIFE General Lafayette Inn (610-941-0600), 646 Germantown Pike, Lafayette Hill. It wasn't Washington, for a change, but the famous French general, who may have hung his hat here. Lafayette and his men successfully fought the Battle of Barren Hill nearby and the inn was supposedly used as headquarters by two of his top generals. The 1732 building was spiffed up in 1996 but managed to retain the feeling of an authentic colonial tavern. If the barroom is too smoky for you, have a house-brewed ale and dinner in the wood-beamed dining room. There's live music on weekends, and open-mic nights on Wed. and Thurs.

Manayunk Brewery (215-482-8220), 4120 Main St., Manayunk. This former textile mill packs them in on summer weekends, when the patio overlooking the canal bank offers the best view around. The multi-room interior has live music and DJs on weekends and some weeknights.

Pitchers Pub (215-482-2269), 4328 Main St., Manayunk. This unpretentious bar is where to go if you want to avoid the "scene" at Manayunk Brewery up the street.

✳ Selective Shopping

Chestnut Hill
Caleb Myer Studio (215-248-9250), 8520 Germantown Ave. Everything in this beautiful shop was made by hand—from the delicate gold and silver earrings to the clay serving bowls.

Kilian Hardware (215-248-3733), 8450 Germantown Ave. Besides the usual assortment of tools, garden supplies, and paint, this old-fashioned corner hardware store sells unique gifts like Liberty Bell showerheads and antique telephones from the early 1900s.

Penzey's Spices (215-247-0770), 8528 Germantown Ave. One of two brick-and-mortar stores in the state (the other's in Pittsburgh) from the Wisconsin-based spice empire.

Monkey Business (215-248-1835), 8624 Germantown Ave. You'll find everything from vintage gowns to barely scuffed Manohlo Blahniks in this upscale consignment shop at the north end of Chestnut Hill.

Manayunk
Bias (215-483-8340), 4442 Main St. This very hip clothing boutique changes its look and merchandise each season and is known for feminine frocks by owner Andre Mitchell and other local designers.

Main Street Music (215-487-7732), 4444 Main St. All the genres are represented at this independent and well-stocked music shop. It also has a good used CD section.

Manayunk Design Group (215-483), 4327 Main St. This unique store digs up, spiffs up, and sells artifacts from Philadelphia's past, such as stained glass from 19th-century churches, paintings of local scenes, and carved fireplace mantles. It's a hoot whether you're looking to buy or just browse.

✳ Special Events

May: **Manayunk Bike Race** (third weekend), Manayunk. Officially known as the Philadelphia International Championship, this race goes all over the city, but Manayunk is one of the best places to cheer and serenade the cyclists on as they head up the steep wall on Lyceum Ave.

June: **Manayunk Arts Festival** (third weekend), Manayunk—huge outdoor street festival featuring live music, food by local restaurants, and handmade arts and crafts by more than 250 artists from all over the country.

October: **Battle of Germantown Reenactment** (first weekend), Germantown—live bagpipe music, lectures by historians, and an actual reenactment of the famous Revolutionary battle by more than a thousand costumed volunteers in and around the gates of Cliveden (see *Historic Sites*).

Southeastern
Pennsylvania

THE MAIN LINE

VALLEY FORGE AREA

THE BRANDYWINE VALLEY

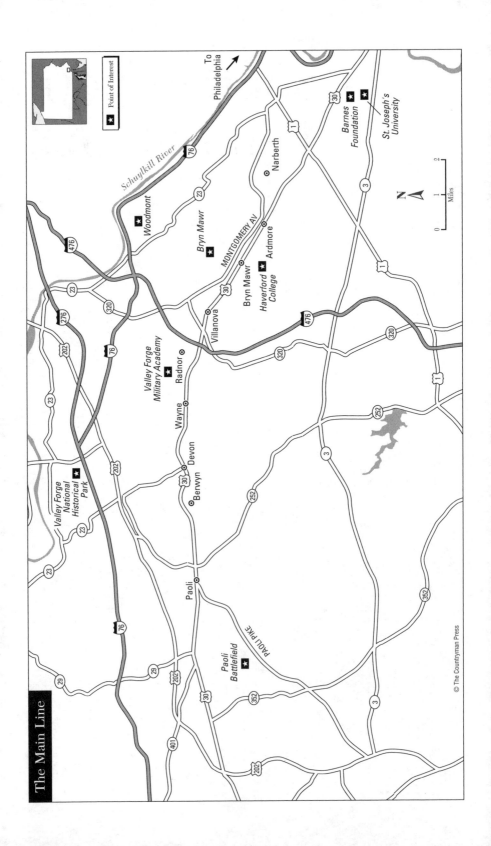

The Main Line

THE MAIN LINE

The Main Line is an affluent western suburb of Philadelphia comprised of a handful of towns along or near US 30 (Lancaster Avenue). There are no skyscrapers or malls or industrial centers; what you'll find are mansions fit for European aristocrats, some of the country's top private colleges, and more families listed on the Social Register than just about anywhere else in the country.

The Main Line takes its name from the local rail line that has run between Center City and Harrisburg and Pittsburgh since the 19th century. Someone came up with the phrase "Old Maids Never Wed and Have Babies, Period" as a way to remember the names of the station stops between Center City and Malvern. They are Overbrook, Merion, Narberth, Wynnewood, Ardmore, Haverford, Bryn Mawr, and Paoli. Bala Cynwyd, Gladwyne, Radnor, Wayne, Villanova, and Malvern are also considered a part or adjacent to the Main Line, and mentioned in this chapter.

Many travel guides and articles mention the Main Line within context of Philadelphia, but it's a destination that increasingly deserves standalone coverage, with stellar shopping and restaurant options and exquisite public gardens. Despite a lingering *Philadelphia Story*–type snobbishness that borders on caricature and golf and cricket clubs that ooze exclusivity, the area offers much to enjoy. Colleges like Villanova and Bryn Mawr have excellent art galleries, gardens, and theaters that are open to the public, and its restaurants and delis are good enough to motivate Philadelphians to abandon the city for an evening or afternoon. Most notably, it has the Barnes Foundation, a large gallery and arboretum in Overbrook with an extraordinary collection of impressionist, post-impressionist, and early modern paintings by Picasso, Matisse, Cézanne, and others. After years of controversy, fund-raising drives, and lawsuits, the foundation announced in 2006 that it was moving ahead with its plan to relocate its collection to a new yet-to-be-built facility on Benjamin Franklin Parkway in Philadelphia, though a move wasn't expected until 2010.

Several towns on the Main Line, including Wayne, Radnor, Devon, and Paoli, are closer to Valley Forge than they are to Bala Cynwyd or Bryn Mawr, but I've included them in this chapter because they are an integral part of the Main Line, and are all located on or near Lancaster Avenue. Some might say the Main Line is more a state of mind than a specific geographic location anyway.

AREA CODE The western Main Line lies within the 610 area code. The eastern edge uses 215.

GUIDANCE While it's several miles from the Main Line, the **Welcome Center at Valley Forge National Historical Park** (610-783-1077; 1400 N. Outer Line Drive), is one of the best sources for brochures and maps of the southeastern Pennsylvania area. For online information, go to www.inwayne.com, an independent Web site with good information on local events, parks, restaurants, and shopping.

GETTING THERE *By car:* US 30 (Lancaster Ave.) cuts an east–west route through the Main Line between Philadelphia and Paoli. From I-76 (the Schuylkill Expressway), exit at City Avenue for the eastern towns of Merion, Bryn Mawr, and Ardmore and follow US 1 to US 30 west. For the western end of the Main Line, take I-76 south to the King of Prussia interchange and follow US 202 south. From the Blue Route (I-476), exit at Villanova.

By air: **Philadelphia International** (215-937-6800) is the closest airport.

By train: **SEPTA's** R5 rail line trains to Paoli/Thorndale (215-580-7800, www .septa.org) run regularly between Center City and the Main Line, with stops in Merion, Ardmore, Bryn Mawr, Villanova, Radnor, Wayne, and other towns. Amtrak trains also run along the same line.

By bus: **SEPTA** bus route 44 to Merion, Ardmore, Narberth, and other Lancaster Avenue towns.

GETTING AROUND You can ride the SEPTA R5 rail line between Merion and Paoli. It's also easy to get around the Main Line by car. Lancaster and Montgomery avenues are major east–west thoroughfares that are often choked with traffic; avoid them during rush hour if possible.

Free trolleys run continuous loops through Ardmore, Haverford, and Bryn Mawr from 5–10 PM on the first Fri. of every month. For more information, visit www.firstfridaymainline.com.

MEDICAL EMERGENCY Bryn Mawr Hospital (610-526-3000), 130 S. Bryn Mawr Ave., Bryn Mawr.

WHEN TO GO Anytime, really. It's quietest on the Main Line in late July and Aug., when most college students are gone and residents have left for the shores.

✳ Villages

Ardmore. Formerly known as Athensville, Ardmore is only three miles from Philadelphia and, like Narberth (see below), tends to be more laid-back than other Main Line towns. It's home to one of the country's first malls, Suburban Square, which was turned into an open-air complex of shops and restaurants in the 1970s. It also has a good farmers market selling everything from sushi and gourmet cheese to Lancaster County produce.

Bryn Mawr. Katharine Hepburn would fit right in dining or shopping in this upscale enclave, where ladies still wear proper suits to lunch. Home to Bryn Mawr College and some of the Philadelphia area's wealthiest citizens, it also has businesses that cater to student budgets and tastes, like pizza joints and The Grog tavern. With its train station, hospital, and proximity to Haverford and other colleges, it is one of the busiest towns along the Main Line; expect grid-lock and allow plenty of time to find street parking.

Gladwyne. Gladwyne still feels like the quiet, walkable country village it was a century ago. Its center at the intersection of Youngs Ford and Righters Mill roads, historically known as Merion Square, includes small shops and single or double houses that were once tenant housing for the laborers or mill workers of nearby Mill Creek Valley. It's home to several parks and historic mansions, including Woodmont Palace.

Narberth is a dinner-and-movie sort of place. Its pretty tree-lined downtown, centered around Narberth and Haverford avenues, has many good restaurants, a historic one-screen movie theater, and hip boutiques and consignment shops that seem to always rate a "Best of Philly" award for something or other.

Merion. Merion is largely a residential neighborhood of expensive old homes, but two reasons to visit are the Barnes Foundation's art collection and Hymie's Deli. St. Joseph's University is just over the town border in Bala Cynwyd.

Wayne. Named after "Mad" Anthony Wayne, a brigadier general known for his insomniac ways, this lively town makes a good base for visiting both the Main Line and nearby Valley Forge, especially if you want a nonchain lodging option. It's home to the handsome Wayne Hotel and lovely Chanticleer "pleasure gar-den." You can easily spend an afternoon shopping and eating in its downtown, which was glammed up in the 1990s and now includes lots of shops selling home furnishings and scented candles.

BRYN MAWR'S ALUMNAE HOUSE

✳ **To See**

MUSEUMS & GALLERIES ↑ **The Barnes Foundation** (610-667-0290; www
.barnesfoundation.org), 300 N. Latches Ln., Merion. Open 9:30–5 Fri.–Sun.;
$10 adults, plus $10 parking. Reservations required; be sure to call at least a
month ahead. Albert Barnes was a local Philadelphian who made a fortune
developing and manufacturing an antiseptic product and used it to amass one of
the grandest and quirkiest art collections in the country. When he retired in the
early 1920s, he devoted the rest of his life to educating the masses about art and
placed his prized pieces in a French Renaissance–style mansion he built at the
north end of the Main Line. Today, the art works are displayed exactly as Mr.
Barnes left them, grouped by common visual elements like brush strokes, rather
than by artist or period. Renoir nudes, Cezanne still-lifes, Matisse murals, more
than 40 works by Picasso, African sculpture and folk art, and Pennsylvania German furniture are some of the treasures you'll find in the rooms of this grand old
mansion. But there is a catch: despite Barnes's wish that his collection remain in
the galleries he built for it, Barnes trustees announced in 2006 that the entire
collection would relocate to new, larger quarters on the Benjamin Franklin Parkway in Philadelphia, with an estimated move-in date of 2010.

Meanwhile, the original building continues to receive up to 1,200 visitors a day.
It's a bit daunting to try to take it in all by yourself. A good investment is the $7
audio-cassette guide or take advantage of the free docent tours that run three
times a day. Either way, plan to spend at least three hours here; there's also a
lovely 12-acre arboretum that surrounds the house and is open to anyone in
good weather.

& ↑ **Cantor-Fitzgerald Gallery** (610-896-1287; www.cantorfitzgeraldgallery
.com), 370 Lancaster Ave, Haverford. Open daily Sep.–May, weekdays June
through Aug.; free. The founder of the Wall Street company helped finance this
sleek gallery space on the campus of Haverford College (in the Whitehead Campus Center). Exhibits change monthly and feature sculpture, photography, print-
making, and other media by professional artists.

& ↑ **Lawrence Art Gallery at Rosemont College** (610-526-2967; www
.rosemont.edu), 1400 Montgomery Ave., Rosemont. Open 9–5 weekdays; free.
Situated against the picturesque backdrop of Rosemont College, this gallery has
quality exhibitions, featuring artists of local and international renown.

GARDENS **Jenkins Arboretum** (610-647-8870, www.jenkinsarboretum.org),
631 Berwyn Baptist Rd., Devon. Open 8–sunset daily. Elisabeth Phillippe Jenkins received part of this natural woodland property as a wedding present from
her father in 1926. Her husband helped turn it into a public arboretum after her
death in 1965. Now 46 acres, it is known for its big-leaved rhododendrons and
evergreen azaleas and usually hits its colorful peak Apr.–June. It has 1.2 miles of
winding paved paths and a 2-acre pond framed by day lilies, wildflowers, and
white pines. You'll come away from here with a newfound appreciation for leaves
and twigs, since gardeners leave them where they fall to act as a sort of natural
mulch.

✈ ♿ ❀ **Chanticleer** (610-687-4163, www.chanticleergarden.org), 786 Church Rd., Wayne. Open Wed.–Sun. Apr. through Oct.; $5 adults. Grounds stay open until 8 on Fri. in the summer. Hip meets elegant at this 35-acre estate and garden tucked into a tony neighborhood south of Lancaster Avenue. To give you a sense of its pedigree, the family residence of Hope Montgomery Scott, the Main Line heiress on whom Katharine Hepburn's character is based in *The Philadelphia Story,* is nearby. Once the estate of pharmaceutical mogul Adolph G. Rosengarten, it is now a pleasure garden with wisteria-draped arbors, a babbling brook, and rolling green hills. In the spring, fields surrounding the main house are awash with 150,000 white and yellow daffodils. There are few signs (plant lists are available in small, whimsical kiosks), and Adirondack chairs and stone couches with cushions are places invitingly around the premises to take advantage of the lovely views. When the horticulturalists aren't tending to the flora and fauna, they are creating furniture, sculptures, and metal bridges for placement around the property. No child, and few adults, will be able to resist rolling down the lush sloping hillside near the main house (it's even encouraged). House tours are given at 11 AM for an additional $5 on Fri.

CHANTICLEER ESTATE AND GARDENS

Haverford College Arboretum (610-896-1101, www.haverford.edu/arboretum), 370 Lancaster Ave., Haverford. Open daily dawn to dusk. Rolling lawns, a 3-acre pond, and hundreds of majestic old trees can be found in this small arboretum on the campus of Haverford College. A 2.2-mile walking and jogging nature trail circles the campus. Maps and self-guided brochures are available at the arboretum office near the main visitors' parking lot.

HISTORIC SITES Woodmont Palace (610-525-5598), 1622 Spring Mill Rd., Gladwyne. Open 1–5 Sunday Apr. through Oct.; free. You've got to see this massive French Gothic–style manor to believe it. Built by a local steel magnate in the 1800s, it's now home to the International Peace Mission Movement, a religious group founded in the early 20th century by an African-American man who renamed himself Father Divine and claimed to be the embodiment of Jesus. His widow, known as Mother Divine, still lives in the manse and allows the public to tour the house or stroll the bucolic grounds one afternoon a week. Tours take about an hour and include a visit to the "Shrine of Life" where Father Divine is buried. Modest dress is required (no shorts or sleeveless shirts).

❧ **Merion Friends Meetinghouse** (610-664-4210), 615 Montgomery Ave., Merion. One of the oldest Quaker meeting houses in America, this 17th-century building counts William Penn among its worshippers. The cherry trees that dot its burying ground have a great backstory: Japanese and American horticulturalists planted them in the early 1900s as a test to ensure that the cherry trees Japan intended to give to Washington, D.C., would survive the climate. They did, and they're still a beautiful sight in the spring. There are worship services on Sun. and rummage sales and art exhibits throughout the year.

Valley Forge Military Academy (610-989-1509), 1001 Eagle Rd., Wayne. This prestigious boarding school, whose graduates include retired army general Norman Schwarzkopf and author J. D. Salinger, played a major role in the 1981 film *Taps* and is home to a Battle of the Bulge monument dedicated to the soldiers who fought in the significant World War II battle. Visitors are welcome to view the monument, located near the parade field next to Eisenhower Hall.

✳ Outdoor Activities

BICYCLING The Radnor Trail is a paved 2.4-mile path with graded shoulders for walkers and horses. It begins at Radnor–Chester Road south of Lancaster Avenue and follows an old railroad line to Sugartown Road. Downloadable maps are available at www.friendsofradnortrails.com. **Bean's Bikes** (610-640-9910), 10 W. Lancaster Ave., Paoli, rents mountain bikes for $25 a day.

HORSEBACK RIDING Greylyn Farm (610-889-3009, www.greylynfarm), Sugartown Rd. and Paoli Pike, Malvern. Private or group instruction in showing horses starting at $35.

✳ Green Space

Saunders Woods (610-520-9197) 1020 Waverly Rd., Gladwyne. Open daily dawn to dusk. A 25-acre nature preserve with hiking and dog-walking trails, open meadows and forested valleys, and good bird-watching opportunities. Pick up a trail map at the information kiosk near the Waverly Road entrance.

ꝏ **The Willows** (610-964-9288), 490 Darby–Paoli Rd., Villanova. Open daily dawn to dusk. Weddings take up much of this grand old estate most weekends, but anyone is welcome to stroll the 47 acres of grounds, which are dotted with stately trees, flowering plants, and a small pond that comes with lots of geese.

✷ Lodging

You'll find many chain hotels in St. Davids, near Radnor, and a few miles away in the King of Prussia area, but there are few independent lodging options on the Main Line.

BED & BREAKFASTS **Tudor House** (610-617-9247, www.tudorhousebandb.com), 207 Bryn Mawr Ave., Bala Cynwyd. You can walk to the Barnes Foundation and St. Joseph's University from this small B&B on the Main Line's northern edge. Retired high-school teacher Len Rosenthal is the innkeeper; he knows the area well and is happy to help with local points of interest. The Carriage House sits apart from the main house and sleeps two; entrance is by spiral staircase and the rate is $140–150 a night. The Loft Room is on the second floor of the main house with a detached private bathroom; it sleeps up to four people and costs $100–140, depending on the number of guests. Both rooms have TVs, refrigerators, and access to a back garden and koi pond. The rate includes a breakfast of cereals, bagels, and fresh fruit.

HOTELS & INNS **Wyndham** (610-526-5236; www.brynmawr.edu/wyndham) 235 N. Merion Ave., Bryn Mawr. Housed in a quaint stone farmhouse that serves as Bryn Mawr's alumnae headquarters, this seven-room inn is one of the best lodging deals you'll find on the Main Line. Rooms are immaculate and decorated in a restrained colonial style; all have private baths and include a continental breakfast. It's within walking distance of the Bryn Mawr train station and many shops and restaurants. Reserve early; the inn often fills up fast with visiting parents and graduates; it closes for a week in Nov., three weeks in Dec., and a couple of weeks in Aug. Rooms $119.

♿ **Wayne Hotel** (610-687-5000; www.waynehotel.com), 139 E. Lancaster Ave.,Wayne. This four-story Tudor Revival building in the center of Wayne's shopping and restaurant district was a retirement home and synagogue before new owners bought it in 1985 and restored it to the handsome inn it was when it opened in 1906. Its 37 rooms and 3 suites have a Victorian feel with comfortable mahogany beds, lace curtains, and flowery wallpaper. It's also home to Taquet, a posh French restaurant (see *Dining Out*). Guests have access to a gym and seasonal swimming pool at the Radnor Hotel a few miles away. Rooms $189–229, includes a light breakfast.

✷ Where to Eat

DINING OUT ♿ 🍸 **333 Belrose** (610-293-1000), 333 Belrose Ave., Wayne. Lunch and dinner Mon.–Fri., dinner Sat. This stylish restaurant has a contemporary American menu that features innovative seafood dishes like

HISTORIC WAYNE HOTEL

salt and pepper calamari, pistachio-crusted trout, and pan-blackened crab cakes. There are good burgers, too, which come with garlic fries and will set you back $11. The bar is often packed during happy hour. Extensive wine list. Lunch $11–17, dinner entrees $24–31.

Margot (610-660-0160), 232 Woodbine Ave., Narberth. Dinner Tues.–Sat. This intimate open-kitchen bistro is off Montgomery Avenue, about a 20-minute drive from Center City. The changing seasonal menu might include warm goat cheese salad, Cuban pulled pork, and sea scallops in a blood-orange glaze. Save room for the chocolate challah-bread pudding. BYO. Entrees $16–28.

& **Taquet** (610-687-5005), 139 E. Lancaster Ave. Lunch and dinner Mon.–Sat. If you'd like to experience the Main Line in all its tweed-jacket and Lilly Pulitzer opulence, this posh French restaurant in the Wayne Hotel is where to go. The contemporary French menu features country duck pate, filet mignon, and seared sea scallops with porcini risotto. Eat on the hotel's grand old front porch,

great for people-watching, or have a seat in the palm-framed dining room. Another option is to sit at the grand mahogany bar and order a martini and something from the less expensive bistro menu. Reservations recommended. Entrees $23–29.

& **Teresa's Café** (610-293-9909), 124 N. Wayne Ave., Wayne. Lunch and dinner Mon.–Fri., dinner Sat. and Sun. This popular neighborhood bistro just off Lancaster Avenue serves gourmet pizzas, pastas, and Italian entrees like veal medallions in a lemon caper wine sauce and mushroom risotto. You can't go wrong with anything made with the housemade pesto. The restaurant serves wine, but you can also bring your own. Lunch $6–13; dinner entrees: $15–26.

& **Wyndham** (610-526-5236, www.brynmawr.edu/wyndham), 235 N. Merion Ave., Bryn Mawr. Lunch Mon.–Fri. Closed July and Aug., and the last week of Dec. This small restaurant at the alumnae house of Bryn Mawr College exudes a "Ladies Who Lunch" vibe, but it's open to anyone and well worth a visit if you're in the area. The buffet is a great value at $13 and includes a choice of soups, salads, and changing entrees such as coconut curry chicken and beef bourguignon. There are also a la carte dishes like pecan-crusted chicken and hot roast beef. Try to get a table on the covered patio overlooking the lawn. You may bring your own wine for a small fee. Dishes $8–14.

EATING OUT & **Hymie's Merion Deli** (610-554-3544), 342 Montgomery Ave., Merion. Breakfast, lunch, and dinner daily. You won't find much in the way of decor at this always-busy spot along a busy stretch of Montgomery Avenue, but you won't care once the food arrives. As much a diner as a deli, it serves amazing matzo ball soup, thin-sliced pastrami sandwiches with homemade coleslaw, and other deli staples. Stop here for a late lunch after a trip to the nearby Barnes Foundation. Expect a wait on weekends. Dishes $4–10.

Landis Catering (610-688-9999), 118 W. Lancaster Ave., Wayne. Lunch Mon.–Sat. Excellent fresh-made Italian hoagies. Sandwiches $5–8.

& **Minella's Diner** (610-687-1575), 320 W. Lancaster Ave., Wayne. A popular 24-hour diner that serves breakfast all day and night. The huge menu includes everything you'd expect from a good diner: eggs every way, pancakes, burgers, salads, fried flounder, moussaka, and more. Breakfast $5–8; lunch and dinner $10–29.

BAKERIES & FARM MARKETS &
Hope's Cookies (215-660-9607), 916 Montgomery Ave., Narberth (other locations in Wayne, Rosemont, and King of Prussia). This small local chain sticks to what it knows best—cookies. Try the caramel pecan or chocolate raspberry.

& **Ardmore Farmers Market** (610-896-7560), Anderson and Coulter aves., Ardmore. Closed Mon. and Tues. This popular market in Suburban Square moved to a spiffy new spot in 2000 and now includes indoor and outdoor dining areas and 20 vendors selling everything from hoagies and sushi to artisanal cheeses to African spices.

Lancaster County Farmers Market (610-688-9856), 289 W. Lancaster Ave., Wayne. Open 6–4 Wed., Fri., and Sat. If you can't make it to Amish country, this large indoor market is

the next best thing. It has more than a dozen stalls selling hand-rolled pretzels, fresh turkeys, wood-smoked hams, silk flower arrangements, and all kinds of seasonal produce. I've also found some unusual pottery and linen gifts here.

BYO Where to buy wine on the Main Line:

You'll find **Wine & Spirits stores** in Bryn Mawr at 922 W. Lancaster Ave. (610-581-4560); in Wayne at 161 E. Swedesford Rd. (610-964-6724); and in the Ardmore Plaza Shopping Center at 56 Greenfield Ave. (610-645-5010).

✳ Entertainment

MOVIES Narberth Theater (610-667-0115), 129 N. Narberth Ave., Narberth. This classic art deco theater has added an additional screen and stadium seating and shows first-run films.

Anthony Wayne Theater (610-225-0980) 109 W. Lancaster Ave., Wayne. Another old theater divided into four screens showing first-run films. It's within walking distance of many shops and restaurants.

Bryn Mawr Film Institute (610-527-9898), 824 W. Lancaster Ave., Bryn Mawr. This restored 1926 movie palace shows independent, documentary, art, and repertory films.

THEATER & **People's Light and Theater Company** (610-644-3500, www.peopleslight.org), 39 Conestoga Rd., Malvern. This venerable theater group produces eight or nine plays per season, mixing world premieres, contemporary plays, and new approaches to classic texts like *Anne of Green*

Gables. The main stage is in a beautifully restored 18th-century barn.

&. **Villanova Theater** (610-519-7474, www.theatre.villanova.edu), Lancaster and Ithan aves., Villanova. Villanova University's well-regarded theater department stages four shows a year, ranging from classic and contemporary plays to musicals.

NIGHTLIFE Main Line nightlife tends to cater to cash-strapped college students. You'll find plenty of beer and pool halls with happy hour deals.

The Grog (610-527-5870), 863 W. Lancaster Ave., Bryn Mawr. This hangout for students from Bryn Mawr, Haverford, and Villanova is an amiable place to relax with a beer and a few friends. Families populate the upstairs nonsmoking dining room in the early evening.

John Harvard's Brew House (610-687-6565) 629 W. Lancaster Ave., Wayne. Part of an East Coast chain of brewpubs, this is a popular after-work and late-night watering hole for Main Line professionals and college students. The beer selection and boisterous ambiance outshine the food.

McShea's (610-667-0510), 242 Haverford Ave., Narberth. A friendly neighborhood pub with a large beer selection and a variety of nightly entertainment, including DJs, open mike nights, and beer pong games.

Rusty Nail (610-649-6245), 2580 Haverford Rd., Ardmore. Specializes in live original music from local bands. There's also satellite TV, pool tables, and a late-night pub menu.

✳ Selective Shopping

Bryn Mawr Hospital Thrift Shop (610-525-4888), 801 County Line Rd, Bryn Mawr. Closed Sun. No thrift-store junkie should miss this sprawling shop stocked with hand-me-downs from some of the area's richest neighborhoods. The main store sells furniture, jewelry, bric-a-brac, and women's clothing on three floors. Across the street are small shops for men's and children's clothing.

Earthworks (610-667-1143), 233 Haverford Ave, Narberth. Closed Sun. and Mon. A fun-to-browse gallery in Narberth's downtown selling handcrafted ceramics, glass, and other high-end gifts.

Ardmore

&. **Suburban Square**, Anderson and Coulter aves., Ardmore. Most of the stores and restaurants in this outdoor mall off Montgomery Avenue are chains (Talbots, Gap, Corner Bakery), but it's an attractive setting for shopping or browsing.

Junior League Thrift Shop (610-896-8828), 25 W. Lancaster Ave. Closed Sun. Frequently named by local papers as the best thrift store on the Main Line, this well-maintained store sells furniture, designer clothing, jewelry, toys, and books.

Wayne

Readers' Forum (610-254-9040), 116 N. Wayne Ave., Wayne. Pleasantly cluttered used bookstore in downtown Wayne with a wide selection and reasonable prices.

&. **Spread Eagle Village** (610-293-2012), Lancaster Ave. and Eagle Rd. A small complex of upscale independent shops, many specializing in home furnishings or women's clothing. It's east of downtown with a large parking lot.

uBead2 (610-688-8842), 105 W. Lancaster Ave. Closed Sun. A very cool neighborhood shop selling beads in all shapes, colors, and sizes. Buy your beads to go or design a piece and assemble it at one of the worktables. Bead soirees and workshops are held regularly.

✳ Special Events

May: **Devon Horse Show** (last weekend and first weekend of June), Horse Show Grounds, Devon—the oldest and largest annual outdoor horse competition in the U.S. features more than 1,200 horses competing for prizes and a county fair with Ferris wheel rides, equestrian-themed crafts, and cotton candy.

June: **Main Line Jazz and Food Festival** (first weekend), Wayne—showcases some of the finest jazz performers in Philly, plus signature dishes from more than 20 Main Line restaurants. Visit www.mainlinejazz .com for information.

VALLEY FORGE AREA

About 20 miles outside Philadelphia, Valley Forge is an unincorporated part of Chester County that is best known for lending its name to the encampment of George Washington's Continental army during the winter of 1777–78. Its 3,600-acre national historic park is undoubtedly the area's most famous attraction, though the nearby King of Prussia Court and Plaza, which claims to be the country's largest shopping mall, draws the most visitors and groupies each year (a whopping 18 million).

King of Prussia takes its name from a local 18th-century tavern called the King of Prussia Inn, which was named for the Prussian king Frederick II, possibly due to his support of George Washington during the American Revolution (another educated guess is the name was a way of attracting the German soldiers who were fighting nearby alongside the Americans). The tavern long ceased operating (it was moved from its original location in 2002 and is now home to the Chamber of Commerce), replaced by rampant commercial and residential development that grew up around the mall.

The Valley Forge area is close enough to Philadelphia to make it a reasonable day trip, but it has enough lodging, eating, and recreational options to spend a night or two. The King of Prussia Court and Plaza are cities unto themselves with hundreds of upscale stores and restaurants. Two of the Philadelphia area's most popular jogging and biking trails, the Perkiomen and Schuylkill River, converge here. And a couple of villages within easy reach of Valley Forge, Skippack and Phoenixville, offer quaint small-town shopping and dining alternatives to your visit. It's also an easy drive to the attractions of the Main Line and Brandywine Valley.

AREA CODE The Valley Forge area lies within the 610 and 484 area codes.

GUIDANCE The **Welcome Center at Valley Forge National Historical Park** (610-783-1077; 1400 N. Outer Line Dr.) has maps and brochures on the park itself and the entire southeastern Pennsylvania area, as well as computer kiosks that let you search for nearby restaurants, attractions, and hotels. For online information and maps, check out the **Valley Forge Convention and Visitors Bureau's** site: www.valleyforge.org.

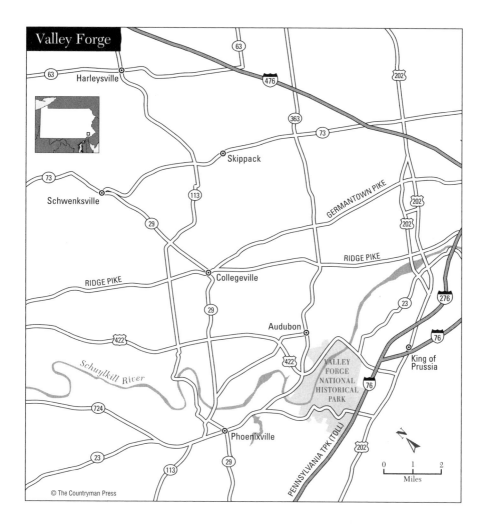

GETTING THERE *By air:* **Philadelphia International** (215-937-6800) is the closest airport.

By car: King of Prussia and nearby Valley Forge sit at a critical junction where US 202 and 422, the Schuylkill Expressway (I-76), and the Pennsylvania Turnpike (I-476) converge. From Philadelphia, take I-76 west to US 422 west and follow signs for Valley Forge. From the Pennsylvania Turnpike, take exit 326 at Valley Forge and follow signs for N. Gulph Road.

By bus: **Capitol Trailways** (800-721-2828) buses run four times a day between King of Prussia and Philadelphia's Greyhound terminal. They stop about 2 miles from the mall and 5 miles from Valley Forge at 234 E. DeKalb Pike (US 202). Buses also run regularly between King of Prussia and York, Harrisburg, and Lancaster.

GETTING AROUND Valley Forge National Historical Park and King of Prussia are within five minutes of each other by car. Phoenixville's main street is perfect for strolling, but you'll need a car to get to other towns and attractions.

MEDICAL EMERGENCY Montgomery Hospital (610-270-2000), 1301 Powell St., Norristown.

WHEN TO GO Spring and fall are good times to visit Valley Forge National Historical Park; there are fewer crowds than in the summer, and its hills and meadows are ablaze with orange and yellow foliage in the fall and tall grass and wildflowers in the spring. The shops and restaurants of King of Prussia, Skippack, and Phoenixville thrive year-round.

✳ Villages

Phoenixville. This small town on the northwest edge of Valley Forge underwent a transformation in recent years from blue-collar steel town to edgy urban neighborhood. Bridge Street, its main thoroughfare, is (so far, at least) a happy coexistence of art galleries, BYO bistros, old-time barber shops, and faded diners. Anchoring the downtown area is the restored Colonial Theater, famous for its role in the sci-fi film *The Blob*.

DOWNTOWN PHOENIXVILLE

Skippack. Once a stop on a 1900s rural trolley route, Skippack added village to its name in the 1990s, opened some antique shops and nice restaurants, and waited for the people to come. They did, and now it is the area's version of Peddler's Village (see *Central Bucks County*) and rarely described without the adjective quaint. It is a nice shopping alternative for those who aren't in the mood for the crowds and choices of the King of Prussia mall. Its main street, however, is busy Skippack Pike and lacks sidewalks, which makes it less pedestrian-friendly than you might expect.

✳ To See

HISTORIC SITES John James Audubon Center at Mill Grove (610-666-5593), 1201 Pawlings Rd., Audubon. Closed Mon. Self-guided house tours $6 adults. Audubon lived in this rambling stone farmhouse when he first moved to America from

JOHN AUDUBON'S HOME AT MILL GROVE

Europe in the early 1800s; it was here that he started studying and painting the birds that would shape his career. Mill Grove attracts a fraction of the traffic that nearby Valley Forge National Historical Park does, but it's worth an hour-long stop, even if you don't want to take the house tour. Situated on a hill with an inviting back porch overlooking Perkiomen Creek, it is filled with original paintings and books by Audubon, including a complete four-volume set of *The Birds of America*, Audubon's famous portrayal of nearly five hundred distinct species of birds. Picnic areas and 5 miles of hiking trails surround the house.

Paoli Battlefield (no phone, www.ushistory.org/paoli) Wayne and Monument aves., Malvern. Open daily mid-May through mid-Oct., weekends Nov.–Apr. During the night of September 20, 1777, the British launched a surprise attack against General Anthony Wayne's troops that is now known as the Paoli Massacre. Using bayonets and swords, they killed between 50 and 100 men and wounded about 150 more. The battlefield is surrounded by development, but has been preserved in its original form as woodland and farm fields. There is no visitor center, but an easy half-mile walking trail leads you past interpretative signs and significant sites.

✦ **Peter Wentz Farmstead** (610-584-5104), Shearer Rd., off PA 73, Worcester. Open 10–4 Tues.–Sat., 1–4 Sun.; free. George Washington stayed on this Pennsylvania German farm twice in 1777, before and after the Battle of Germantown. Tours include a glimpse at the room in which he was believed to have slept. Front desk service can be laid back, but it's worth a brief stop if you're looking for a dose of history after a morning of shopping and eating in nearby Skippack.

MUSEUMS ✦ **Wharton Esherick Museum** (610-644-5822), 1520 Horseshoe Trail Rd., Malvern. Open Mar. through Dec.; one-hour tours on weekends; group tours weekdays; $9 adults, $4 ages 12 and under. You'll never look at a

Valley Forge National Historical Park (610-783-1077; www.nps.gov/vafo), 1400 N. Outer Line Dr., Valley Forge. Welcome center open 9–5 daily, until 6 in summer) Grounds open year-round 6 AM–10 PM. No battles were fought here, but this 3,600-acre property is considered a critical turning point of the Revolutionary War. It's where George Washington chose to settle his weary and ill-equipped army for the winter of 1777–78. Despite the fact that as many as 2,000 Continental soldiers (out of a total 12,000) died of hunger, disease, and frostbite while here, it's also where Washington, with the help of Prussian drill master Friedrich von Steuben, eventually shaped his beleaguered army into a force to be reckoned with that would go on to defeat the British. Today the area is marked by rolling hills and woodlands, earthen forts, reconstructed log cabins, towering war memorials, and miles of hiking and biking trails.

Begin your visit at the welcome center, where you can catch a short film and talk to Park Service staffers about what's going on that day. The whole park and its highlights can be covered in a couple of hours by car (self-guided driving tours are available here), or you may opt to take one of the two free 40-minute walking tours offered daily at 11:50 and 1:50. In 2007, the park added three storytelling benches, open-air trolley tours, and after-hours picnics with actors playing George and Martha Washington and Continental soldiers. Call the welcome center for specific times and days.

Another option is to proceed independently and leave your car at the piece of timber the same again after visiting the studio and home of one of America's greatest and perhaps least appreciated woodworkers. Wharton Esherick was a Philadelphia-born artist who turned his attention to woodcraft after failing at a string of illustrating jobs. Lucky us. His stone and wood home and studio, just as he left it since his death in 1970, is located along a crest overlooking Valley Forge and is a hobbitlike wonderland of irregular plank floors, dropleaf oak desks, sculptures, and hand-carved coat hooks. Three of the four levels are connected by a stunning spiral staircase made from massive pieces of red oak.

& ⑂ **Philip and Muriel Berman Museum of Art** (610-409-3500; www.ursinus .edu/berman), 601 E. Main St., Collegeville. Closed Mon.; free. This gem of a small art museum on the campus of Ursinus College features paintings and prints by Charles Willson Peale, Walter Baum, Andy Warhol, Roy Lichtenstein, and Susan Rothenberg; Japanese block prints; and Pennsylvania German artifacts such as almanacs, pottery, and quilts. An impressive collection of more than 40 outdoor sculptures peppers the campus.

Washington Memorial Chapel on the north side of the park. The chapel itself, built in 1917 and home to an active Episcopalian church, is worth a stop for its soaring stained glass windows and hand-carved choir stalls. It also features a carillon of 58 bells that represent the U.S. states and territories (concerts are held every Sunday and weekday evenings during summer) and the Justice Bell, a replica of the Liberty Bell that was used to promote the women's suffrage movement in the early 1900s.

Behind the chapel is a tiny used book shop and a gift and snack shop that sells homemade soup, sandwiches, and shoofly pie for reasonable prices. From here you can pick up the main park trail for a short hike to the fields where Washington trained his army, and the Isaac Potts house (see below), one of the park's top attractions.

The area around the Isaac Potts house, which served as Washington's headquarters during that fateful winter, underwent a large renovation in 2007 that included restoring a 1911 train station near the house and adding exhibits aimed at better capturing the misery and pressure that permeated the encampment and Washington's state of mind, according to park officials.

With nearly 30 miles of moderate trails, Valley Forge is also a haven for bicyclists, equestrians, and walkers. On spring and summer evenings, the 5-mile Multi-Use Trail, which begins on Outer Line Drive near the welcome center and passes rows of log cabins, the National Memorial Arch, and the chapel, is filled with exercise hounds. The Web site (see facing page) has good downloadable trail maps.

✳ Outdoor Activities

BICYCLING/RENTALS The Schuylkill River Trail follows the river 25 miles west from Philadelphia's Fairmount Park, crosses through Valley Forge, and ends at Lower Perkiomen Valley Park, where it links with the 19-mile Perkiomen Trail, which continues west through the towns of Collegeville, Schwenksville, and Green Lane. Several bike shops near the route rent bikes and can offer guidance, including **Bikesport** (610-489-7300, 325 W. Main St., Trappe) and **Indian Valley BikeWorks** (215-513-7550, 500 Main St., Harleysville).

Valley Forge National Historical Park has several miles of moderate bike trails. City bikes for kids and adults are available for rent in the lower parking area of the welcome center and the **Betzwood Picnic Area** (610-783-4593).

FISHING The lower half of Little Valley Creek near Washington's headquarters at Valley Forge National Historical Park is stocked with brown trout and popular for fly-fishing, though all caught fish must be released back into the creek.

Skippack Creek is stocked with brown and rainbow trout Mar. through Memorial Day and warm-water fish such as smallmouth bass, catfish, and eel throughout the year. An accessible fishing dock is on Lewis Road in Evansburg State Park (see *Green Space*).

GOLF **Jeffersonville Golf Course** (610-539-0472), 2400 W. Main St., Jeffersonville. A well-maintained 18-hole, par-72 municipal course designed by architect Donald J. Ross. **Pickering Valley Golf Club** (610-933-2223), 450 S. White Horse Rd., Phoenixville. A no-frills yet challenging 18-hole course featuring 6,572 yards of golf from the longest tees with a par of 72.

HORSEBACK RIDING **Red Buffalo Ranch** (610-489-9707), 1093 Anders Rd., Collegeville. Leads one- to four-hour guided trail rides through adjacent Evansburg State Park (see also *Green Space*). They also give lessons to all levels of riders. Rates start at $35.

✴ Green Space

PARKS **Evansburg State Park** (610-409-1150), 851 Mayhall Rd., Collegeville. These 3,300 acres of woodlands and meadows were first settled by Mennonite farmers; remnants of water mills can still be found along the creek that runs through the property. You'll also find four baseball fields, dozens of picnic tables, fishing and hunting options, a golf course, and 26 miles of hiking, biking, and equestrian trails. The visitor center, in an early 18th-century Mennonite farmhouse, is a great place for bird watching.

Lower Perkiomen Valley Park (610-666-5371), 101 New Mill Rd., Oaks. The Perkiomen and Schuylkill River trails intersect in this landscaped 107-acre park near the John James Audubon Center at Mill Grove (See also *To See*). Besides hiking and biking trails, it also has a kids' playground, picnic areas, and basketball courts. Fishing is allowed in Perkiomen Creek.

✴ Lodging

Just about every chain hotel you can think of can be found near the mall in King of Prussia, but the area also has several well-regarded B&Bs and inns.

HOTELS ♿ **Hotel Fiesole** (610-222-8009; www.hotelfiesole.net), 2046 Skippack Pike, Skippack. This attractive 16-room luxury inn opened in 2006 as Skippack's only upscale lodging option. Located along its thriving main street, it was once a popular restaurant known as the Trolley Stop. All that's left is the original trolley that now serves as a dining room for one of the hotel's three restaurants. Its rates are on the high side for this area, but the luxury level is high: rooms are large and have marble baths, flat-screen televisions, and sitting areas. Try to get one facing Perkiomen Creek. Rooms $179–375, includes continental breakfast.

BED & BREAKFASTS **General Warren Inne** (610-296-3637; www.generalwarren.com), Old Lancaster Hwy., Malvern. This historic inn off

US 202 was a popular stage stop and Tory stronghold during the American Revolution. It has eight comfortable colonial-style suites with sitting areas, private baths, and TVs. There's a well-regarded restaurant and tavern on the ground floor (see also *Dining Out*). No children or pets. Suites $120–170, including a light breakfast.

Great Valley House (610-644-6759, www.greatvalleyhouse.com), 1475 Swedesford Rd., Valley Forge. Also near US 202 and a mile from Valley Forge Park, this 17th-century stone farmhouse has three guest rooms, each with quaint Victorian touches like clawfoot bathtubs and canopy beds as well as TVs, refrigerators, and wireless Internet access. The down-stairs common areas are filled with owner Pattye Benson's collections of antique dolls, quilts, and vintage clothes from the late 1800s. Breakfast is served in the pre-Revolutionary kitchen in front of a walk-in stone fireplace. The 4 acres of grounds are a nice touch, and the tree-fringed swimming pool makes you feel like you are lounging at a friend's home. Rooms $99–125, two-night minimum on weekends with some exceptions.

Morning Star Bed and Breakfast (610-935-3289; www.morningstar bandb.net), 610 Valley Forge Rd., Phoenixville. You'll share common areas with owner Rebekah Ray, her husband and teenage daughter, city folk (a.k.a. Philadelphians) who bought this rambling 19th century house about 3 miles from Valley Forge Park in 2004. The four rooms are large and attractive with queen beds (two of them have private baths), and there's a pool table in the living room and fabulous old wood-work everywhere. Ray will tailor

breakfast accordingly to guests with allergies or on special diets. Rooms start at $105, or you can reserve two rooms with a shared bath for $150.

MOTELS ✿ ⬥ **French Creek Inn** (610-935-3838, www.frenchcreekinn .com), 2 Ridge Rd., near PA 23 and 724, Phoenixville. A good option for budget travelers, this family-owned motel has 22 large, sparsely furnished rooms with refrigerators, microwaves, and TVs. It's 5 miles to Valley Forge and 2 miles to Phoenixville's Main Street. Rooms $70.

✳ Where to Eat

King of Prussia has plenty of popular chain restaurants from Maggiano's Little Italy to Outback Steakhouse. You'll find the best independent options in the towns of Skippack, Malvern, and Phoenixville.

DINING OUT ⬥ ⅄ **General Warren Inne** (610-296-3637), Old Lancaster Hwy., Malvern. This restaurant on the ground floor of a B&B (see *Lodging*) offers old-school dishes like beef Wellington, chateaubriand for two, Caesar salad, and Long Island duck breast in two colonial-style dining rooms. Desserts are decadent; try the champagne mascarpone or chocolate peanut butter roulade. The adjacent tavern has a full bar, tasty appetizers, and live oldies and top-40 music on Thurs. nights. Entrees $25–34.

Phoenixville
⬥ ⅄ **Black Lab Bistro** (610-935-5988), 248 Bridge St., Phoenixville. Lunch Tues.–Fri., dinner Tues.–Sun. The food is consistently fab-ulous at this upscale bistro near the Colonial Theatre. The dinner menu might feature braised short ribs,

artichoke-crusted salmon, and pep-per-seared ostrich filet. For lunch, there's butternut squash gnocchi, a lump crab omelet, and tasty sand-wiches. BYO. No reservations are taken Fri. and Sat. Lunch $8–15, din-ner entrees $18–32.

Skippack
&. ⅋ **Mistral** (610-222-8009), 2046 Skippack Pike. Dinner daily, Sun. brunch. This special-occasion restau-rant in the Hotel Fiesole opened in late 2006. The main dining room is elegant and inviting with a stained-glass ceiling, white tablecloths, and a large fireplace. The northern Italian menu features a wide range of pastas, seafood, and meats, including braised rabbit, buffalo, and free-range chicken. A less-expensive and abbreviated menu is available at the more casual Bella Rossa downstairs. Entrees $26–42.

&. ⅋ **Roadhouse Grille** (610-584-4231), 4022 Skippack Pike. Lunch and dinner daily, Sun. brunch. Lo-cated in a renovated 18th-century home, this handsome restaurant is a local favorite for steaks and seafood. Portions are huge. Lunchtime brings a large business crowd, and the prices reflect it. Reservations recommended. Leave time for a cocktail at the long mahogany bar. Lunch $11–15. Dinner entrees: $21–32.

EATING OUT Appetites Delight (610-688-2129), US 202 and PA 252 (in the Gateway Shopping Center). Lunch daily. Stop by this casual deli on the way to Valley Forge Park for a picnic lunch of hoagies or cheeses-teaks. The milkshakes are awesome. Sandwiches $6–8.

Phoenixville
🐾 **Irish Joe's Café** (610-935-3625),

180 Bridge St. Breakfast and lunch Tues.–Fri., breakfast Sat. and Sun. This everybody-knows-your-name diner was here long before gentrification set in and still has the low prices to prove it; it's known for its ample portions (try the Western omelet) and brick-size portions of scrapple. Dishes $2–7.

Steel City Coffee House (610-933-4043, www.steelcitycoffeehouse.com), 203 Bridge St., Phoenixville. Open daily. Everything you'd want in an independent coffeehouse: a loftlike space, four different special roasts on tap at any given time, and a wide selection of panini, salads, and scones. (See also *Entertainment*.)

✳ Entertainment

MUSIC Steel City Coffee House (610-933-4043, www.steelcity coffeehouse.com), 203 Bridge St., Phoenixville. This hip cafe turns into a happening place to hear live music on Fri. and Sat. nights. There is a BYO policy during live-music events.

MOVIES & THEATER &. **Colonial Theatre** (610-917-1228, www.the colonialtheatre.com), 227 Bridge St., Phoenixville. A 1903 theater that was the site of the Blob's last supper in the 1958 sci-fi film starring Steve McQueen. It was restored by a non-profit group in the 1990s and now shows art and independent films and children's classics. Every July, the the-ater celebrates its 15 of minutes of fame with a Blobfest (see *Special Events*).

Forge Theatre (610-935-1920), 241 First Ave., Phoenixville. Located in a former funeral home, this company has been staging Broadway and off-Broad-way shows for more than 45 years. Ticket prices are absurdly reasonable.

✳ Selective Shopping

Skippack Pike in Skippack is lined with quaint clothing boutiques, antiques dealers, and home decor shops. Phoenixville's Main Street has hip art galleries and independent shops selling soy candles, incense, books, unusual crafts, and vintage clothes.

&. **King of Prussia Court and Plaza** (610-265-5727; www.kingofprussia mall.com) 160 N. Gulph Rd., King of Prussia. When I was a kid, my friends and I would brag to out-of-towners that this sprawling shopping complex was the biggest mall in the world. Not quite, but it comes awfully close—with a square footage equaling two Louisiana Superdomes and enough marble flooring to cover the entire flight deck of an aircraft carrier. The Plaza was refashioned in the 1990s to better match the swankier Court across the parking lot. Today, the two malls are linked by a pedestrian walkway and have more than four hundred shops and restaurants, including Bloomingdale's, Nordstrom, Versace, Cartier, Hugo Boss, Old Navy, Sephora, and Urban Outfitters. An estimated 25 percent of its visitors are tourists. Serious shoppers could easily spend an entire weekend here.

✳ Special Events

July: **Blobfest** (second weekend), Bridge St., Phoenixville—this small town celebrates its prominent role in the 1958 film with a two-day festival of *Blob* screenings, scene reenactments, a tinfoil hat contest, and a street festival.

December: **March-in of the Continental Army** (second or third weekend), Valley Forge National Historical Park. Costumed soldiers reenact the Continental army's arrival in Valley Forge, followed by musket and artillery demonstrations. In mid-June, there's a similar march-out event marking the army's departure.

THE BRANDYWINE VALLEY

An easy drive from Philadelphia and Baltimore via I-95, the Brandywine Valley follows the Brandywine River from southeastern Pennsylvania into northern Delaware. Featuring dozens of excellent restaurants and some of the states' best B&Bs, it's a popular weekend getaway for Philadelphians and Washingtonians, though one could easily spend a week here and find plenty to do and see. This is where the Battle of Brandywine Creek was fought and a young French soldier named Lafayette made his auspicious military debut. It's where the du Pont family made its fortunes and built the extraordinary mansions and gardens that now draw millions of visitors. It's where N. C. Wyeth, one of America's top illustrators, got his start as an artist at Howard Pyle's Brandywine School of Illustration, and where his eccentric son Andrew and grandson Jamie, who now live in Maine, took inspiration for their own acclaimed landscape and portrait paintings.

The Brandywine Valley was an important paper-milling center in the 18th century, supplying paper to Ben Franklin's print shop in Philadelphia and throughout the colonies. William Penn's influence was prominent and can still be seen today in the many Quaker meetinghouses that dot the valley.

Today, US 1 and US 202 are two main routes that cut through the heart of the Brandywine Valley, each with its share of strip malls and chain hotels. But turn off these thoroughfares and you'll soon find yourself surrounded by rolling farmland, old gristmills, antiques shops, and even a glass-blower's studio. Closer to the Maryland border west of Kennett Square is mushroom country, where nearly half of the country's mushrooms originate from greenhouses and special buildings that once grew carnations. The industry has seen its share of labor conflicts and residential complaints over the years, but the town vigorously celebrates its heritage each year with a big street party.

While the Brandywine Valley tends to be geared toward grownup getaways, it has its share of kid-friendly places, such as Linvilla Orchards, Jimmy John's hot dogs, and children's gardens at Winterthur and Longwood.

GUIDANCE You'll find maps, history exhibits, and information on Philadelphia and surrounding areas at the **Chester County Visitors Center** (610-388-2900, www.brandywinevalley.com), Kennett Square. It's just outside the gates of Long-

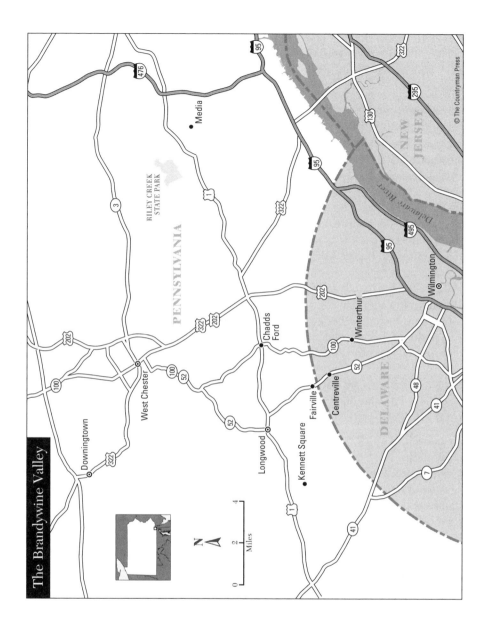

The Brandywine Valley

wood Gardens in a Quaker meeting house that once served as a stop on the Underground Railroad. In Chadds Ford just south of US 1, the **Brandywine Conference and Visitors Bureau** (610-565-3679, www.brandywinecvb.org) has maps and brochures of Delaware County and other attractions and a helpful staff. In Delaware, the **Greater Wilmington Convention and Visitors Bureau** has two offices, downtown at 100 W. 10th St., and in the Delaware Travel Plaza along I-95.

GETTING THERE *By air:* The center of the Brandywine Valley is about a 20- to 30-minute drive from **Philadelphia International Airport** (215-937-6800) via I-95. **Baltimore-Washington International Airport** is about 100 miles away, also via I-95.

By car: I-95, via Philadelphia or Delaware, cuts to the west of the Brandywine; US 202 between West Chester and the Maryland border cuts right through it.

By train: The R3 line of the **Southeastern Pennsylvania Transportation Authority**, or SEPTA, (215-580-7800, www.septa.org) runs regularly between Philadelphia's 30th Street Station and Media.

GETTING AROUND The easiest way to navigate the Brandywine Valley is by car. Try to avoid US 1 and US 202 during rush hour; both are popular truck routes that connect to I-95. US 30, which runs east–west above West Chester, is also a main route into Philadelphia and is best avoided at rush hour.

WHEN TO GO The fall and Christmas seasons are particularly attractive in the Brandywine Valley. Unlike some areas of eastern Pennsylvania, many of its attractions, including Longwood Gardens and Winterthur, stay open year-round. Jan. and Feb. bring a melancholy (but no less beautiful) starkness to the area and mean fewer crowds and lines.

MEDICAL EMERGENCY **Riddle Memorial Hospital** (610-566-9400), 1068 W. Baltimore Pike, Media. Farther west along US 1 is **Jennersville Regional Hospital** (610-869-1000), 1015 W. Baltimore Pike, West Grove.

✳ Towns & Villages

Centreville, Delaware. This small village is at the center of hunt country, between Longwood Gardens and Winterthur on PA 52. Named after the nearby Quaker Friends Center Meeting House around 1750, it was a popular spot for Chester County farmers and cattle ranchers to stop on their way to market at the river port of Wilmington, Delaware. It has several antiques shops, galleries, and cafés, including a favorite local watering hole, Buckley's Tavern.

Chadds Ford takes its name from a small stretch of the Brandywine Creek that was once forded by travelers and John Chads, who started a ferry business nearby to carry passengers when conditions were rough. US 1 passes right through town, making it a popular base for visiting the entire valley. It's home to the Brandywine Battlefield, the Brandywine River Museum, and many antiques shops and B&Bs.

Kennett Square. This hamlet at the west end of the Brandywine Valley calls itself "the mushroom capital of the world." Its pretty downtown includes many mom-and-pop shops and restaurants and is surrounded by rural B&Bs and farms that produce nearly half of the country's mushroom supply.

Media. The county seat of Delaware County, Media has a population of about six thousand and an attractive main street with good restaurants, shops, an arts theater, Trader Joe's, and a small veterans' museum. It's on the eastern edge of the Brandywine Valley and is connected to the Upper Darby section of Philadelphia by the 101 trolley, which runs down the middle of its main street.

West Chester. A settlement since 1692, this historic town of about 18,000 people has served as the Chester county seat since 1786. It is one of the largest towns in the Brandywine Valley and offers the widest options for dining, nightlife, and shopping. US 30 and 202 are busy thoroughfares that cross through or near the center, but it maintains an attractive and walkable downtown with shops, small cafés, and preserved Victorian homes. It is also home to a 130-year-old state college and the QVC shopping network.

KENNETT SQUARE

✳ To See

HISTORIC SITES ♿ **Brandywine Battlefield State Historic Park** (610-459-3342, www.ushistory.org/ brandywine) US 1 (east of Chadds Ford). Open Tues.–Sun., Mar. through Nov. and Thurs.–Sun., Dec.–Feb. The largest single-day battle of the Revolutionary War took place here on September 11, 1777, marking the first military action for a certain young Frenchman, the Marquis de Lafayette. Today, what's left of the battlefield is surrounded by residential homes and traffic-heavy US 1, but you can still get a sense for what colonial-era life was like. Watch a 20-minute video in the visitor center, then take a tour of the two modest farmhouses that served as headquarters for Washington and Lafayette. Tours are $5 for adults, but anyone may wander the 50 acres of rolling tree-dotted grounds. Every Sept., the park hosts a reenactment of the battle.

Chester Courthouse (610-872-0502), 412 Avenue of the States, Chester. Open 9–4 Mon.–Fri. This beautifully restored 1724 courthouse was the official court of Chester County until 1789 when the county was split and Delaware County was created. It claims to be the oldest continually operating building in the country and features original chairs, wainscoting, and woodworking. The Delaware County Historical Society offers occasional guided tours of the interior; call ahead for a schedule.

MUSEUMS ♿ **Brandywine River Museum** (610-388-2700, www.brandywine rivermuseum.org), Chadds Ford. Open 9:30–4:30 daily. $8 adults, $5 ages 6–12. This former 1800s gristmill on the banks of the Brandywine River houses works by

GARDENS Two of the biggest attractions in the Brandywine Valley are Longwood Gardens in Kennett Square and Winterthur, about a 15-minute drive across the Delaware border. Both belonged to members of the du Pont family and have lush gardens and grand estates, and both are money and time well spent. They are also very different. Here's the rundown on each one. A tip: don't ever, ever attempt to visit either property on Mother's Day.

✐ ♿ **Longwood Gardens** (610-388-1000, www.longwoodgardens.com). $16 adults, $6 students ages 5–22. On Tues., the adult entrance fee drops to $12. Established by Pierre S. du Pont, the former chairman of General Motors and a big fan of freely running water, Longwood Gardens resembles a formal 20th-century European pleasure garden with its ornate marble fountains and shrubs clipped to perfection. Highlights include a conservatory that shelters 20 indoor gardens and 5,500 types of plants, a flower garden walk that blooms with thousands of tulips in the spring, and a main fountain garden with more than 350 water jets that soar as high as 130 feet. For kids, there's an indoor children's garden, expanded in 2007, with bamboo mazes and plenty of water-based activities. The gardens stay open until 10 PM on Tues., Fri., and Sat. in the summer. Don't miss the poinsettia display at Christmas.

♿ ✐ Less than 10 miles away lies **Winterthur** (302-888-4600, www .winterthur.org), the country estate of collector and horticulturist Henry du Pont until 1951. If Longwood is the proper Sorbonne-educated uncle, Winterthur (the "h" is silent) is its slightly nuttier and laid-back second cousin. Whimsical displays of wildflowers, azaleas, daffodils, and magnolia and quince trees surround the estate; inside exhibits include an entire wall of hanging Windsor chairs and a collection of unusual soup tureens. The marquee attraction here is the 175-room house, where the du Ponts lived and entertained for more than 20 years, which features their splendid collections

three generations of Wyeths—N. C., Andrew, and Jamie—as well as such renowned illustrators as Howard Pyle, Maxfield Parrish, Reginald Marsh, and Theodor Geisel. Plan to spend an hour in the galleries and another hour wandering the wildflower gardens and browsing the marvelous gift shop. From Apr.–Nov., the museum offers one-hour tours of N. C. Wyeth's nearby studio and home for an additional $5. Andrew Wyeth's witty and forthright granddaughter Victoria leads anecdote-filled tours of her grandfather and uncle's galleries in spring and fall.

✐ ♿ **American Helicopter Museum** (610-436-9600, www.helicoptermuseum .org), 1200 American Blvd., West Chester. Closed Mon. and Tues. $6 adults. A tribute to the rotor-blade industry and its roots in southeastern Pennsylvania, this of antique American furniture and other artifacts that were made in America between 1640 and 1860. The one-hour tours change throughout the year; a popular one is the "Elegant Entertaining" tour of the grand dining room, sitting rooms, and other public rooms. In Dec. and early Jan., the "Yuletide" tour includes 18 festively decorated rooms and sells out quickly. Free trams run every few minutes from the visitor center through the gardens to the main house and often include banter from witty drivers. A ticket for only the galleries and gardens is $15, tours of the house are $20 each and include access to all the grounds.

WINDSOR CHAIRS AT WINTERTHUR

QVC neighbor has more than 35 aircraft on display, including the evacuation helicopter from TV's *M°A°S°H* and the V-22 Osprey currently used by the Marine Corps. Kids can climb in and take the controls of some of the aircraft; there's also a toddler area to keep the preschool set occupied. Helicopter rides are sometimes available to the public for $35 a person; call for a schedule.

SCENIC DRIVES For a pleasant alternative to US 202 south, head west on PA 926 and follow it past rolling hills to PA 100, which will take you south past the John Chads House to the center of Chadds Ford. Or continue straight on PA 926 past the Brandywine River and an old train depot to PA 52. Turn left, and this will lead you back to US 1 and the entrance to Longwood Gardens.

❋ Outdoor Activities

BOAT EXCURSIONS/RENTALS The Brandywine River tends to be calm and meandering, perfect for self-guided canoeing and kayaking trips. **Northbrook Canoe Company** (610-793-2279, www.northbrookcanoe.com), 1810 Beagle Rd. in West Chester, rents one-person canoes and kayaks starting at $25 an hour. Inner tubes are also available for $15 an hour or $20 for three hours. Canoeing is also offered at **Brandywine Creek State Park**; call 302-655-5740 for fees and a schedule.

FISHING Ridley Creek State Park in Media and **Newlin Grist Mill Park** are two good spots for trout fishing. Anglers may also fish for smallmouth bass, bluegill, crappie, and trout at **Brandywine Creek State Park**. A fishing license and trout stamp are required, and can be obtained at any of the park offices (see *Green Space*).

HORSEBACK RIDING At Ridley Creek State Park, **Hidden Valley Farms** (610-892-7260) operates a stable that offers trail rides and lessons. **Viking Horse** (610-517-7980, www.vikinghorse.com) in West Chester offers year-round guided treks through the Chester Country countryside on Icelandic horses. Ninety-minute rides start at $75 a person.

❋ To Do

QVC Studios Tour (800-600-9900, www.qvctours.com), 1200 Wilson Dr., West Chester. Tours are offered on the hour daily between 10 and 4. $7.50 adults, $5 kids 6–12. Though it's heavy on trivia about the 24-hour shopping network, anyone with an interest in how a major television network operates will enjoy this hour-long tour. It includes a peek at the various QVC sets, a stop at the Hall of Records featuring retired QVC products, and a visit to the 150-seat performance studio, where you might glimpse Paula Abdul, Suzanne Somers, or another celebrity hawking jewelry, skin-care systems, or other products. No reservations are needed, but you must have valid identification. Tickets for some of the shows are available but require advance reservations; call 1-800-600-9900, or check the website for more information.

FOR FAMILIES ✐ **Linvilla Orchards** (610-876-7116), 137 W. Knowlton Rd., Media. This 300-acre family farm has seasonal hayrides, a massive wooden play-ground, and animal feeding areas featuring deer, sheep, goats, and emus. For parents, there's fresh corn, peaches and blackberries in the summer, apples and pumpkins in the fall, and fresh-baked pies year-round. There always seems to be a weekend festival celebrating whatever the current crop is.

WINERIES The Brandywine Valley has several wineries set on picturesque farm-land and operating out of century-old buildings and barns. Visit www.bvwine trail.org for information on events and a complete listing of wineries.

Chadds Ford Winery (610-388-6221, www.chaddsford.com), 632 Baltimore Pike (US 1). Open 12–6 daily. One of the first large wineries to open in Chester

County, this scenic estate sells features a variety of wines, including Chambourcin, Syrah, and Pinot Noir, and has evolved into a true destination with daily tastings, cellar tours, wine-education classes, and live concerts and other events in the summer. It's just down the road from the Brandywine River Museum.

Kruetz Creek Vineyards (610-869-4412), West Grove. Open 11–6 Sat. and Sun. Jim and Carol Kirkpatrick grow 13 varieties of grapes on 8 acres of farmland southwest of Kennett Square. Free tastings, plus there's often live music on weekends throughout the year.

❋ Green Space

✿ 🐾 **Brandywine Creek State Park** (302-577-3534), 41 Adams Dam Rd., Wilmington, Delaware. Open daily 8–sunset. Once a dairy farm owned by the du Pont family, this 933-acre park has 14 miles of trails, open meadows that encourage picnicking and kite-flying, and plenty of recreational water activities like fishing and canoeing. A nature center has maps, a gift shop, and an observation deck. Rocky Run is a popular 2-mile trail that winds along the creek and through pine forest and meadows. It begins at Thompson Bridge parking lot.

✿ 🐾 **Newlin Grist Mill Park** (610-459-2359), 219 S. Cheyney Rd. This small park off US 1 is home to several miles of trails and the oldest operating 18th-century gristmill in the state. The visitor center is located in a restored 1850s train station. The easy 1.5-mile Water Walk follows the west banks of Chester Creek past dense woodland, trout ponds, and a three-hundred-year-old dam to the gristmill, then loops back around to the visitor center.

✿ 🐾 **Ridley Creek State Park** (610-892-3200) 1023 Sycamore Mills Rd, Media. This 2,600-acre park has 12 miles of hiking, biking, and equestrian trails, 14 picnic areas, and fishing platforms. Its crown jewel is the **Colonial Plantation** (610-566-1725), a working farm restored to its late 18th-century appearance. On weekends Apr. through Nov., there are costumed demonstrations of open-hearth cooking, food preservation, field plowing, and other chores of the era. Open 11–4 Wed.–Sun. $6 adults, $4 children. Enter from West Chester Pike (PA 3). Be sure to check out the Belgian horses, Devon milking cows, and other animals that live on the property; they all represent the types of breeds that were around in the late 1700s.

❋ Lodging

INNS & MOTELS ♿ **Brandywine River Hotel** (610-388-1200, www .brandywineriverhotel), US 1 and PA 100, Chadds Ford. A European-style inn along busy US 1 that combines the amenities of a business hotel with homey bed-and-breakfast touches like afternoon tea and cookies. The 40 rooms and suites are handsomely decorated; many have queen or king beds, convertible sofas, and jacuzzi tubs. There's also a fitness center and cocktail bar on the premises. Rooms and suites $129–179.

♿ **Steak & Mushroom Motel** (610-444-5085, www.kennettsteakand mushroom.com), 201 Birch St., Kennett Sq. Attached to the Steak & Mushroom restaurant, this small motel opened in 1999 and has 13 clean and basic rooms with queen beds, televisions, and coffeemakers. Downtown Kennett Square is a few blocks away. Rooms $90.

BED & BREAKFASTS ♿ **Fairville Inn** (610-388-5900; www.fairvilleinn .com), 506 Kennett Pike (PA 52). A longtime favorite for romantic weekend getaways, this pretty three-building complex is just above the Delaware border and five minutes from the Winterthur estate. The five rooms in the 1820s Federal residence, with queen or king beds and private baths, are a good value at $150 a night. There's also a carriage house with four rooms and two large and quiet suites and a springhouse with four rooms with fireplaces and private decks that face a rolling meadow. New owners Rick and Laura Carro took over the inn in mid-2007, but had no plans to change things. No children under 10. Rooms $150–250, with a two-night minimum on Sat. **Hamanassett** (610-459-3000; www .hamanassett.com), 725 Darlington Rd., Media. Owner Ashley Mon, who was raised in New Orleans, infuses this 1856 mansion with Southern charm and her exquisite taste in antique furniture and collectibles. It can be found at the top of a hill of a residential development a few blocks from US 1 near the Brandywine Battlefield. The seven rooms are spacious with queen or king beds, large bathrooms, and top-quality linens. Be sure to check out Mon's antique toy collection and sip sherry amid the books and grand piano in the great room. Breakfast is a gourmet delight here, featuring such items as pesto pinwheel omelettes and homemade crawfish bread. There's also a two-bedroom carriage house behind the main house, where kids and pets are allowed. Rooms $150–235; carriage house $350–500.

◯ **Sweetwater Farm** (610-459-4711; 800-793-3892; www.sweet waterbnb.com), 50 Sweetwater Rd., Glen Mills. This former Quaker farmhouse on 50 bucolic acres 2 miles off US 1 is now a luxurious bed and breakfast owned by Grace Kelly's nephew. With seven handsome guest rooms, five cottages, and amenities like a landscaped swimming pool, fitness center, and massage room, it's geared toward couples looking for a complete weekend escape with minimal use of the car keys. The royal blue master bedroom is a guest favorite, with its meadow views and large fireplace; the Dormer Room, a large exposed-brick attic room, served as an infirmary during the Civil War. The farm is a popular site for wedding receptions. Rooms $135–220, cottages $135–295.

CAMPGROUNDS KOA of West Chester (610-486-0447; 800-562-1726), 1659 Embreeville Rd., Coatesville. Open late Mar. through early Nov. About 7 miles west of West Chester this attractive property skirts the Brandywine River and has 28 tent sites, 75 RV sites, and 15 one- and two-room cabins. There's a large swimming pool, playground, and fishing pond. Tent sites start at $35, cabins are $72–86.

✳ Where to Eat
DINING OUT

West Chester
♈ ♿ **Dilworthtown Inn** (215-399-1390), 1390 Old Wilmington Pike. Open daily for dinner. This restored

18th-century tavern and boarding house seats two hundred, but its three floors of separate candlelit dining rooms, many with walk-in fireplaces, make for an intimate and romantic dining experience. They don't even allow highchairs. The menu leans toward American with Asian influences; try the almond-dusted Chilean sea bass or the chateaubriand for two. There's also an exceptional wine list. Reservations recommended. Entrees $28–40.

Gilmore's (610-432-2800), 133 E. Gay St. Open for dinner Tues.–Sat. with seatings at 6 and 8. A classic French restaurant that lets you bring your own wine? Believe it. Chef owner Peter Gilmore was the chef de cuisine at Philadelphia's Le Bec Fin for 22 years before opening this romantic bistro in downtown West Chester. The menu changes regularly and might include scotch-flavored lobster bisque, veal scaloppini in a madeira cream sauce, and Caribbean butter fish coated with coconut and almonds. Desserts are just as decadent; try the milk-chocolate mousse or amaretto souffle. Reservations recommended. BYO. Entrees $25–29.

♧ 🕶 **Simon Pearce** (610-793-0948, www.simonpearce.com) 1333 Lenape Rd. (PA 52), West Chester. Open daily for lunch and dinner. Renowned glass blower Simon Pearce expanded his unique Vermont glass blowing in this picturesque creekside setting. With its water views, elegant dining room, and first-floor glass-blowing demonstrations, it's a good choice for a romantic dinner or leisurely lunch with a friend. The menu is innovative and the portions ample: Try the crispy roast duckling in mango chutney sauce or divine mushroom strudel.

The wine list includes more than 20 by-the-glass options. After your meal, you can purchase the glassware and ceramic plates on which you just ate (among many other items) in the adjacent retail shop. Lunch: $10–15. Dinner: $20–28.

🕶 **Fellini's Café** (610-892-7616), 106 W. State St., Media. Lunch and dinner Mon.–Fri.; dinner Sat.–Sun. A festive Italian trattoria with Old Country wall murals, live opera music on Mon. nights, and a huge selection of pastas. Daily specials might include penne tossed with veal tips and chopped tomatoes or grilled ahi tuna with lump crabmeat. Entrees $11–20.

State Street Grille (610-925-4984), 115 W. State St., Kennett Square. Dinner Mon.–Sat.; Wed.–Sat. during summer. An always reliable lunch or dinner choice, this noisy family-friendly bistro is known for its optional $32 prix-fixe dinner menu. Menu highlights include pistachio-crusted rack of lamb, farfalle with wild Kennett Square mushrooms, and grilled New York strip steak. BYO. Lunch $8–16, dinner entrees $21–32.

EATING OUT 🕶 **Buckley's Tavern** (302-656-9776), 5812 Kennett Pike, Centreville, Delaware. Open daily for lunch and dinner; Sun. brunch. Patrons of this 19th-century watering hole include employees of Winterthur (it's right down the road), out-of-towners, and the ascot-wearing horse set. The Southern-influenced menu features everything from wild mushroom calzone and burgers to shrimp and grits and seared gaucho steak with sweet potato fries. Sun. brunch entrees, such as smoked salmon quiche and blueberry johnnycakes, are half-price for anyone wearing pajamas. The adjoining tavern is a lively local gathering place. Dishes $10–21.

& **Hank's Place** (610-388-7061), Baltimore Pike at PA 100, Chadds Ford. Breakfast and lunch daily, dinner Tues.–Sat. An old-school diner known for its calories-be-damned breakfasts—shiitake mushroom omelets, eggs Benedict topped off with chipped beef, and crispy scrapple are a few favorites. For lunch and dinner, there's homemade meatloaf, chicken pot pie, and macaroni and cheese with stewed tomatoes. Cash only. Dishes $6–$11.

🐾 & ♈ **Kennett Steak & Mushroom** (610-444-5085), 201 Birch St., Kennett Square. Owned by local mushroom growers Lou Caputo and Herb Guest, this boxy gray building may not look like much from the outside, but it has some of the best mushroom dishes around, plus a wide selection of top-quality steaks. Try the wild mushroom soup or the steak and exotic mushroom egg roll appetizer before moving onto a rib-eye topped with mushroom and onion marmalade. There are free samples of exotic mushrooms on Sat. nights. Lunch $7–14, dinner entrees $14–26.

West Chester

🐾 & **Jimmy John's** (610-459-3083), West Chester Pike (US 202). Open daily for breakfast, lunch, and dinner. This institution on US 202 has been serving "pipin' hot sandwiches" to omnivores since 1940. It's an ideal rest stop for families traveling on 202 between Philadelphia and Baltimore. The specialty is hot dogs, but you can also get burgers, cheesesteaks, and pork roll sandwiches. You can add bacon on anything for an extra 50 cents. Kids will love the electric trains that dominate the dining area. Sandwiches $2–$5.

& **Three Little Pigs** (610-918-1272), 131 N. High St. Open 10–3 Mon.–Fri. This small deli serves salads, soup, and a dozen types of gourmet sandwiches including shrimp and crab salad, honey ham and Brie, and corned beef and coleslaw. Service is usually fast and no-nonsense. Dishes $6–7.

CAFES & FARM STANDS Talula's Table (610-444-8255), 102 W. State St., Kennett Square. Open daily from 7 AM. Named after the toddler daughter of owners Aimee Olexy and Bryan Sikora, this gourmet food shop specializes in takeout prepared foods like goat cheese gnocchi and chicken pot pie; you may also eat in at the long communal table in the back. In the morning, there are croissants, lemon ginger scones, sticky buns, and all kinds of coffee and tea drinks.

Haskell's SIW Vegetables (610-388-7491), 4317 S. Creek Rd. (PA 100), Chadds Ford. Open daily June through Oct. Sweet corn, melons, peppers, and dozens of varieties of heirloom tomatoes, all grown across the street at Hill Girt Farm.

BYO Where to buy wine in the Brandywine Valley:

Collier's (302-656-3542); 5810 Kennett Pike, Centreville, Delaware, has a large selection of local and international wines. There's also a **Wine & Spirits store** (610-436-1706) at 933 Paoli Pike, West Chester.

✴ Entertainment

MUSIC The Brandywine Valley isn't known for its active night life or live-music scene. The best late-night options are in downtown Media or West Chester along Gay and High sts., where stores stay open until 9 on the first Fri. of every month.

Ⓨ **Brickette Lounge** (610-696-9656), 1339 Pottstown Pike, West Chester. A fun bar and restaurant featuring live country bands like the Double Clutchin' Weasels. There's karaoke on Wed. and line dancing on Tues. and Thurs.

& Ⓨ **Iron Hill Brewery** (610-738-9600), 3 W. Gay St., West Chester. This popular local brewery has live music on Wed. nights from 9 to 11.

THEATER **Media Theatre** (610-891-0100, www.mediatheatre.org), 104 E. State St. A former vaudeville house that stages five Broadway shows a year.

✴ Selective Shopping

Chadds Ford
Brandywine River Antiques Market (610-388-2000), 878 Baltimore Pike, Chadds Ford. Closed Mon. and Tues. Local antiques shoppers like this large multi-vendor warehouse for its reasonable prices and wide selection of pottery, glass, books, and country and Victorian furniture. It's near the busy intersection of US 1 and PA 100 and right in front of the Brandywine River Hotel.

Chadds Ford Gallery (610-459-5510), 1609 Baltimore Pike (US 1). This two-story gallery features a huge selection of prints by N. C., Andrew, and Jamie Wyeth, including signed limited editions. It also holds exhibits by local artists.

Pennsbury-Chadds Ford Antique Mall (610-388-1620), 641 E. Baltimore Pike (US 1). More than a hundred dealers selling everything from Civil War artifacts and vintage clothes to antique dolls and Oriental rugs. The upper level is open Thurs. through Mon.; the lower level Sat. and Sun.

R. W. Worth Antiques (610-388-4040), 810 Baltimore Pike. Exquisite (and expensive) furniture and decorative arts from the 18th and 19th century. You might find a 1790 mahogany sideboard, a dozen New York Sheraton chairs made between 1800 and 1820, or portraits of 18th-century men and women.

Kennett Square
Marion's Room (610-444-8312), 107 W. State St. Framed photographs of Chester County, horse figurines, and locally made hot sauces are some of the items you'll find in this eclectic gift shop.

McLimans (610-444-3876, www.mclimans.com), 940 W. Cypress St. Two stories of used and antique furniture at reasonable prices.

The Mushroom Cap (610-444-8484), 114 W. State St. This small store in downtown Kennett Square is devoted to the local mushroom industry. You'll find mushroom magnets, charm necklaces, and cookbooks, plus fresh-picked shiitake and white mushrooms from owner Kathi Lafferty's family farm.

Quilt Sampler (610-444-1887), 719 W. Baltimore Pike, Kennett Square. A consignment shop for local quilters and artisans, this unique store in a red-shuttered stone house features a changing inventory of antique quilts, pillows, table-top runners, toys, and blankets.

West Chester

Baldwin's Book Barn (610-696-0816), 865 Lenape Rd. (PA 100). This former dairy barn is now a book lover's utopia with nearly half a million used and rare books crammed into five floors of crooked shelves and creaky planked floors. It also has a large collection of antique maps and drawings. A must for readers of all ages.

QVC Outlet (610-889-3872) US 30 and Malin Rd. (in the Lincoln Park Shopping Center). One of a handful of outlets run by the shopping network. Everything's heavily discounted, but the selection is hit or miss—one day you might find a treasure trove of 18-karat jewelry; another might feature little more than shoes or pots and pans.

✳ Special Events

September: **Mushroom Festival** (first or second weekend), Kennett Square. The mushroom is the star of this two-day event featuring tours of local farms, a mushroom soup cook-off, an antiques and art show, and food offerings like pumpkin-mushroom ice cream. Also in Sept. is the **Revolutionary Times at Brandywine** (second weekend), when costumed soldiers reenact the 1777 Battle of Brandywine at the battlefield site.

December: **Candlelight Christmas in Chadds Ford** (first weekend)—the Chadds Ford Historical Society (610-388-7376) sponsors a driving tour of fieldstone farmhouses, Victorian mansions, and other historic buildings decorated in 18th-century style.

Bucks County

LOWER BUCKS

CENTRAL BUCKS

UPPER BUCKS

INTRODUCTION

Situated in the southeastern corner of Pennsylvania and less than an hour's drive from Philadelphia, Bucks County has long been associated with old farmhouses, rolling green hillsides, and a peaceful *Green Acres* way of life. It was one of three original Pennsylvania counties founded by William Penn in 1862 and takes its name not from the deer that still populate its forests and rolling hillsides, but from the Penn family's native village of Buckinghamshire, England. Its place in history was cemented on Christmas Day 1776, when George Washington rallied his troops to cross the Delaware River in lower Bucks County in the middle of a fierce winter storm. The Continental army then headed downriver and surprised the British soldiers camping out in Trenton, New Jersey, marking a major turning point of the Revolutionary War.

The river dominates the county's east side and separates Bucks County from central New Jersey. A historic 60-mile towpath parallels the river between Bristol to the south and Easton in the Lehigh Valley. Once trod by mule teams pulling cargo-laden boats along the canal, the towpath is used today by walkers, joggers, bicyclists, and cross-county skiers. Ever since Dorothy Parker bought 40 acres in Pipersville and took up gardening in the 1930s, burnt-out city dwellers have been coming to Bucks County, especially the central and northern parts, to decompress and listen to the grass grow. The area has been home to lyricist Oscar Hammerstein II, writers Pearl S. Buck and James A. Michener (who was raised in Doylestown), anthropologist Margaret Mead, and Stan and Jan Berenstain, authors of the popular children's book series. Residential development over the last couple of decades has changed the landscape of central and upper Bucks County (for the worse, if you ask any local who predates 1985), but the bucolic feel remains on its backcountry roads and in its quaint stone inns, and keeps visitors coming back again and again.

Just about every B&B here will claim that Washington slept, ate, tippled, soaked his feet, or hatched a battle in the very spot where you are standing. Quite often, they are right. Fortunately, many of the inns have been upgraded since the general's visits with luxuries like indoor plumbing, three-hundred-thread-count bed linens, and whirlpool tubs. The ones that remain on the rustic side often have their own appeal, like very reasonable rates, and a chance to encounter the many "friendly" ghosts of soldiers and other Revolutionary

War–era figures said to haunt the streets of New Hope and its vicinity.

Unlike Washington and his troops, many business owners in Bucks County have no interest in braving a freezing winter along the Delaware and shut down for the better part of Jan.y or Feb. I mention this whenever possible in the listings, but it's a good idea to call ahead during this slow time of year.

Bucks County has a total population of more than 600,000 and tends to be viewed in three parts: Lower Bucks, easily accessible via I-95, is the most urban of the three, and home to Pennsylvania's second-largest casino, a Sesame Street–themed amusement park, and the many chain hotels that come with these attractions. Central Bucks has the hip, urban village of New Hope and the brilliant museums and county-seat bustle of Doylestown. Upper Bucks remains largely rural and sleepy, with family-friendly campgrounds, old-fashioned general stores, and narrow, winding country roads that make perfect Sun. drives but that you wouldn't ever, ever want to drive under the influence of anything stronger than a cup of tea.

It's tough to cover all three parts of Bucks County in one trip; the rural, two-lane roads that give much of the area its beauty also mean that drives can take two or three times longer than a map or online program suggests. For many visitors, that's part of the charm.

LOWER BUCKS

AREA CODE The entire Lower Bucks region lies within 215.

GUIDANCE Bucks County Conference and Visitors Bureau (800-836-2825; www.buckscvb.org), 3207 Street Rd., Bensalem. This shiny new center in the southeast corner of Bucks County is a good source of information for the entire region. Their annual visitor guide offers detailed listings of many of the area's attractions, lodging, and eating options.

GETTING THERE *By car:* I-95, via Philadelphia or Trenton, New Jersey, cuts right through the lower end of Bucks County. The Pennsylvania Turnpike has three exits for Bucks County: exit 343 for PA 611 north (Doylestown), exit 351 for US 1 north (Quakertown), exit 358 for US 13 north.

By train: **SEPTA**'s R3 line (215-580-7800, www.septa.org) runs regularly between Philadelphia's 30th Street Station and Yardley; the R2 stops in Warrington.

By bus: **SEPTA** bus route 14 to Bensalem and Langhorne.

By air: Lower Bucks County is accessible from two major airports, **Philadelphia International** (215-937-6800) and New Jersey's **Newark International** (800-397-4636).

GETTING AROUND *By car:* The small towns of Yardley and Newtown are pedestrian-friendly, but a car is your best way of getting around the south end of Bucks County. Major sights like Pennsbury Manor, Sesame Place, and Washington Crossing are reached easiest by car.

By foot: Lower Bucks County's many parks offer a variety of hiking trails for all fitness levels (see *Green Space*). For an urban walking experience, head to Newtown's historic district. Many people like to walk the Delaware Canal towpath between Yardley and Washington Crossing, a 3-mile stretch.

WHEN TO GO The fall brings a riot of color to the area's forests and rolling hills, while Dec. means a flood of lights and festivals in places like New Hope, Peddler's Village, and Byers' Choice. If you plan to be here in early spring, check

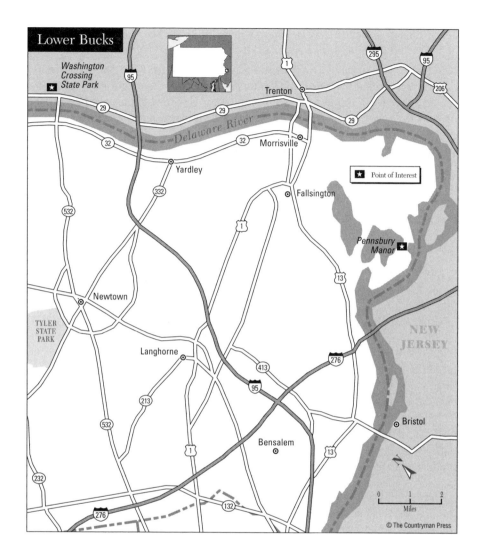

with local sources about the condition of roads and towns near the Delaware River, which is prone to flooding.

MEDICAL EMERGENCY **Frankford Hospital, Bucks County Campus** (215-949-5000), 380 N. Oxford Valley Rd., Langhorne. The **Bucks County Rescue Squad** (215-788-0444) is a nonprofit ambulance squad serving the Lower Bucks area.

✳ Villages

Bristol. First settled in 1681, Bristol is one of the oldest towns in Bucks County and home to the venerable King George Inn, which claims to be the oldest continuously run inn in the country. The focal point of the town is a waterfront area near Mill and Radcliffe streets, where you will find the King George, a number of stores and cafés, a theater, and a pretty waterfront promenade.

Newtown. This thriving town was the county seat from 1725 to 1813. Its historic district, intersected by State and Washington streets, is lined with many preserved colonial-era residences, taverns, and inns. Newtown sponsors a pedestrian-friendly bash on the first Fri. of the month, when many downtown shops and galleries stay open late.

Yardley. Anchored by a restored gristmill, this quaint town south of I-95 has several good restaurants, a man-made pond, and a pretty main street lined with trees and Victorian homes. It was a station for the Underground Railroad during the Civil War and is home to the family-owned Cramer's Bakery and the Yardley Inn. The Delaware River, bordering the town to the east, adds to its beauty.

✷ To See

HISTORIC SITES & **Pennsbury Manor** (215-946-0400, www.pennsburymanor .org), 400 Pennsbury Memorial Rd., Morrisville. Open 9–5 Tues.–Sat., 12–5 Sun.; $5 adults, $3 ages 6–17. As much as William Penn contributed to this state in name and philosophy, there are few sites or museums that offer a window into his time here. That's why this 43-acre site, to which the Quaker governor and his family retreated to escape the "city life" and political mayhem of Philadelphia, is more than just an English gentleman's 18th-century country estate. The red brick manor house that Penn designed and built fell into ruin in the early 1700s but was reconstructed painstakingly by historical architects in the 1930s. It includes an herb garden, one of the state's largest collection of 17th-century furnishings, and views of the Delaware River. On weekends, costumed artisans demonstrate open-hearth cooking, woodworking, sheep shearing, and other trades and crafts of the time. Don't forget to check out Penn's personal sailing barge in a covered garage near the main house. A shiny new visitor center, which unfortunately doesn't match the regality of the estate, opened in 2007. Tours of the house are given several times each day during the summer, and twice a day on weekends in winter.

PENNSBURY, WILLIAM PENN'S COUNTRY HOME

✏ **Washington Crossing Historic Park** (215-493-4076, www.ushistory.org/washingtoncrossing) 1112 River Rd., Washington Crossing. Open 9–5 Tues.–Sat, 12–5 Sun.; free. Of all the Washington-slept-here places in Bucks County, this is the place history buffs will most want to witness. It was here that George Washington rallied his troops to cross the Delaware River in the middle of a fierce winter storm on Christmas Day 1776, which resulted in surprising the British soldiers over in Trenton and one of the most significant battles of the Revolutionary War. Even on a gentle summer day, it's easy to stand at the spot where Washington's demoralized troops embarked on their 11-hour journey, gaze across the powerful river, and marvel at the determination it must have taken to pick up those oars. The park is spread out along River Road and home to several picnic areas, easy walking trails, and 13 historic buildings, including **McConkey's Ferry Inn**, the guard outpost where General Washington and his aides ate dinner and made plans prior to the crossing, and the **Thompson-Neely House**, a private home that served as a convalescent hospital in the winter of 1776 and 1777. Start at the visitor center on River Road north of PA 532, where you can watch a short film, pick up maps, and check out the digitally mastered photomural of Emanuel Leutze's famous painting *George Washington Crossing the Delaware* (staffers will grumble that New York's Metropolitan Museum of Art has the real thing). Just outside the visitor center is the stone marker that commemorates the spot where the troops crossed and a 20th-century barn with several replica Durham boats that were used to transport soldiers, horses, and equipment across the river on that famous night. A short drive north on River Road is **Bowman's Hill Tower**, a 125-foot tower that was built in 1931 as a monument to the Revolutionary War and offers sweeping views of the Delaware River Valley. It's open May to December, though the hours can be erratic. Guided tours are $5 and include entrance to the tower and tours of McConkey's Ferry Inn and the Thompson-Neely House. Also worth a stop is the memorial grave site of 40 to 60 unknown soldiers who died during that bitter winter. It can be accessed via the Delaware Canal towpath east of the Thompson-Neely House. The park is visited most often in Dec., when dozens of "soldiers" cross the river in an annual reenactment of the event.

SITE OF WASHINGTON'S CROSSING THE DELAWARE RIVER

WINERIES Bucks County's wineries may be light years away from matching the Rhone or Napa valleys in terms of quality, but its boutique wineries have expanded and upgraded in recent years and many are producing drinkable wines, much to the pleased surprise of everyone involved. And what they lack in quality or selection, they more than make up for in earnestness and historic setting.

♿ **Buckingham Vineyards** (215-794-7188; www.pawine.com), 1521 PA 413, Buckingham. Open 11–6 Tues.–Sat., 12–5 Sun. One of Pennsylvania's largest and oldest wineries was begun in the 1970s by two University of Pennsylvania graduates. The Forest family still runs the place, offering a selection of wines from deep, oak-aged reds to dry whites as well as self-guided tours.

♿ **Crossing Vineyards** (215-493-6500; www.crossingvineyards.com) 1853 Wrightstown Rd., between Washington Crossing and Newtown. Open 12–6 daily. The Carroll family began selling wines in 2003 and has already won awards for their 2004 Viognier and 2005 Chardonnay. Set on a 200-acre estate, the facility has separate barrel and bottling rooms and a tasting room overlooking 15 acres of vineyards. It also serves as a community gathering place, with evening lectures, singles events, and "meet the winemaker" dinners.

♿ ⚛ **Rose Bank Winery** (215-860-5899), 258 Durham Rd., Newtown. Open 11–5 Fri.–Sun. Even teetotalers will be charmed by this 1790 manor estate north of Newtown. Besides a winery, it's a sheep farm and a popular setting for weddings. Its specialty is a sweet wine made with New Jersey blueberries.

♿ **Sand Castle Winery** (800-722-9463), 755 River Rd., Erwinna. Open 10–6 Mon.–Sat. The 11,000-square-foot main facility really looks like a sand castle. Located just beyond the Golden Pheasant Inn, it features Johannesburg Riesling, Chardonnay, Cabernet, and Pinot Noir. Tours of the barrels and underground wine cellar are available for $5–10.

✳ To Do

GAMBLING ♿ **Philadelphia Park and Racetrack** (215-639-9000; www.philadelphiapark.com), 3001 Street Rd., Bensalem. Dubbed a "racino" because it houses both a casino and thoroughbred horse racetrack, this five-story betting parlor 25 miles east of Philadelphia opened in late 2006 after the Pennsylvania Gaming Board voted to grant permanent casino licenses to six existing horse-racing facilities. It can't compete with Atlantic City's glitz and high-stakes jackpots, but local crowds fill up the parking lot on weekends and keep the 2,100 slot machines clanging. There's also an all-you-can-eat buffet and plans to tack on a hotel, spa, and golf course. The adjacent racetrack hosts throroughbred races year-round, including the $750,000 Pennsylvania Derby over Labor Day weekend.

FOR FAMILIES ✦ ♿ **Sesame Place** (215-752-7070; www.sesameplace.com), 100 Sesame Rd., Langhorne. Open May through Oct.; $44.50 adults and kids 2 and up; parking $10. Let's face it: most sane adults would rather get a root canal than come here on a summer weekend and put up with the long lines and elbow-to-elbow crowds. But if you catch this 14-acre theme park on a weekday or early in the day when the lines are manageable and the noise levels bearable, there is fun to be had. It's the only theme park around featuring Elmo and his *Sesame Street* pals in live dance shows, a twice-a-day parade, and 28 different rides and water attractions that splash, climb, bounce, and twirl. Most attractions are geared toward ages 2–12. There are also regular breakfasts with Elmo, lunches with Cookie Monster, and dinners with Big Bird (for an extra fee).

✴ Green Space

✍ ❧ **Churchville Nature Center** (215-357-4005, www.churchvillenature center.com), 501 Churchville Ln., Churchville. Open 10–5 Tues.–Sun. Despite its proximity to busy roads and new housing developments, this 54-acre preserve is an oasis of wild gardens, dense woodland, and salt marshes with 2 miles of hiking trails and a large picnic grove. There's also a visitor center and a re-created Lenape Indian village with traditional wigwams and elm-bark wickiups (the Lenni-Lenape were the original residents of the Delaware River Valley). It's about a 15-minute drive from Bensalem and a 10-minute drive from Newtown.

❧ **Neshaminy State Park** (215-639-4538), 263 Dunks Ferry Rd., Bensalem. Neshaminy Creek meets the Delaware River at this 330-acre park just south of I-95. The short River Walk Trail has a wonderful view of the Philadelphia skyline and is a favorite trail for dog-walkers. Pick up a brochure at the park office for more information on the estuary. There's also a swimming pool and picnic areas.

✍ ❧ **Tyler State Park** (215-968-2021) 101 Swamp Rd., Newtown. Neshaminy Creek winds through this popular 1,700-acre park, which was once the estate of the Tylers, a wealthy farming family that developed one of the finest Ayrshire dairy herds in the county. It has 10 miles of hilly bike trails, seven picnic areas, and walking trails that lead past original stone buildings and the longest covered bridge in Bucks County. Not enough? You can also rent canoes, fish for carp and smallmouth bass, play disc golf, or spend the night in an 18th-century farmhouse (see also *Lodging*).

GOLF **Makefield Highlands Golf Club** (215-321-7000; www.makefieldhigh lands.com), 1418 Woodside Rd., Yardley. An 18-hole par-72 course featuring 7,058 yards of golf from the longest tees.

TENNIS **Frosty Hollow Tennis Center** (215-493-3646) New Falls Rd., Levittown. Ten indoor public courts.

✴ Lodging

Lower Bucks has more hotels than anywhere else in the county, though the majority tend to be run-of-the-mill chains catering to I-95 travelers and Sesame Place visitors. There are, however, some interesting, comfortable sleeping options for intrepid travelers who don't mind staying off the beaten path or sharing a yard with a potbellied pig.

BED & BREAKFASTS ▼ ◐ **Inn to the Woods** (215-493-1974, www .inn-bucks.com), 150 Glenwood Dr., Washington Crossing. This small B&B

is notable for its quiet woodsy location, special romance packages, and personalized attention. Each of the seven rooms is unique and named after a literary figure: favorites are the antiques-filled D. H. Lawrence Room and the Henry David Thoreau Room, which opens to a terrific view of the woods. Owners David Gerard and Brady Barr will arrange in-room massage or yoga sessions, pack custom picnic baskets, and steer you to all the best area restaurants and sights. The rate includes a full breakfast, plus treats like brownies in bed and evening cocktails in the garden or by the fireplace. They also host corporate meetings, weddings, and commitment ceremonies for gay couples. There's a two-night minimum for a Sat.-night stay. Rooms $129–$225.

🐾 **Temperance House** (215-860-9975; www.temperancehouse.com), 5 South St., Newtown. First opened as an inn in 1772, this red-shingled brick building in the heart of downtown Newtown has served as a gathering place for those fighting colonists' causes and a teetotaling restaurant whose hardest drink was lemonade. Today, "the Temp" is attached to a full-service bar and restaurant (see also *Dining Out*) and has 11 unique rooms and suites with private baths that are modern and comfortable while still retaining the inn's historic feel. Breakfast is included in the rate. Light sleepers might want to avoid the rooms facing State Street. Rooms start at $120, and suites with fireplaces are $150–185.

👓 **Bridgetown Mill House** (215-752-8996; www.bridgetownmillhouse .com), 760 Langhorne-Newtown Rd. (PA 413), Langhorne. One of the few luxury lodging options in lower Bucks County, this former gristmill property has five guest rooms, eight acres of lawns and gardens, and a first-rate restaurant (see also *Dining Out*). Kim and Carlos DaCosta bought the place in 1995 and spent three years converting it into a high-end bed and breakfast, preserving the Federal architecture that exemplifies many of Bucks County's historic rural estates. Rooms have four-poster canopy beds, private baths, and TVs, and include breakfast. Guests also have access to the library, solarium, formal dining room, sitting room, brick patio, and quarter-mile jogging track that winds past Neshaminy Creek. Rooms $140–175.

OTHER LODGING ✒ **Cottage at Kabeyun** (215-736-1213; www.bucks countycottage.com), 699 River Rd., Yardley. Alfred and Emily Glossbrenner own this white-shingled riverfront cottage about 2 miles south of downtown Yardley. It's perfect for families or couples looking for a home-away-from-home getaway. The 700-square-foot cottage has one master bedroom, one bathroom, a full kitchen, and an office or second bedroom with a twin bed and pop-up trundle. The Glossbrenners, who live next door, are on hand to answer questions and keep the place stocked with towels, fireplace logs, books, and other amenities. Another bonus: access to the Delaware Canal towpath is a quarter-mile away. It sometimes books up for a month at a time, so reserve early if you can. A three-night minimum stay, at $195 a night, is required. The weekly rate is $1,000.

✒ 🐾 🐷 **Ross Mill Farm** (215-322-1539; www.rossmillfarm.com), 2464 Walton Rd., Rushland. Owners

Richard and Susan Magidson call their farm north of Newtown the world's only boardinghouse for pet potbellied pigs. But they also let humans stay on the premises in a 17th-century cottage for the bargain price of $100 a night. The rustic cottage sleeps up to six people and has a full kitchen, working fireplace, and 30 surrounding acres that guests are welcome to share with the pigs. It's a great place for families (though the upstairs bedroom can be accessed only via spiral staircase), and pets are welcome. Unlike the piggy spa, the cottage doesn't come with pool or daily maid service, though the Magidsons sometimes let guests borrow one of the pigs for the night.

Tyler Hostel (215-968-0927), P.O. Box 94, Tyler State Park, Newtown. Open year-round. Budget travelers will love this 23-bed hostel in an 18th-century stone farmhouse within Tyler State Park. Run by Hostelling International, it has a full kitchen, bunk beds divided into gender-specific rooms, and strict policies for check-in time (between 6 and 9 PM) and supplies (bring your own sheets and towels). House parents Susan Thomson and Jim Witmoyer live on the premises. Rooms $18–21.

✳ Where to Eat

DINING OUT ☥ **Bridgetown Mill House** (215-752-8996; www.bridge townmillhouse.com), 760 Langhorne-Newtown Rd (PA 413), Langhorne. Lunch Tues.–Fri., dinner Tues.–Sat. This is a special-occasion restaurant that's well worth the splurge; reservations are recommended. The wait staff dress in tuxedoes, tables are set with fine white linens and crystal stemware, and large picture windows framed in oak line the main dining room. *Philadelphia Inquirer* food critic Craig LaBan awarded it 3 out of 4 bells and praised chef Matthew Levin for being among the region's most experimental young chefs. The classic continental menu changes every three months; among the standouts are crispy veal sweetbreads, carmelized sea scallops with purple cauliflower, and a milk-fed veal chop with pancetta-flavored risotto. Most entrees are in the $30 range, but a three-course prix-fixe menu is available for $26 at lunch. There's also a summer tapas menu, where nothing costs more than $12, served on the patio.

⅏ ☥ **King George II Inn** (215-788-5536), 102 Radcliffe St., Bristol. This 17th-century landmark was a stagecoach stop for travelers between New York and Philadelphia. Its menu still seems geared toward royalty, in both prices and dishes like filet mignon crowned with crabmeat, grilled venison, and stuffed mushrooms imperial. There's also a casual tavern menu available and early-bird specials for $17.95. Entrees $25–36.

KING GEORGE II INN ON THE DELAWARE

Ⴤ **Temperance House** (215-860-9975), 5 South St., Newtown. Bargain lunch and Tues. through Thurs. dinner specials keep this place buzzing on weekday afternoons and evenings. The classic American menu includes shrimp scampi, veal Oscar, filet mignon, roast beef sandwiches, burgers, and pizza. Wed. is all-you-can-eat crab night for $19.95 a person, and Fri. brings "the largest seafood buffet in Bucks County" for $34.95 a person.

Ⴤ ∞ Ⴤ ▼ **Washington Crossing Inn** (215-493-3634), PA 32 and PA 532, Washington Crossing. Open daily for lunch, dinner, and late-night snacks. Not long ago, this 18th-century inn around the corner from the site of Washington's historic crossing was known more for its quirkiness—a parrot greeted patrons at the entrance and portraits of Elvis hung on the walls—than its culinary attributes. There are still better places to lift your fork around here, but it's a good choice if you like pomp and history with your meal. The classic American dinner menu includes French onion soup, veal medallions, shrimp in a brandy cream sauce, stuffed flounder, and prime rib. Request a table in the inn's anteroom, a step-down former porch featuring murals of Bucks County's covered bridges. Staffers will tell you that General Washington ate one of his last meals here before heading over to Trenton. Lunch $8–15. Entrees $19–30

Ⴤ Ⴤ **Yardley Inn** (215-493-3800), Afton Ave. at River Rd., Yardley. Lunch and dinner daily, Sun. brunch. Locals favor this circa-1890 restaurant across from the Delaware River for its classic modern decor, friendly environment, and an upscale menu that includes grilled New Zealand lamb, Long Island duck, and mushroom-crusted salmon. The reasonably priced bar menu features sirloin burgers, salads and a variety of tasty appetizers, including lobster mac and cheese and crab quesadillas. Reservations are recommended on weekends. Entrees $24–38, bar menu, $6–18.

EATING OUT Ⴤ ♂ ☸ **Casino Tony Goes** (215-428-3480), 53 E. Trenton Ave., in the Morrisville Shopping Center, Morrisville. Closed for dinner Mon. This third-generation family restaurant serves breakfast, lunch, and dinner, and splits its business between takeout and casual table service. Its trademark sandwich is the Jersey Dog, an Italian-style hot dog on a torpedo roll brimming with fried potatoes and green peppers. You pretty much can't go wrong with anything on the soup-to-nuts menu, from the mushroom omelets at breakfast to the vodka rigatoni and baby back ribs at dinner. They also make a respectable cheesesteak and ship in New York–style cheesecake from Brooklyn. BYO. Breakfast and lunch $4–10; dinner $9–17.

♂ Ⴤ Ⴤ **Faherty's** (609-737-0766), 1339 River Rd. (New Jersey side) at Washington Crossing Bridge. A central meeting place for towpath hikers and bicyclists, Faherty's is also one of the few places to grab a quick bite around Washington Crossing State Park. It's an easy walk across the bridge from the Pennsylvania side. Order a beer on tap and a burger, and grab a table on the deck overlooking the Delaware River. Dishes $7–15.

Ⴤ Ⴤ **Isaac Newton's** (215-860-5100) 18 S. State St., Newtown. The burger, pizza, and salad menu is decent, but it's the stellar selection of microbrews and Belgian-style beers that keeps this place buzzing every night. It's in a two-story building in the municipal parking lot behind State Street. Domestic pints are half-price on weeknights 10–midnight. The outside deck is a popular spot on summer evenings.

Jack's Cold Cuts (215-639-2346) 1951 Street Rd., Bensalem. This New York–style deli near Philadelphia Park Casino features 80 different varieties of sandwiches (turkey with roasted peppers, hot brisket, roast pork and sauerkraut, and white fish salad, to name a few). The prices are as reasonable as the sandwiches are tasty. Sandwiches: $4–7.

BYO Where to buy wine in Lower Bucks:

Wine & Spirits stores are in Yardley at 635 Heacock Rd. (215-493-3182) and Morrisville at 229 Plaza Blvd. in Pennsbury Plaza (215-736-3127).

CAFES & BAKERIES ♪ ઙ **Cramer's Bakery** (215-493-2760) 26 E. Afton Ave., Yardley. Specialties at this venerable bakery include seven-layer cake, raisin bars, and pumpkin chocolate cookies. They also sell a deliciously rich German butter cake, a yeast-based cake with a pudding center that was a popular Philadelphia dessert until people started to realize its calorie count was higher than the state deficit.

♪ ઙ **Zebra-Striped Whale** (215-860-4122), 12 S. State St., Newtown. Named after a children's book written by owner Shari F. Donahue, this inviting cafe serves micro-roasted coffee, frozen hot chocolate, and custom-made ice cream "whirlwinds" of

candy, fruit, or nuts. There's live jazz in the back room on Thurs. evenings.

✳ Entertainment

MUSIC ઙ ⍟ **Washington Crossing Inn** (215-493-3634), PA 32 and PA 532. The piano bar features live performances (usually on the mellow side) every weekend and some weeknights.

THEATER ઙ **Bristol Riverside Theatre** (215-785-0100; www.bristol riversidetheatre.com) 120 Radcliffe St., Bristol. This restored three-hundred-seat theater hosts professionally staged musicals, dramas, and art exhibits.

Langhorne Players (215-860-0818; www.langhorneplayers.org) stages five plays a season at the Spring Garden Mill at Tyler State Park.

✳ Selective Shopping

Another Time Antiques (215-788-3131), 301 Mill St., Bristol. Fun-to-browse shop selling period lamps, vintage jewelry, and a large selection of furniture.

Bucks Gallery of Fine Art (215-579-0050), 201 S. State St., Newtown. Two floors of artworks by contemporary and traditional Bucks County painters and sculptors.

Delaware River Gallery (215-321-3285), 19 E. Afton Ave., Yardley. This 25-year-old gallery across from Cramer's Bakery represents local and national artists and displays original paintings and limited edition prints, ranging from landscapes by Bucks County artists to exotic wildlife art and historical events.

Dragonfly (215-579-8888), 110 S. State St., Newtown. Whimsical gift shop selling handcrafted pottery, mixed-metal jewelry, and garden flags. There's also a great selection of baby gifts.

Magic Sojourn (215-788-5755), 32 Mill St., Bristol. Located in a two-hundred-year-old building in down-town Bristol, this is the go-to place for all things magic, from disappearing card tricks to Houdini videos. Every Fri. night, local magicians gather here to socialize and show off new tricks; novices are welcome.

✳ Special Events

August: **Middletown Grange Fair** (third weekend), Wrightstown fair grounds—real country agricultural fair, with farm products, livestock judging, horse shows, and barbecue dinners.

October: **Fall Fine Craft Festival** (third weekend), Tyler State Park, Newtown—the Pennsylvania Guild of Craftsmen's biggest outdoor exhibition features more than 180 displays of paintings, sculptures, and other works, plus live music and fine foods.

December: **Reenactment of Washington's Crossing** (Christmas Day), Washington Crossing State Park—Thousands of people gather on the banks of the Delaware to watch costumed volunteers re-create General George Washington's historic boat ride across the icy river. The reenactment begins around 1 PM and finishes across the river in Titusville, New Jersey. Musket-firing ceremonies and speeches are held on both sides of the river.

CENTRAL BUCKS

AREA CODE The entire Central Bucks region lies within the 215 area code.

GUIDANCE New Hope Information Center (215-862-5030; www.newhope informationcenter.org), 1 Mechanic St. Open daily. Housed in New Hope's first city hall, school, and jailhouse, this is a great source for free walking maps, calendars, gallery schedules, and local newspapers. If you're really smitten with the town, there are New Hope–emblazed mugs, shot glasses, tote bags, and snow globes available for purchase. Across the river, visit the **Lambertville Chamber of Commerce** (609-397-0055; www.lambertville.org), 60 Wilson St., for maps and other info. **Doylestown Business Alliance** (215-340-9988; www.doyles alliance.com), 17 W. State St., offers detailed walking maps and visitor guides.

GETTING THERE *By car:* I-95, via Philadelphia or Trenton, New Jersey, cuts right through the lower end of Bucks County. To get to points north, take the River Road/PA 32 exit and head toward New Hope. US 202 is also a good way to reach New Hope or Doylestown from the east.

By bus: **Trans-Bridge Lines** (800-962-9135; www.transbridgebus.com) operates daily bus service to Lambertville from New York City and from Newark and JFK airports. The bus stops at Main and Bridge streets in Lambertville, New Jersey.

By train: **SEPTA** regional R5 line runs between Philadelphia's 30th Street Station and downtown Doylestown.

By air: Bucks County is accessible from two major airports, **Philadelphia International** (215-937-6800) and New Jersey's **Newark International** (800-397-4636). **Lehigh Valley International Airport** in Allentown (888-359-5842) is about an hour's drive away from the central region.

GETTING AROUND *Exploring by car:* The two-lane roads that link New Hope with Doylestown and other Central Bucks towns are easy to navigate and lined with antiques shops and farm estates. US 202 runs east–west across central Bucks County, passing through the towns of New Hope, Lahaska, Doylestown, and Chalfont. PA 611 is the easiest way to reach Doylestown from Philadelphia and points west.

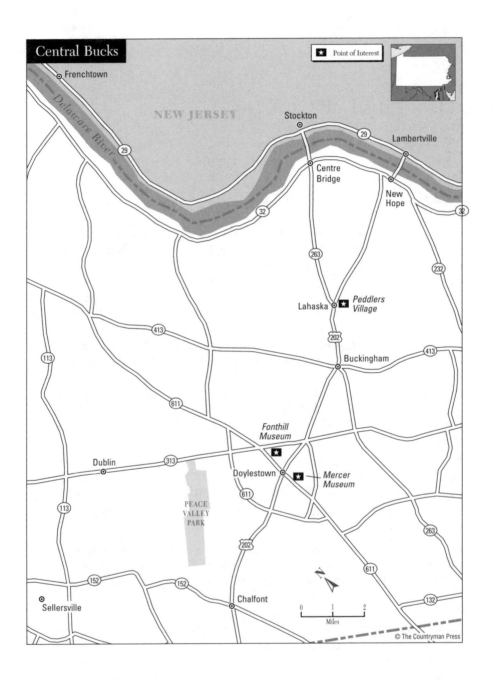

Central Bucks

Point of Interest

Frenchtown

NEW JERSEY

Delaware River

Stockton

Lambertville

Centre
Bridge

New
Hope

Peddlers
Village

Lahaska

Buckingham

Fonthill
Museum

Dublin

Doylestown

Mercer
Museum

PEACE
VALLEY
PARK

Sellersville

Chalfont

N

0   1   2
Miles

© The Countryman Press

Exploring by foot or bicycle: ⚲ ♿ **Delaware Canal State Park** (610-982-5560; www.dcnr.state.pa.us). The Delaware Canal runs parallel to the Delaware River and was used to transport coal and other cargo from inland Pennsylvania to Philadelphia and New York in the 19th century. Its 60-mile towpath makes a fine bicycle or walking route that runs between Bristol and Easton and passes through Washington Crossing, New Hope, and other river towns. Parking is easiest (read: free and unlimited) at Washington Crossing State Park (see *Lower Bucks*) and Virginia Forrest Recreation Area, on River Road north of Centre Bridge. Many cyclists like to cross the bridges at Lumberville or Upper Black Eddy over to New Jersey, then take the Jersey-side towpath south back to Lambertville or Washington Crossing. An easy 8-mile loop begins in New Hope and follows the towpath north to Centre Bridge, then crosses over to Stockton, New Jersey, and takes the path south past an 18th-century gristmill to Lambertville and crosses the bridge back into New Hope. Sometimes the bridges are closed due to maintenance or flooding damage, so it's a good idea to check with the state park office before setting out.

MEDICAL EMERGENCY Doylestown Hospital (215-345-2200), 595 W. State St., Doylestown.

✳ Villages

Doylestown. Driving west on US 202, you will find this bustling county seat, birthplace of James A. Michener and Margaret Mead and home to several good museums. Courthouse and other office workers fill its streets on weekdays, but weekends and evenings bring more of a hip, urban feel to the its restaurants and coffeehouses.

Lahaska. This small town between New Hope and Doylestown is most often associated with Peddler's Village, a quaint shopping village that once housed a chicken farm known as Hentown. You'll also find a cluster of outlet stores directly across from Peddler's Village, and a smattering of mom-and-pop antiques shops.

Lambertville, New Jersey. This town of about four thousand is an easy walk or drive from New Hope via a two-lane car and pedestrian bridge. Once called Coryell's Ferry, after the ferry service used by George Washington and his troops, it was renamed Lambertville after the town's postmaster in 1810. Today, its wide streets are lined with Victorian-era homes, a few inns and B&Bs, and many independent shops and restaurants. It's easier to find free parking here than it is in New Hope, and the streets always seem a little quieter on weekends than they do across the river. The Shad Festival in Apr. is one of its biggest events of the year.

New Hope. Situated on a picturesque spot next to the Delaware River, this is perhaps the best known of central Bucks County's tourist destinations. Gay and straight vacationers like the creative vibe of its downtown, with its hodgepodge of antiques shops, art galleries, noisy bistros, and Washington-slept-here B&Bs. Others find the packed sidewalks and lack of parking intolerable, and prefer to seek out the country flea markets, horse farms, and wide-open parks that fringe the northern and western parts of town.

✹ To See

MUSEUMS ⚲ **Fonthill Museum** (215-348-9461; www.fonthillmuseum.org), 84 S. Pine St. Open daily for guided tours. $9 adults, $4 ages 5–17; a $12 "Mercer experience" pass gets you into both Fonthill and the Mercer Museum. There's a bit of Hearst Castle in this imposing early-20th- century mansion, once the home of Henry C. Mercer, a wealthy Benjamin Franklin–like character. Just about every inch of the 44 rooms is covered with handcrafted, multicolored tiles; there are also 18 fireplaces, 32 stairwells, and 200 windows.

⚲ **Mercer Museum** (215-345-0210, www.mercermuseum.org). Open daily. $8 adults, $4 ages 5–17. Henry Mercer believed that the story of human progress and accomplishments was told by the tools and objects that people used, and he set about collecting and preserving those tools with extraordinary perseverance. His exhaustive collection of blacksmith's anvils, ox yokes, apple grinders, whale oil lamps, and thousands of other items are on display in this medieval-like six-story castle, which was designated a National Landmark in 1985. Exhibits and tours geared toward kids ages three and up are held throughout the year. Though all the Doylestown museums mentioned here are worth a visit, this would be my top choice if I had time to hit only one.

♿ ⚲ **The James A. Michener Museum** (215-340-9800; www.michener museum.org), 138 S. Pine St., Doylestown. Open Tues.–Sun. Apr. through Dec.; closed Tues. Jan. through Mar.; $5 adults, $2 ages 6–18. Bucks County native son James Michener funded this small-but-notable art museum, which features changing exhibitions of Pennsylvania impressionist painters and other contempo-rary and historic artists from the area. Don't miss the Japanese-style reading room featuring furniture by renowned woodworker George Nakashima. There's also a small room dedicated to the Pulitzer Prize–winning author featuring books and records from his personal collection and the typewriter and desk on which he wrote *Sayonara* and *A Floating World*. A satellite branch is in downtown New Hope (215-862-7633).

⚲ **Moravian Pottery and Tile Works** (215-345-6722), 130 Swamp Rd., Doylestown. Open daily; $3.50 adults. When he wasn't collecting artifacts or building castles, Henry Mercer designed tiles. Not just any tiles, as you will see on a visit to the Spanish-style building that served as his studio. These tiles were forged in three-dimensional relief and depicted scenes from folktales, the Bible, and Dickens novels. Tours run hourly and include a movie and the chance to observe full-time ceramicists who continue to produce tiles according to Mer-cer's designs.

✹ To Do

✪ **Locktender's House Interpretive Center** (215-862-2021), 145 S. Main St., New Hope. Open daily. Boats can't go uphill or downhill, so Delaware Canal engineers installed 23 locks to raise and lower them on stretches of level water.

ARTISAN AT MORAVIAN TILE WORKS

Learn how they did this through the center's exhibits, murals, and artifacts.

FOR FAMILIES ✎ ⍑ **Giggleberry Fair** (215-794-8960), Peddler's Village, Doylestown. Open daily. Kids will love this indoor playground, with its wooden-horse carousel, indoor obstacle course, and discovery room for the under-5 set. The place can be quite loud on weekends, when birthday groups show up. A $14 pass gets your child into all the attractions (parents are free), but there's also an á la carte option.

✎ **New Hope and Ivyland Railroad** (215-862-2332; www.newhoperailroad .com), 32 W. Bridge St., New Hope. Open daily late May through Oct., weekends only winter and early spring; $13 adults, $8 ages 2–11. Vintage steam- and diesel-powered engines carry passengers between New Hope and Lahaska several times a day. There are also regular theme rides for kids and adults; reservations are recommended for these.

✳ Green Space

Bowman's Hill Wildflower Preserve (215-862-2924; www.bhwp.org), 1635 River Rd., between New Hope and Washington Crossing. Open 8:30–sunset daily; $5 adults, $2 ages 4–14. Established in 1934 to preserve Pennsylvania's native flora and fauna, Bowman's Hill features more than a thousand species of plants and flowers, 26 walking trails, and a bird observatory.

✎ ♿ ☙ **Peace Valley Park and Nature Center** (215-345-7860), 170 Chapman Rd, Doylestown. A 1,500-acre park with a lake framed by rolling hills, 14 miles of walking trails, and a bird blind that is frequented by cardinals, woodpeckers, finches, and sparrows. The 6-mile paved biking/walking trail around the lake is arguably the prettiest bike path in the county. Stop at the nature center at 170

PEACE VALLEY LAVENDER FARM

Chapman Rd. for maps, birdseed, and information on guided hikes. At the north end of the park is **Peace Valley Lavender Farm** (215-249-8462), where visitors may wander across violet-hued fields and witness how lavender is harvested and dried. Admission is free, but the gift shop sells tough-to-resist soaps, oils, and sachets.

BICYCLE RENTALS The mostly flat 60-mile Delaware Canal towpath is popular with all levels of cyclists. **New Hope Cyclery** (215-862-6888), 186 Old York Rd., rents every kind of bike and support item. On the Jersey side, try **Cycle Corner of Frenchtown** (908-996-7712), 52 Bridge St., Frenchtown, New Jersey.

BOAT EXCURSIONS Coryell's Ferry Historic Boat Rides (215-862-2050), 22 S. Main St., New Hope.
Capt. Robert Gerenser leads half-hour excursions on a Mississippi-style stern paddlewheel pontoon boat. Rides leave roughly every 45 minutes 10–5:30, May through Sept.

FLY-FISHING The catch in the Delaware River includes shad in Apr., striped bass in May, and small- and largemouth bass in Oct. **Gary Mauz** (215-343-1720, www.flyfishingguideservice.com) has been fly-fishing along the Delaware for 25 years and offers half- or full-day excursions, plus lessons. Book early for summer outings.

GHOST TOURS Adele Gamble (215-343-5564) leads lantern-lit walking tours through New Hope every Sat. night at 8 June through Nov. for $10 per person. She assures her charges that all her ghosts are friendly. Tours begin at the corner of Main and Ferry streets.

MULE-BARGE TOURS The last commercial boat passed through the canal in 1931, but Leo Ramirez and George Schweidkhardt of the **Delaware River Canal Boat Co.** (215-862-0758) run regular one-hour excursions daily May through Oct. A folk singer/historian peppers the trip with guitar strumming and canal lore.

SCENIC DRIVES A classic Sunday drive, the **Delaware River Loop** rambles along winding roads that hug the river and pass by dense woodlands, antiques stores, and inns that have hosted presidents and founding fathers. Begin in

Pennsylvania near Morrisville and follow PA 29 (River Road) north past Washington Crossing State Park. Stop in New Hope for some shopping or a stroll along the Delaware Canal towpath, then continue 7 miles to Lumberville, where the **Black Bass Hotel** (215-297-5770) serves a lavish brunch in a room overlooking the Delaware. Continue a few more miles north to Upper Black Eddy, where you can cross the truss bridge into Milford, New Jersey, and browse the reasonably priced **Allen's Antiques** (908-995-8868; 49 Bridge St.), or stop for coffee and pastries at the **Lovin' Oven** (908-995-4040; 17 Bridge St.). From here, head south along NJ 519 to NJ 29, which passes through the tiny towns of Frenchtown and Stockton. At Lambertville, make a right on Bridge Street and cross back into New Hope. Cap the day with a drink or decadent dessert on the river-view deck of **The Landing** (215-862-5711). It can take as little as an hour or up to four to drive the loop, depending on how much eating and shopping you do along the way.

✳ Lodging

INNS & MOTELS 🍴 ♿ ⊚ 𝐘 **Inn at Lambertville Station** (609-397-4400; www.lambertvillestation.com/inn), 11 Bridge St., Lambertville, New Jersey. This riverfront inn just over the bridge from New Hope has 45 antiques-filled rooms with nice views of the Delaware, but it's the high standard of service that really sets it apart. Want to check in early or have breakfast delivered to your room? The staff will do everything they can to accommodate you. There's also an honor bar, a creekside deck off the lobby, and wireless Internet access in every room. It's a popular spot for weekend weddings; guests who book a first-floor room should take note that their hallway serves as the main entrance way to the ballroom. Rooms $125–220; suites $165–300.

🐾 **Logan Inn** (215-862-2300, www.loganinn.com) , 10 W. Ferry St., New Hope. This centrally located hotel, which fronts Main Street, opened in 1727 and claims to be the longest continually running inn in Bucks County. All 16 rooms were refurbished in 2001 and feature colonial-style antiques, cable television, and private baths. Rumor has it that Room 6 is haunted by a former owner who lost the inn at a sheriff's sale. The ghost of Aaron Burr, who fled to New Hope after his famous duel with Alexander Hamilton, is also suspected of roaming the premises on occasion. Standard and premium rooms $100–185; deluxe rooms $125–200.

🍴 ✐ ♿ 🐾 **Inn at the Room** (215-862-2800; 400 W. Bridge St., New Hope. Travelers who appreciate a good bargain will love this small motel a half-mile outside of town. Located on 5 woodsy acres, it has a duck pond, heated outdoor pool, and 28 spacious rooms with air conditioning and working fireplaces. A common lounge offers a big-screen TV, microwave, daily newspapers, and unlimited coffee, ice, and soda. It's one of the few nonchain places in New Hope that truly welcomes kids. Rooms $109–149.

♿ **Doylestown Inn** (215-345-6610; www.doylestowninn.com), 18 W. State St., Doylestown. This elegant century-old inn underwent a major renovation and expansion in 2001. The 11 understated rooms have four-poster beds, jetted tubs, and cable television. Premium rooms are larger with turreted sitting areas and gas fireplaces. The rate includes a voucher for breakfast at Starbucks across the street. Rooms $185–220.

BED & BREAKFASTS ✎ **Aaron Burr House** (215-862-2570; www.aaron burrhouse.com), 80 W. Bridge St., New Hope. Burr, the nation's third vice president, hid on this site after shooting Alexander Hamilton in their infamous pistol duel. Only the foundation of the original building remains, but this consistently good Victorian-style inn has retained an aura of safe haven despite its central location in the heart of downtown. It's part of the Wedgewood Inns complex, and the 10 attractive rooms have canopy or four-poster beds, brass ceiling fans, and private baths or showers. Room 5 (the Sleigh Bed Room) is a favorite. Rooms $90–189; suites $159–249, including breakfast, two-night minimum on weekends.

∞ ▼ **Ash Mill Farm** (215- 794-5373; www.ashmillfarm.com), 5358 York Rd. (US 202). Six sheep and two pygmy goats named Gizmo and Billy Jean, along with owner David Topel, live on this working 11-acre farm between Peddler's Village and Doylestown. The circa-1790 house underwent a major renovation in 2003, and the six rooms are tastefully decorated with colonial antiques, Andrew Wyeth prints, and flat-screen TVs. A reflexology expert gives on-site massages at $60 a pop. Breakfast is served in the home's original dining room next to a huge cooking fireplace. Rooms $140–175.

&. ▼ **Mansion Inn** (215-862-1231; www.themansioninn.com), 9 S. Main St. George Washington rested on the front lawn here before mounting the Battle of Trenton, according to the plaque outside. Walk inside this 1865 Victorian mansion in the heart of downtown New Hope, and you'll feel like you stepped into a world of hoop skirts and top hats. A polished-wood staircase leads to the comfortable second- and third-floor rooms, which have four-poster feather beds, down comforters, and whirlpool baths. There's also a swimming pool and a gazebo out back to escape the sidewalk crowds in summer. If you like abandoning your car for the weekend and being in the center of the action, this is the place to stay. Rooms $195–225.

&. ▼ **Porches on the Towpath** (215-862-3277; www.porchesnewhope .com), 20 Fisher's Alley. Hidden away at the end of a quiet lane that fronts the Delaware Canal, this two-story Federal house was once the home of "Pop" and Ethel Reading, who ran a popular sandwich shop out of it in the 1930s. Now owned by interior designer John Byers, the 10 rooms (four of which are located in a restored carriage house) have nice touches like claw-foot bathtubs, antique furnishings, and canal views. A country breakfast is served each morning in the chandelier-lit dining room. Those looking for absolute privacy and quiet might not appreciate the stream of walkers and cyclists who use the adjacent towpath, but most guests enjoy hanging out on the hotel's wide, inviting porches. Rooms $95–195; two-night minimum for Sat. stays.

✳ Where to Eat

DINING OUT Domani Star (215-230-9100), 57 W. State St., Doylestown. Lunch Mon.–Sat., dinner daily. Bring your own wine to this boisterous awning-topped bistro down the street from the Doylestown Inn. There is little elbow room and the noise levels can be high, but the "cucina Italiana" by chef Chris Oravec is consistently good. Highlights include crispy pan-fried tilapia, roasted red pepper soup, and filet of beef grilled in balsamic pignoli butter. Don't miss the chocolate pudding for dessert. BYO. Entrees $18–25.

Lambertville, New Jersey

&. **Ota-Ya** (609-397-9228), 21 Ferry St. Lunch Tues.–Fri., dinner Tues.–Sun. For years, this was Bucks County's only Japanese restaurant. It's still a local favorite for sushi and outdoor patio dining. BYO. Dishes $17–27.

Siam (609-397-8128), 61 N. Main St. Sleek Thai restaurant behind a modest storefront with moderate prices. Try the crispy duck or chicken curry. Reservations recommended. BYO. Entrees $10–15.

New Hope/Lahaska

⍨ **Earl's Prime** (215-794-4020), US 202 and Street Rd., Lahaska. This sleek steakhouse and bar (formerly Jenny's) is a fine addition to the Peddler's Village shopping and eating complex. At lunch, expect to see a mix of office workers, ladies who lunch, and families noshing on crab chowder, chopped salads, sirloin burgers, and gourmet hot dogs, most of which are under $10. The dinner menu features a wide selection of steaks and chops, plus a raw oyster bar. This is also one of the few places around that serves ice cream from Penn State's renowned creamery. Entrees $24–42.

Inn at Phillips Mill (215-862-9919), 2590 N. River Rd. Dinner daily French-inspired country cooking and romantic Old World ambiance make up for leisurely service at this four-room inn and restaurant. Daily pates, locally smoked salmon, and rosemary-infused lamb chops are a few of the menu highlights. Desserts such as lemon-curd pie and vanilla mousse rarely disappoint. No credit cards. Reservations only. BYO. Entrees $18–28.

⍨ **The Landing** (215-862-5711), 22 N. Main St. Lunch and dinner daily. Known for its large deck overlooking the river, the Landing also has good food to match its primo views. Its all-day menu includes a prime rib sandwich with mushroom gravy, peppercorn-crusted tuna, lobster ravioli, and a long list of gourmet salads and appetizers. The extensive wine list changes frequently. In the cooler months, grab a table by the roaring fireplace. Dishes $8–33.

⍨ ▼ **Marsha Brown's** (215-862-7044), 15 S. Main St. Open for lunch Sat. and Sun., dinner daily. Ecclesiatical roots meet culinary excellence at this Methodist-church-turned-restaurant in the center of town. The menu specializes in prime beef and seafood, as well as Creole recipes from the New Orleans–raised owner's family stash. Reservations recommended. Entrees $22–36.

EATING OUT ⍨ **Mesquito Grille** (215-230-7427) 128 W. State St., Doylestown. Open for lunch and dinner daily except Tues. This unpretentious bar and restaurant serves the best Buffalo chicken wings outside of New York state, plus steaks, pork spareribs, and barbecue chicken. The esteemed beer menu boasts 150 different bottles and is available for takeout. There are separate smoking and nonsmoking bars and lots of sports on the wide-screen TVs. Dishes $7–22.

New Hope

🦞 🐚 ♿ **El Taco Loco** (215-862-0908), 6 Stockton Ave. Open daily. One of Bucks County's few Mexican restaurants, this is a pleasant place for a quick burrito or quesadilla. The Mexican BLT is a steal at $3.25. Dishes: $3–9.

♿ 🍸 **Mother's** (215-862-5857), 34 N. Main St. Lunch and dinner daily. This New Hope institution is known for its huge portions and window seats overlooking New Hope's street scene. The large menu includes burgers, smoked salmon risotto, filet mignon, and many vegetarian options. There is live jazz on weekends in the bar. Owners and oenophiles Theresa Rubio and Lenore Picariello host free wine tastings on Wed. evenings. Dishes $10–24.

🍸 **Via Vito Ristorante** (215-862-9936) 26 W. Bridge St. Lunch and dinner daily. This family-owned restaurant serves big salads and decent cheesesteaks and pastas, but it's the delicious thin-crust pizza that make it worth a visit. Try the white spinach or sausage. The cheesesteaks aren't bad either. Dishes $6–12.

🦞 🍸 **Wildflowers** (215-862-2241) 8 W. Mechanic St. The over-the-top 12-page menu sounds like the employee buffet at Epcot Center: Yankee pot roast, chicken cordon bleu, Polish kielbasa, pad see ew, taco salad. But it works. This casual eatery off Bridge Street is always busy, thanks to reasonable prices, a secluded patio, and consistently good food. The wait can be long during peak times, but the owners recently added a full bar and lounge to make the time go by faster. Dishes $7–20.

CAFES & BAKERIES 🍨 **Gerenser's Exotic Ice Cream** (215-862-2050) 22 S. Main St., New Hope. Stephen and Julia Gerenser and their descendents have been scooping out dozens of unique flavors, from German Peach Brandy and Spanish Rum Raisin to cinnamon-infused Jamaican Tree Bark, for more than 55 years. Some complain that the service has gone downhill in recent years, but no one ever challenges the quality of the product.

Bucks County Coffee (215-345-0795), 22 N. Main St., Doylestown. Pennsylvania's top micro-roaster began life in a carriage house in Langhorne and has proliferated to 33 locations. The Doylestown branch has art-covered brick walls, high ceilings, and couches.

Night Kitchen (215-348-9775), 45 E. State St., Doylestown. Stop here for a pick-me-up walnut tart or a mocha-iced cupcake after a visit to the Mercer or Michener Museum.

BYO Where to buy wine in Central Bucks:

In New Hope, try the **Wine & Spirits store** (215-862-4650) in Logan Square Shopping Center.

✳ Selective Shopping

New Hope's Main Street is lined with shops, many of which shout "tourist trap" from the tops of their refinished 18th-century eaves. The best discoveries can be had by exploring the alleys and roads that branch off the main strip, like Mechanic and Union streets, or stopping at the many antiques shops along York Road (US 202) between New Hope and Buckingham.

5th Season (215-862-2780), 30 W. Bridge St. The scent of lavender infuses this shop across from the New Hope Railroad Station. It sells soap, candles, and oils made from a local lavender farm, plus gift and garden items.

Farley's Bookshop (215-862-2452), 44 S. Main St. An old-fashioned, independent bookshop with more than 70,000 titles and a great section on local culture and history, this shop is a must visit for anyone who loves to read.

Golden Door Gallery (215-762-5529), 52 S. Main St. This two-story wood-paneled gallery in front of the Bucks County Playhouse is worth a stop whether you're looking to buy or not. The upstairs Bucks County Room features rural landscapes and river scenes by local artists.

Heart of the Home (215-862-1880), 28 S. Main St. The perfect place to shop for the person who has everything, this customer-centered shop sells elephant birdhouses, leaf-embossed leather handbags, porcelain teapots, and jewelry.

Integrity Studio (215-534-1500, www.IntegrityStudio.com), 40 W. Bridge St. Owner Carl Christensen is a photographer and woodcrafter who, in 2001, founded Integrity Studio to present his fine art photography of Bucks County landscapes in his hand-crafted frames. He and his wife are active supporters of land conservation and charitable organizations in the local region. Integrity Studio has donated more than $50,000 of Carl's work to local charities since 2003.

Love Saves the Day (215-862-1399), 1 S. Main St. The East Village branch of this vintage toy and clothing shop was featured in the film *Desperately Seeking Susan*, and has developed something of a cult following among teenagers. The New Hope branch is a browser's paradise of feather boas, vintage T-shirts, and Betty Boop lunch boxes.

Elsewhere in Central Bucks

Byers' Choice (215-822-0150; www.byerschoice.com), 4355 County Line Rd., Chalfont. Open 10–5 Mon.–Sat., 12–5 Sun. It's Christmas all year at the headquarters of Byers' Choice, maker of handcrafted caroler figurines that are sold at specialty shops around the country. Here, you can shop for doe-eyed Kindles (elves), Christmas tree cookie molds, and red velvet Santas at the gift emporium and watch the company's 180 artists put the finishing touches on the figurines (each one is unique) at the Christmas Museum.

Doylestown Bookshop (215-230-7610), 16 S. Main St., Doylestown. A homegrown bookstore with a helpful staff, wide selection, and one of the most comprehensive collections of *Berenstain Bears* titles around.

Peddler's Village (215-794-4000; www.peddlersvillage.com), US 202 and PA 263, Lahaska. Inspired by the village of Carmel, California, this former chicken farm opened in 1962 with seven shops and one restaurant. It's now home to 70 independent shops selling everything from Lladro figurines and lace lingerie to soy candles and apple dumplings. With its landscaped brick pathways and easy, free parking, it's a low-maintenance alternative to New Hope's busier streets. It plays host to many different events throughout the year, including a Strawberry Festival in May and a scarecrow-making contest in Oct.

PEDDLER'S VILLAGE

Lambertville, New Jersey

The People's Store (609-397-9808) 28 N. Union St. Three floors of antique lamps and furniture, books, art displays, and vintage clothing.

The Sojourner (609-397-8849) 26 Bridge St. The ever-changing merchandise includes embroidered cottons from China, sterling silver jewelry from Mexico and Italy, and sapphire swirl lamps from Istanbul. You never know what exotic items co-owner Amy Coss might bring back from her regular trips abroad. It's also known for its large bead collection.

FLEA & FARM MARKETS Delaware Valley College Farm Market (215-230-7170), 2100 Lower State Rd., Doylestown. Open 9–7 daily. An abundance of produce (and vinegars and honey and sausages) straight out of the adjacent 500-acre teaching farm.

Golden Nugget Flea Market (609-397-0811, www.gnmarket.com), 1850 River Rd., Lambertville. Open 6–4 Wed., Sat. and Sun. Roseville pottery, 1950s pinball machines, comic books, and vintage jewelry are some of the items you'll find at this indoor-outdoor market south of downtown Lambertville.

Rice's Sale and Market (215-297-5993; www.ricesmarket.com), 6326 Greenhill Rd., New Hope. Open 7–1 Tues. year-round, Sat. Mar. through Dec. Bargain hunters and avid collectors won't want to miss this seven-hundred-vendor market about 6 miles northwest of downtown New Hope. It began as a livestock auction in 1860 and evolved into an indoor-outdoor extravaganza of fresh produce, woodcrafts, antique furniture, Amish pastries, used CDs, and dried-flower arrangements. Those in the know skip Sat. and show up on Tues. (the earlier the better), when all the vendors are present and accounted for. There is a small fee for parking.

✳ Entertainment

THEATER ♿ Bucks County Playhouse (215-82-2041; www.buckscountyplayhouse.com), 70 S. Main St., New Hope. Closed Jan. Grace Kelly and Julie Harris made their theatrical debuts here in 1949 and 1964, respectively. The theater continues to stage

CARVERSVILLE

Once a Lenni-Lenape Indian gathering place, Carversville today is a classic Bucks County hamlet of 18th-century stone homes anchored by an old mill, a storybook stream, and waterfall. A center of commerce in the 1700s, it was home to gristmills and a factory that made roram hats, fur-covered caps worn by Revolutionary-era boys. Today, the town claims toy historian Noel Barrett, a longtime host of PBS's *Antiques Roadshow,* as an enthusiastic resident. Its general store, located in a former livery stable, is the place for local gossip, homemade donuts, and reasonably priced sandwiches and soup—you also may spot Barrett, a regular. Across the way, the **Carversville Inn** (215-297-0900) serves an innovative Cajun-influenced lunch and dinner menu in formal 1813 surroundings. On the last Mon. night of the month during the summer, the village runs underappreciated films like *Joe Versus the Volcano* on the side of the general store. To get to Carversville from River Road, head west on Fleecydale Road in Lumberville to the intersection of Aquetong Road. It's a beautiful, though narrow and curvy, ride that follows a tree-shaded stream.

CARVERSVILLE INN

crowd-pleasers like *Miss Saigon* and *Ragtime* in a renovated gristmill.

MUSIC ℡ **John and Peter's** (215-862-5981; www.johnandpeters.com). 96 S. Main St., New Hope. Bucks County's largest newspaper calls this intimate night club "the musical heart and soul of New Hope." A must stop for music lovers, it has hosted Norah Jones, George Thoroughgood, and countless other artists. Burgers and other bar food are served all day.

♿ ℡ ▼ **Triumph Brewing Company** (215-862-8300; www.triumph brew.com), 400 Union Square, New Hope. This busy microbrewery stays open late with a varying entertainment slate of karaoke, acoustic guitar, and Texas Hold 'Em.

CABARET ♿ ∞ ℡ ▼ **Stockton Inn** (609-397-1250), 274 S. River Rd., Stockton, New Jersey. This three-hundred-year-old inn and restaurant just north of Lambertville hosts a popular cabaret night on Mon.

DANCING ℡ ▼ **The Raven** (215-862-2081; www.theravenresort.com), 385 Bridge St., New Hope. A popular gay night spot any night of the week, this oak-paneled bar and restaurant transforms into a huge dance party Sat. and every other Thurs.

MOVIES **County Theater** (215-345-6789,www.countytheater.org), 20 E. State St., Doylestown. Current independent releases screened in a restored 1938 art deco theater in the center of town.

✳ Special Events

February: **Winter Festival** (first weekend), New Hope and Lambertville, New Jersey—includes ice-carving demonstrations, a chili cook-off, and folk sing-a-longs.

April: **Shad Festival** (last weekend), Lambertville, New Jersey—includes crafts displays, culinary tents, and live music, all in celebration of the silvery fish's spring appearance in the Delaware River.

May: **Mercer Museum Folk Fest** (second weekend), Doylestown—a hundred skilled artisans demonstrate early American crafts; **New Hope Gay Pride Festival** (third weekend), street festival that attracts thousands of local and out-of-state visitors.

UPPER BUCKS

Development has found its way to Upper Bucks in recent years, but it remains the least trammeled and traffic-plagued area of the county. It has more covered bridges and state parks than anywhere else in Bucks County, and its two-lane roads make perfect Sunday drives. The region attracts a good deal of nature-seekers from New York and northern New Jersey because of its easy access via I-287 and I-78. Many of its B&Bs are hidden at the end of unpaved roads or within dense woodlands, but they are no less gracious and comfortable than lodgings elsewhere in the county, and tend to be less expensive to boot.

AREA CODE Except for the northernmost corner, which uses 610, Upper Bucks region lies within 215.

GUIDANCE Bucks County Visitor Center (800-836-2825; www.experience buckscounty.com), Quakertown Train Station. This branch of the tourism bureau's Bensalem office has maps, visitor guides, and information on the area's attractions, lodging, and eating options.

GETTING THERE *By car:* From New York and northern New Jersey, take I-287 south to I-78 west. From Philadelphia or points south, take the Northeast Extension of the Pennsylvania Turnpike to the Quakertown exit.

By bus: **Carl Bieber Tourways** (800-243-2374) runs an express bus from New York City's Port Authority to Hellertown, about 25 minutes north of Quakertown.

By air: Upper Bucks County is about an hour's drive from **Philadelphia International** (215-937-6800) and New Jersey's **Newark International** (800-397-4636). **Lehigh Valley International Airport** in Allentown (888-359-5842) is about a 45-minute drive.

MEDICAL EMERGENCY St. Luke's Quakertown Hospital (215-538-4500), 1021 Park Ave., Quakertown.

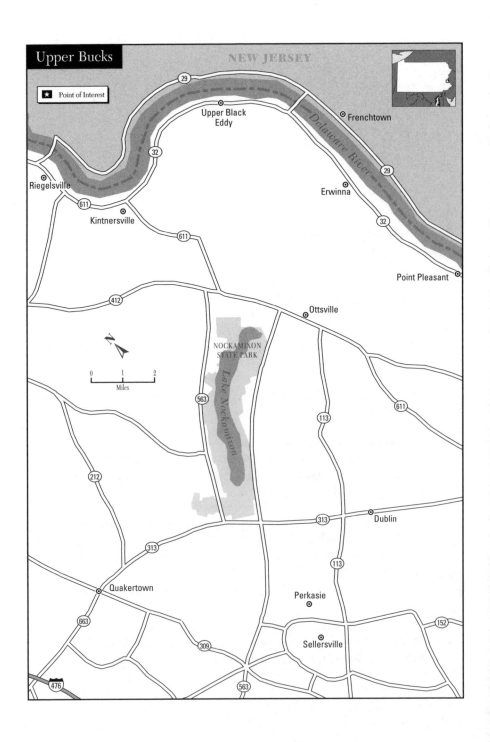

Lumberville. George Washington most decidedly did *not* sleep in this tiny Tory-sympathizing river town 7 miles north of New Hope. Named after the lumber mills that operated here in the late 1800s, it is today anchored by a general store, a footbridge that connects it with New Jersey, and the Black Bass Inn, a charming, if faded, 18th-century inn and restaurant still steeped in Tory memorabilia.

Point Pleasant. A few miles north of Lumberville, this river village was a popular fishing spot for the Lenapi Indians; later its inns and taverns catered to the rafters and canalmen who transported goods along the Delaware River and Canal. Today it's home to River Country and known for its recreational water activities. You'll also find a general store and shops selling garden accessories and antiques here.

Quakertown. This growing bedroom community serves both the Delaware Valley and the Lehigh Valley to the north. In the 18th century, it was home to a community of Welsh and German farmers and these roots are evident today in the hex signs that decorate barns, and the funnel cakes and chow-chow for sale at the local farmers market. Its quaint downtown, centered around Broad and Main streets, is a pleasant mix of historic buildings, mom-and-pop stores selling everything from Italian ice to antiques, and even an old-fashioned 5-and-10.

Just as the southern part of Bucks County likes to tout its Washington-slept-here connections, Quakertown and its environs can't help but brag that the Liberty Bell slept there—at least for a night on its way to its hiding place in the Lehigh Valley during the Revolutionary War.

Riegelsville. A National Historic District in the northern reaches of Upper Bucks, Riegelsville is a sleepy river town overlooking the Delaware River and spanned by a 1904 Roebling bridge with a walkway crossing to New Jersey. Once a booming mill town, it is home to antiques shops, a mid-19th-century inn, and

GRISTIE'S ANTIQUES, RIEGELSVILLE

PEARL S. BUCK HOUSE

rows of stately stone residences that were built by Riegel Paper Company executives in the late 1880s. For paddlers, Riegelsville has put-in for easy river access.

✳ To See

HISTORIC SITES ⬥ **Pearl S. Buck House** (215-249-0100; www.psbi.org), 520 Dublin Rd. Guided tours Tues.–Sun.; closed Jan. and Feb.; $7 adults. Pearl Buck used to say this house's solid stone walls and 1835 age symbolized her strength and durability. The author of *The Good Earth* and numerous other books lived with her family on this farmstead, known as Green Hills, from 1933 to 1973, and her gravesite sits just off the main driveway. The China-born Buck's love for Asia comes through in many of the rooms, which are decorated with Chinese screens, Chen Chi paintings, and a silk wall hanging given to Buck by the Dalai Lama. There is also a rich collection of Pennsylvania country furniture and a room dedicated to all of Buck's awards, including the Nobel and Pulitzer prizes.

Liberty Hall, 1235 W. Broad St., Quakertown. The Liberty Bell slept in this 1772 house on September 23, 1777, after being evacuated from Philadelphia to protect it from the approaching British Army. It was on its way to its wartime hiding place of Allentown. A replica of the famous bell (pre-crack) sits out front.

SCENIC DRIVES About 6 miles north of New Hope off River Road, Cuttalossa Road is a rambling 2-mile drive past wooded hills, fieldstone estates, sheep pastures, and a gushing creek that once powered several mills along its run to the Delaware River. Turn off River Road at the Cuttalossa Inn. After the paved road turns to packed dirt, look for a small mill and pond on the left side of the road. Across the road is the white-shingled former home and studio of Daniel Garber, a Pennsylvania impressionist painter known for his vibrant Bucks landscapes. (It is privately owned and not open to the public.) From here, you can cross a small one-lane bridge to N. Sugan Road, turn left and follow it as it turns into Phillips Mill Road back to River Road.

✳ To Do

BOAT RENTALS At Lake Nockamixon, **Nockamixon Boat Rental** (215-538-1340; www.nockamixonboatrental.com) rents canoes, motorboats, rowboats, sailboats, paddleboats, kayaks, and pontoon boats during the summer.

FLYING Sport Aviation Inc. (610-847-8320), Van Sant Airport, 516 Cafferty Rd., Erwinna. I know someone who comes here every year on his birthday and takes an aerobatic glider ride over Bucks County. It sure beats a cupcake. They also offer rides in biplane barnstormers, plane and glider rentals, and flying classes.

GOLF Fox Hollow Golf Club (215 538-1920), 2020 Trumbauersville Rd., Quakertown. Eighteen holes featuring 6,613 yards of golf from the longest tees for a par of 71.

Sylvan Golf Center (215 348-5575), 1208 Swamp Rd. (PA 313), Fountainville, has a driving range and two miniature golf courses. There's also miniature golf at **Ottsville Golf Center** (610-847-2547), 22 Tohickon Valley Rd., Ottsville.

HORSEBACK RIDING Haycock Stables (215-257-6271; www.haycockstables .com), 1035 Old Bethlehem Rd., Perkasie. Trail rides are $25 an hour.

HUNTING About 3,000 acres are open to seasonal hunting and trapping at **Nockamixon State Park**. Common game are deer, pheasant, rabbit, and turkey. Call the **Pennsylvania Game Commission** (717-787-4250) for more details.

RIVER EXCURSIONS ⚓ **Bucks County River Country** (215-297-5000; www .rivercountry.net), 2 Walters Ln., Point Pleasant. Open mid-May through Oct. This veteran river outfitting operation offers rentals, plus two- to four-hour guided trips down the Delaware; all-day outings and season passes are also available.

⚓ **Delaware River Tubing** (866-938-8823; www.delawarerivertubing.com), 2998 Daniel Bray Hwy., Frenchtown, New Jersey, just across the Uhlerstown Bridge. The tubing and rafting rides include a free lunch or dinner at what may be the world's only swim-up hot dog stand.

✳ Green Space

⚓ ♿ ❀ **Lake Nockamixon** (215-529-7300, www.dcnr.state.pa.us), 1542 Mountain View Rd., Quakertown. This 5,300-acre park 4 miles east of Quakertown is a scenic and popular recreation spot for locals and nature-loving out-of-towners. Its centerpiece is a 1,450-acre reservoir that allows sailing, boating, windsurfing, and fishing (but no swimming). Surrounding the lake are picnic areas, several miles of biking and hiking trails, 20 miles of equestrian trails, and 10 modern log cabins (see *Lodging*). In the winter, this is a popular spot for ice-skating, sledding, and cross-country skiing. There's also a great swimming pool overlooking the lake that's open to the public during summer.

Quakertown Swamp is the largest freshwater inland wetland in southeastern Pennsylvania, with more than 500 acres of cattail marshes, ponds, and gnarled tree groves. It's home to the largest breeding colony of great blue herons in eastern Pennsylvania, as well as a variety of songbirds, turtles, frogs, ducks, muskrats, and beavers. Since much of it is on private property, the **Bucks County Heritage Conservancy** has created a self-guided walking tour that steers visitors to public areas. For a free copy, call 215-345-7020 or download the map online at www.heritageconservancy.org.

♪ ❀ **Ringing Rocks Park** (215-757-0571), Ringing Rocks Rd. at Bridgeton Hill Rd., Upper Black Eddy. Open 8–sunset daily. This has to be the only park around that encourages its visitors to pack hammers along with their picnic baskets and bird binoculars. That's because smack in the middle of it lies an 8-acre field of large boulders, many of which ring like bells when struck lightly by hammers. According to park history, these are diabase rocks that 175 million ago were formed by fire and cooled underground, meaning they solidified at superfast speed. This put the bonds composing the rocks under a great deal of stress and, just like with the tightening of a guitar string, caused them to produce a high-pitched sound when tapped. Not surprisingly, this park is very popular with families, who can be seen trudging toward the boulder field on weekends like Snow White's dwarves going off to work. It's a bit challenging to find, so be sure to bring a good map.

LAKE NOCKAMIXON

RINGING ROCKS PARK

✄ ♿ 🐾 **Ralph Stover State Park** (610-982-5560), 6011 State Park Rd., Pipersville. This 47-acre park 2 miles north of Point Pleasant is best known for its sheer rock cliff and stunning views of Tohickon Creek and the dense woodland surrounding it. Experienced rock climbers may scale the 200-foot sheer rock face, but anybody can enjoy the safety-railed view from the top, thanks to a nearby parking area off Tory Road and a generous grant from the late James A. Michener. The park also has a pretty picnic area and a couple of short hiking trails. Whitewater kayaks and canoes may be launched from Tohickon Creek. The trails here link up with nearby Tohickon Valley Park, which is owned by the county.

✄ ♿ 🐾 **Tohickon Valley Park** (215-757-0571), Cafferty Rd. Crowds flock to this park in late Mar. and early Nov., when water flows from Lake Nockamixon to the north flow at a rate of 500 cubic feet per second and the normally staid Tohickon Creek turns into a raging whitewater playground. It also has a playground, a trout fishing stream, and tidy cabins that book up fast in the spring and summer (see also *Lodging*). Its hiking and biking trails are among the most challenging in Bucks County and connect with **Ralph Stover State Park**.

✷ Lodging

INNS, BED & BREAKFASTS

Inland

⊙ **Bucksville House** (610-847-8948, www.bucksvillehouse.com), 4501 Durham Rd., Kintnersville. Built in 1795, this old-fashioned inn on 4 landscaped acres has five guest rooms and a history of friendly ghosts. Rooms are furnished in 19th-century antiques, Asian rugs, and colorful quilts; several have fireplaces. Guests have access to a deck, screened gazebo, herb gardens, and a fish pond. Rooms $125–$150, two-night minimum on weekends.

🐸 **Frog Hollow Farm** (610-847-3764; www.froghollowfarmbnb.com), 401 Frogtown Rd., Kintnersville. One of Upper Bucks' newest B&Bs, this intimate three-room inn is about 20 miles from Quakerstown. Petie's Room (named after the resident dog) is the showcase room, but I'm partial to the Cathedral Room with its sunlit loft, exposed stone walls, and a bathroom that overlooks the barn and sheep pasture. Sun tea or mulled cider is served on the outdoor deck every afternoon and port is served in the reading room in the evening. Owners Patti and Mitch Adler can also arrange a dinner package at the nearby Ferndale Inn, which includes a chauffered ride in a restored 1931 Ford Coupe. Rooms $100–155.

🐾 **Stone Ridge Farm** (215-249-9186; www.stoneridge-farm.com), 956 Bypass Rd., Dublin. Just down the road from the Pearl S. Buck House, this 10-acre farm used to belong to the Buck family, who raised prize-winning Guernsey cows on it. Now it's a horse farm and eight-room B&B with a swimming pool and what could be the most inviting barn-turned-living room in all of Bucks County. Guests are welcome to bring their horses but should check with owner Jackie Walker before bringing any kids under the age of 12. Horseback riding packages are available. The four "hayloft" rooms have private entrances overlooking horse pastures and are $125–$175 a night. Suites that sleep four are $185–$235.

On River Road

🐸 **1836 Bridgeton House** (610-982-5856, www.bridgetonhouse .com), 1525 River Rd., Upper Black

Eddy. This riverfront B&B is the perfect antidote for stressed-out city dwellers looking to get away from it all. The only thing old about the place is the 1836 building; everything else, from the staff's attentiveness to the whimsical styles of the rooms, is as modern as it gets. All 12 rooms have private baths, televisions, plank floors, and feather beds. Many have private balconies and fireplaces. Guests may have breakfast in their rooms or next to a cooking fireplace in the dining room. There's also a private dock and an outdoor living room that's great for an afternoon of reading or lounging. Rooms are $139–$249, suites start at $239. A detached one-bedroom cottage, known as the Boathouse, is also available for $349–429.

🐾 **Golden Pheasant Inn** (610-294-9595; www.goldenpheasantinn.com), 763 River Rd., Erwinna. Built as a mule-barge rest stop in the late 1800s, this six-room inn is located right on the Delaware Canal and a short walk from the Sand Castle Winery. It is perhaps best known for its excellent French restaurant (see *Dining Out*), but its simple upstairs rooms, furnished with antiques and canopy beds, are a good value at $95. Pets and children are allowed in a detached cottage suite for an additional $20 a night. A hearty breakfast is included. Cottage suite $175–225.

CAMPGROUNDS, CABINS, & HOSTELS

🚣 **Lake Nockamixon** (888-727-2277; www.dcnr.state.pa.us), 1542 Mountain View Rd., Quakertown. Ten modern cabins that sleep six to eight people can be rented at weekly rates starting at $348.

Colonial Woods Family Camping Resort (610-847-5808, www .colonialwoods.com), 545 Lonely Cottage Dr., Upper Black Eddy. Open mid-April through Oct. Known as the Four Seasons of campgrounds, this facility has 208 tent and RV hookup sites, plus a swimming pool, playground, laundry facilities, stocked fishing lake, and air-conditioned community lodge. Tent sites $30–35.

Tohickon Family Campground (866-536-2267, www.tohickoncamp ground.com), 8308 Covered Bridge Dr., Quakertown. Full-service campground with more than two hundred tent and hookup sites, a swimming pool, and lots of free kid and adult activities. Tent sites $30–36.

Weisel Youth Hostel (215-536-8749), 7347 Richlandtown Rd., Quakertown. This country estate-turned-hostel makes a perfect base for budget travelers who want to take advantage of Lake Nockamixon's recreational activities. There are 25 bunk beds and one dorm-style room for families. Three-day maximum stay. Beds cost $12 for members and Bucks County residents, $15 for anyone else.

✳ Where to Eat

DINING OUT

On River Road

Bucks Bounty (215-294-8106) 991 River Rd., Upper Black Eddy. Open for lunch and dinner Tues.–Fri. Breakfast, lunch, and dinner, Sat. and Sun. You'll find rustic-lodge-meets-Southwest-adobe decor and a simple menu (slow-roasted prime rib, salmon and chicken saltimbocca). The small bar is a popular local gathering place, and there's usually a selection of

homemade pies available.

Golden Pheasant Inn (610-294-9595, www.goldenpheasantinn .com), 763 River Rd., Erwinna. Dinner Tues.–Sat., brunch Sun. Michel Faure, a former chef at Philadelphia's Le Bec Fin, specializes in gourmet French cuisine with a seasonal menu that features trout, venison, pheasant, and frog legs in an array of intensely flavored sauces. The Faures added a modern glass-enclosed dining room, but the original Tavern Room, with its fireplace, antique chandeliers, and hanging copper pots and pans, couldn't be more warm and welcoming. Entrees $22–28.

Indian Rock Inn (610-982-9600, www.indianrockinn.com), 2206 River Rd. Dinner Wed.–Sun., lunch Sat. and Sun. This 1812 inn is a fine place to stop for a hearty dinner on a chilly winter evening; one dining room boasts a large stone hearth fireplace, a second has views of the river. The menu includes a creative selection of appetizers and entrees. Try the mozzarella *en carroza* with garlic cream sauce or the crisp Sicilian duck. The changing dessert menu sometimes features a raspberry almond frangipane tart and white chocolate bread pudding. Lunch and bar menu: $7–10; dinner entrees $18–28.

Nearby

Ferndale Inn (610-847-2662) 551 Church Hill Rd., at PA 611, Ferndale, 2 miles south of Kintnersville. Dinner Wed.–Mon. The traditional menu features clams casino, filet mignon with horseradish sauce, scallops in curry cream sauce. Packages available for guests of Frog Hollow B&B (see also *Lodging*). The wine list includes selections from Sand Castle Winery. Entrees $12–29.

& Ϋ **Milford Oyster House** (908-995-9411) 92 NJ 519 (Water St). Dinner daily, except Tues. Seafood and attentive service are the specialties of this converted 18th-century stone mill on the New Jersey side of the river across from Upper Black Eddy. A *New York Times* critic called chef Ed Coss's Crab Norfolk "one of the most simple and sublime crab dishes" she'd ever had. There are nightly specials and a regular menu that includes shellfish stew, poached salmon, and beer-batter shrimp. A less-expensive tavern menu features burgers, Buffalo wings, and a raw bar selection. Entrees $18–28.

EATING OUT Ϗ & **Dublin Diner** (215-249-3686) PA 313, Dublin. Open daily. Everything you want in a diner–low prices, gruff waitresses, and a salad bar big enough to satisfy a football team-in-training. For a real Pennsylvania breakfast, try the pork roll with eggs.

Ϗ Ϗ & Ϗ **Luberto's Brick Oven Pizza and Trattoria** (215-249-0688), 169 N. Main St., Dublin. Next door to the Dublin Diner. Heaping portions and good simple Italian food served in unfancy surroundings. Order the prosciutto white pizza or anything that comes with pink vodka sauce. There can be a long wait on weekends. BYO. Dishes $5–14.

BYO Where to buy wine in Upper Bucks:

In Ottsville, just south of Ferndale, there's a **Wine & Spirits store** at 8794 Easton Rd. (610-847-2472).

✳ Entertainment

Ϗ & ♈ **Sellersville Theatre** (215-257-5808, www.st94.com), Main and Temple sts., Sellersville. Eclectic lineup of entertainment featuring classical ballet and children's theater matinees to Don McLean and the Bacon Brothers.

& Ϋ **Washington House** (215-257-3000; www.washingtonhouse.net), 136 N. Main St., Sellersville (next to the Sellersville Theatre). George Washington may have slept in this restored 18th-century inn; today, it's known for its lively bar, which features free live music on select weekdays and regular wine and beer tasting events.

✳ Selective Shopping

For a fun old-fashioned shopping experience, head to downtown Quakertown, a mix of antiques shops, bookstores, bakeries, and cafés anchored by **McCoole's Red Lion Inn** (215-538-1776), 4 S. Main St. **Sine's 5 and 10 Cent Store** (215-536-6102), 236 W. Broad St. sells bulk candy, Christmas knickknacks, and other items; a lunch counter serves creamy milkshakes and homemade soups. **Lion Around Books** (215-529-1645; 302 W. Broad St.) has a wide selection of new and used books. On the outskirts of town is the **Quakertown Farmers Market** (215-536-4115), 201 Station Rd., a huge indoor-outdoor affair whose motto is "bargains are our business" and where more than four hundred vendors sell everything from antique armoires and premium cigars to three-for-$1 toothbrushes.

ANTIQUES Antiques lovers will want to head to the northeast towns of Riegelsville and Kintersville.

COVERED BRIDGES

With due respect to Robert James Waller, Bucks County would win handily if its covered bridges went head to head with the bridges of Madison County, Wisconsin. It has 11 picturesque bridges dating from 1832 (compared to Madison's six) and, except for a little graffiti here and there, they are a historic preservationist's dream. A twelfth bridge, Mood's in Perkasie, was destroyed by arsonists in 2004, but was in the process of being rebuilt at this writing.

The best way to view the bridges is by weather-permitting driving tour. Here's one that covers five of them in the northwest region of the county between Doylestown and Upper Black Eddy. Begin your tour at Durham Road (PA 413) and Stump Road, just east of Plumsteadville. Head east on Stump Road and make a left on Wismer Road. **Loux Bridge**, a small white structure surrounded by farmhouses and a scenic valley, is 1 mile ahead. After crossing the bridge, turn right onto Dark Hollow Road to Covered Bridge Road and make a right. This runs into the brick-red **Cabin Run Bridge**, which crosses Cabin Run Creek. Return to Dark Hollow Road and head straight past the Stover-Myers Mill to Cafferty Road. Make a left and follow 0.6 mile to **Frankenfield Bridge**, one of the county's longest bridges at 130 feet. Drive across the bridge to Hollow Horn Road and make a right. Continue 1.3 miles to Headquarters Road, make a right and continue 1 mile to Geigel Hill Road. Turn right and soon you will reach the **Erwinna Bridge**, which crosses Lodi Creek. From here, you will want to return to Geigel Hill Road and head west about .5 mile to River Road. Make a left and go 1.7 miles to **Uhlerstown Bridge**, the only covered bridge that crosses a canal instead of a creek. This shouldn't take more than two hours total, with time figured in for photographs; be mindful that the bridges can be dangerous to cross in icy weather conditions.

COVERED BRIDGE

Antique Haven (610-749-0230),
1435 Easton Rd., Riegelsville.
A variety of antiques and collectibles,
from vintage cocktail shakers and
old books to late 19th-century furniture.

Gristie's Antiques (610-847-1966),
9730 Easton Rd., Kintnersville. A
co-op of about 25 dealers selling
antique and vintage furniture in an
old gristmill.

✳ Special Events

*May:***Arts Alive! Quakertown** (third
weekend)—art exhibits, sidewalk
sales, strolling performances, and
cooking and glass-blowing demonstrations take over Quakertown's center.

*July:***Tinicum Art Festival** (second
weekend), Tinicum Park—annual two-
day party of arts and crafts displays by
local artists, live music, a white elephant barn, and book signings.

Pennsylvania Dutch Country

LANCASTER COUNTY/AMISH
COUNTRY

READING & KUTZTOWN

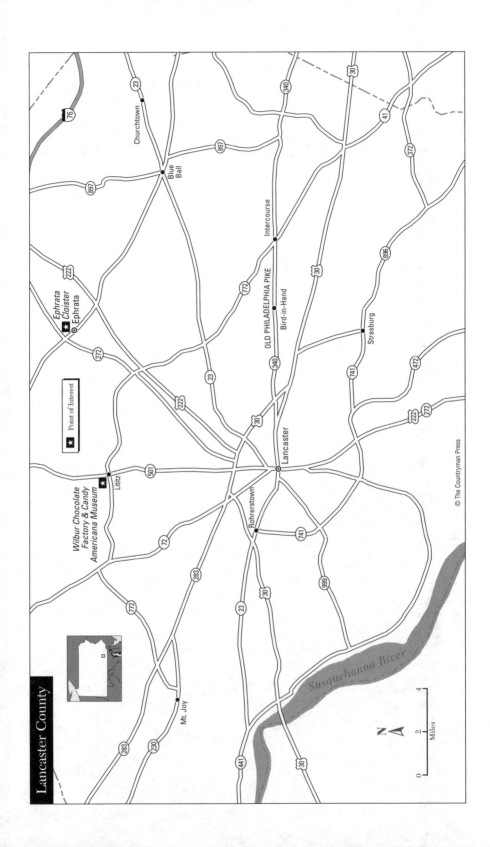

Lancaster County

Point of Interest ★

Ephrata Cloister
★ Ephrata
Cloister

Wilbur Chocolate
Factory & Candy
Americana Museum

Churchtown

Blue
Ball

Intercourse

OLD PHILADELPHIA PIKE

Bird-in-Hand

Strasburg

Lancaster

Lititz

Rohrerstown

Mt. Joy

Susquehanna River

N

0   2   4
    Miles

© The Countryman Press

LANCASTER COUNTY/AMISH COUNTRY

L ancaster County, about 65 miles west of Philadelphia, was settled in the early 1700s by the Amish, Mennonites, and the Brethren, Anabaptist Christian communities who trace their roots back to 16th-century Europe. Referred alternately as Pennsylvania Dutch Country and Amish Country, it is home to one of the country's biggest Amish populations. The Amish are known for their plain dress, pacifism, and avoidance of modern conveniences like electricity and cars. Most, however, have accepted, even embraced, the tourism industry that dominates the area, allowing visitors to eat dinner in their homes (for a small fee), selling their crafts and baked goods in commercial shops and out of their homes, and even leading and narrating buggy rides through the countryside.

The city of Lancaster is the county seat and hub of Lancaster County, with a population of more than 60,000 and an urban downtown with nifty attractions like the Quilt and Textile Museum and Fulton Opera House. The heart of Amish Country, however, lies east of here in the rural towns of Bird-in-Hand, Intercourse, and Paradise. This is where you'll find fourth-generation Amish farms, the largest concentrations of craft and quilt shops, hand-painted ROOT BEER FOR SALE signs, and large commercial operations, from buggy rides to F/X theaters, that are squarely aimed at tourists.

You don't have to spend much time in Lancaster County to realize tourism is the dominant industry. While the area still has an attractive rural backdrop of farms and rolling green hills, it is also home to dozens of souvenir shops, all-you-can-eat smorgasbords, and just about every chain motel in existence. I would suggest that first-time visitors do some advance research and planning about Amish Country before heading there. If you wind up seeing the area from development-crazy Lincoln Highway (US 30), you may wonder what all the fuss is about and leave before ever sampling some of the state's tastiest soft pretzels or viewing the amazing selections of handcrafted Windsor chairs, farm tables, and quilts.

One of the best ways to enjoy the area is to slow down your pace (don't honk when the horse and buggy trots along in front of you at 12 miles an hour, for instance) and follow the winding back roads as much as possible. It's difficult to get lost, and some of the best views, shops, and ice cream can be found away from the crowds and traffic.

SHARING THE ROAD IN AMISH COUNTRY

Today, families from New York, Philadelphia, and the Washington, D.C., area come to Lancaster to give their citified kids a chance to milk cows, romp through corn fields, ride in horse-led buggies, and climb around old steam engines. Bus tours are big, too, filling the area's family-style restaurants, biblical-themed theaters, and farm markets and auctions. Individuals and couples looking for a quiet getaway of antiques shopping and romantic dinners will also find that here—most notably in the quaint northern towns of Lititz and Ephrata.

AREA CODE Except for the southeastern edge, which uses 610, Lancaster County lies within the 717 area code.

GUIDANCE Amish Mennonite Information Center (717-768-0807), 3551 Old Philadelphia Pike, Intercourse. Closed Sun. Near Kitchen Kettle village, it has maps and local tourist information, and sells postcards and books on the Amish and Mennonites.

Pennsylvania Dutch Country Visitor Center (717-299-8901; 800-723-8824), 501 Greenfield Rd., Lancaster. Just off US 30, this large facility has rest rooms, maps and brochures, and a staffed information desk.

Southern Market Center (717-392-1776; 100 S. Queen St., Lancaster) has free maps and brochures and changing art and history exhibits. It also runs daily downtown walking tours Apr. through Oct.

Lititz Springs Welcome Center (717-626-8981), 18 N. Broad St., Lititz. This center, located in a replica of an old railway station, can provide you with details on Lititz and other Lancaster County towns and attractions.

Ephrata Chamber of Commerce (717-738-9010), 16 E. Main St., Ephrata. Maps, brochures, postcards, and more are available at this old train depot.

GETTING THERE *By air:* **Lancaster Airport** (717-569-1221), on PA 501 south of Lititz, has limited service. The nearest full-service airports are **Philadelphia**

International (215-937-6800), about 65 miles away, and **Harrisburg International**, about 40 miles away.

By car: Three main thoroughfares run through Lancaster County. US 30 runs from Philadelphia's Main Line through the city of Lancaster, then west toward York County. US 222 runs north–south through Lancaster between Reading and the Maryland border. From Hershey, take US 322 east.

By bus: **Capitol Trailways** (800-333-8444) runs bus service to and from Philadelphia.

By train: **Amtrak** trains to Philadelphia and New York run several times a day from the Amtrak station (717-291-5080), 53 McGovern Ave., Lancaster.

GETTING AROUND Most people drive between destinations within the Lancaster area. You can join the Amish and take a horse-led buggy ride around the backroads, but these tend to be leisurely tours that return you to the same.

Red Rose Transit (717-397-4246; www.redrosetransit.com) runs buses all over Lancaster County. Pick up a schedule and tickets at the downtown visitor center.

MEDICAL EMERGENCY Lancaster General Hospital (717-544-5511), 555 N. Duke St., Lancaster.

WHEN TO GO The Lancaster area is busy throughout the year, with Aug. and Oct. attracting the largest crowds. Those in the know visit in May and early June, when the weather's usually good and there are fewer crowds. Keep in mind that many shops and restaurants, especially those owned by Amish and Mennonites, are closed on Sun. It's a great day to see locals out and about on walks or buggy rides or attending hymn sings, but you won't find many commercial activities open, except at large tourist attractions like the Amish Homestead and Kitchen Kettle.

✳ Towns & Villages

Bird-in-Hand. Despite a population of just three hundred residents, Bird-in-Hand is home to several of Lancaster's biggest tourist attractions, including the Plain & Fancy Farm and Restaurant and the Bird-in-Hand Farmers Market, and several midsize hotels and inns. Most of these are located along busy Old Philadelphia Pike, but it is also surrounded by scenic farmland and two-lane country roads. It's about 5 miles east of Lancaster city, and takes its name, according to legend, from a debate between two road surveyors about whether they should stay at their present location or push ahead to Lancaster. One of them supposedly responded: "A bird in the hand is worth two in the bush." So they stayed. One of the best things about Bird-in-Hand is its bake shop, a sticky bun and whoopee pie mecca that should not be missed.

Ephrata. Considered a hub of northern Lancaster County, Ephrata (pronounced EH-fra-ta) was founded by Conrad Beissel, the German-born man who also started the town's famous religious cloister. Its name means fruitful in old Hebrew, and it has less of a tourist feel than other towns in the area. Besides the monastery, the town boasts a pedestrian-friendly downtown lined with shops, restaurants, and homes with wide front porches. It is also home to one of the area's largest and best farm markets, the Green Dragon, which features antiques and animal auctions, flea-market finds, Pennsylvania Dutch food, and Donecker's, an upscale shopping complex, restaurant, and inn.

Intercourse. No one seems to know for sure how the town got its name, though it has certainly been the butt of countless jokes and postcards. A likely guess is that it stems from the town's location at the intersection of two busy roads, which also explains its earlier name, Cross Keys. This is perhaps Lancaster's busiest town and one that is heavily geared to tourists, though its dry goods and fabric stores also attract many local Amish and Mennonites. About 2 miles east of Bird-in-Hand, it's home to Kitchen Kettle shopping village, the People's Place Museum complex, plus dozens of independent quilt and crafts shops. Expect traffic, even gridlock, along this stretch of PA 340 most weekends.

Lititz. Founded as a Moravian community in 1756 and named after a castle in Bohemia, this town of about nine thousand people has one of the most charming main streets you'll ever find. It's about 6 miles north of Lancaster and makes a good base for a visit to Amish Country with many good B&Bs, parks, independent shops, and restaurants. It is also home to one of the oldest pretzel bakeries in the nation, as well as the Wilbur Chocolate Factory and Linden Hall, the country's oldest female boarding school. Many of its attractions and shops are within walking distance of one another.

LANCASTER'S BUSIEST TOWN

Mount Joy. Located on Lancaster County's western edge, this town of eight thousand people can also be visited in context with trips to Hershey, Harrisburg, and York. It is home to several well-regarded farm-stay inns and B&Bs, and its revitalized main street has many antiques and gift shops and restaurants. You'll also find Bube's Brewery, a 19th-century brewery-turned-theme-park of sorts, here.

Strasburg. Trains are the main theme in this village south of Lancaster, though it traces its roots back to 17th-century French hunters and traders who named it after the town of Strasbourg in France. Today, it's a small child's dream, with several different train-themed attractions and even a motel that lets you sleep in spiffed-up cabooses. Its anchor is the Strasburg Railroad, which dates to 1832 and is touted as the oldest continually operating public utility in the state. Unless you have a child between the ages of 2 and 7, avoid the town by any means possible when the railroad hosts Thomas the Train events in spring and fall. Strasburg is also home to Sight & Sound Theater complex, a live theater company known for its massive Biblical-themed stage extravaganzas. You'll notice that many of Strasburg addresses list only the street or route name, but it's nearly impossible to get lost here; almost everything is within throwing distance of PA 741 (Gap Road) and PA 896.

✳ To See

HISTORIC SITES ❦ **Ephrata Cloister** (717-733-6600; www.ephratacloister.org), 632 W. Main St. (US 322), Ephrata. Open daily Mar. through Dec., closed Mon. Jan. and Feb; $7 adults, $4 ages 6–17. Founded in 1732 by the German-born Conrad Beissel, this somewhat radical religious community practiced celibacy and asceticism and was known for its calligraphy, *a capella* music, and printing and bookbinding skills. Today, you can visit the cluster of preserved medieval-style buildings where its nearly three hundred members lived, in a grassy area near downtown Ephrata. You may opt for a self-guided tour, but the guided tours (included in the admission price) include access to more buildings and insights into the austere lifestyle and habitat. Plan to spend about two hours here, and leave time to browse the gift shop.

Hans Herr House (717-464-4438), 1849 Hans Herr Dr., Lancaster. Open 9–4 Mon.–Sat. Apr.–Nov.; $5 adults, $2 ages 5–12. Andrew Wyeth, a descendent of Herr, painted many pictures of this 1719 stone structure, which served as the first Mennonite meetinghouse in America and is considered to be the oldest structure in the county. The property also includes a blacksmith's shop, orchards, and gardens.

✐ ☂ **Wilbur Chocolate Company** (717-626-3249), 48 N. Broad St., Lititz. Open 10–5 Mon.–Sat. This century-old candy maker is one of Lititz's top attractions. It runs a large gift shop and chocolate memorabilia museum in the front of its huge brick factory on PA 501. There's a fabulous display of antique chocolate pots and hundreds of unusual tins and molds. You can also watch candy makers create peanut butter meltaways, chocolate-covered strawberries, and other treats in the glass-walled kitchen in back.

WILBUR CHOCOLATE COMPANY

♿ **Wheatland** (717-392-8721; www.wheatland.org), 1120 Marietta Ave. (PA 23), Lancaster. Open 10–4 daily Apr. through Oct., call for hours other times of year; $6.50 adults, $1.75 ages 6–12. The 15th U.S. president, James Buchanan, lived in this 1828 Federal house for 20 years until his death in 1868. Costumed guides lead tours of the home, which contains many of Buchanan's original belongings.

MUSEUMS ❀ ♿ ⊘ **Landis Valley Museum** (717-569-0401; www.landisvalley museum.org), 2451 Kissel Hill Rd., Lancaster. Open Mon.–Sat. 9–5, Sun. 12–5; $9 adults, $6 ages 6–17. George and Henry Landis started a small museum in north Lancaster to exhibit family heirlooms in the 1920s; the state acquired it in the 1950s and expanded it into a 21-building village that showcases Pennsylvania German culture, folk traditions, decorative arts, and language. The best time to visit is in summer and early fall, when costumed clock makers, tavern keepers, farmers, and others demonstrate their trades throughout the complex. The Weathervane gift shop sells beautiful handcrafted gifts and books on local history and farming.

❀ ⛨ **Quilt and Textile Museum** (717-299-6440; www.quiltandtextilemuseum .com), 37 Market St., Lancaster. Open Mon.–Sat. 9–5. $6 adults, free ages 17 and under. Housed in a beautiful Beaux Arts building, this young museum combines a rich and diverse collection of quilts, rugs, and other textiles with stories about the south-central Pennsylvanians who created many of them. It opened in 2004, then underwent an expansion in 2007 that added more exhibit space, an elevator, and an ice cream parlor.

❀ ⛨ **Lancaster Heritage Museum** (717-299-6440; www.lancasterheritage .com), 5 W. King St. Open 9–5 Mon.–Sat.; free. It will take you less than an hour to walk through this worthy history and culture museum across from the downtown farmers market. Housed in an 18th-century Masonic Lodge Hall, it features displays of folk art, quilts, furniture, and toys produced by generations of Lancaster County craftsman, plus an impressive restored 1933 ceiling mural.

⛨ **Demuth Museum** (717-299-9940), 120 E. King St., Lancaster. Open Tues.– Sun., closed Jan.; donations. This museum was the childhood home and painting studio of Charles Demuth, the acclaimed artist known for his watercolors and cubist-derived cityscapes. It contains more than 30 original Demuth works, plus holds exhibits showcasing the work of artists who influenced him.

✿ ♿ ⛨ **Railroad Museum of Pennsylvania** (717-687-8628; www.rrmuseum pa.org). PA 741, Strasburg. Open daily Apr. through Oct.; Tues.–Sun. Nov. through Mar.; $7 adults. The main attraction of this train lover's mecca is the Rolling Stock Hall, home to four railroad tracks and two dozen preserved locomotive and passenger cars dating from 1875 to the 20th century. There are also displays of train tickets, art, uniforms, and tools; kids will love Stewart Junction and its hands-on electric train set-ups. It is directly across the street from the Strasburg Railroad.

Intercourse

❀ **People's Place Quilt Museum** (800-828-8218), 3518 Old Philadelphia Pike, Intercourse. Open 9–5 Mon.–Sat. Not to be confused with the Quilt and Textile Museum in downtown Lancaster, this small second-story exhibit features modern quilts made after the year 2000. It's an oasis of calm from the busy car and pedestrian traffic on PA 340. The downstairs gift shop, the Old Country Store, sells wooden Shaker-style boxes, folk dolls, hand-dyed cotton pillows, and, yes, all types of quilts (see *Selective Shopping*).

PEOPLE'S PLACE QUILT MUSEUM

American Military Edged Weaponry Museum (717-768-7185), 3562 Old Philadelphia Pike, Intercourse. Open 10–5 Mon.–Sat. May through Nov.; $3 adults, $1.50 ages 5 and up. Military history buffs will want to check out the comprehensive collection of military knives on display, from swords and sabers to fencing bayonets and Ka-Bars. There are also displays of old recruiting posters and weapons and artifacts from the Spanish-American War, the Vietnam War, and Desert Storm.

✳ To Do

Amish Homestead and Experience (717-768-3600), 3121 Old Philadelphia Pike (PA 340), Bird-in-Hand. Open daily. It's hokey and a bit faded, but this is a good place for those who know little about the Amish to start their visit to Lancaster. There's a an easy-to-digest multimedia show (complete with 3D sound and special effects) about an Amish family struggling with their teenage son's desire to leave the church, as well as guided tours of a replica of a typical Amish homestead. Combo deals are available for $14; if you must do only one, take the house tour—guides are knowledgeable and full of anecdotes about the Amish lifestyle. Be sure to pick up a couple of hot buttered soft pretzels at Sarah Mae's bakery before you leave—they cost $1 and are as rich as French toast.

FOR FAMILIES 🐾 ♿ **Dutch Wonderland** (717-291-1888; www.dutchwonder land.com), 2249 Lincoln Hwy. east, Lancaster. $29 adults and kids ages 2 and up, $44 two-day flex passes. Beyond the flamboyant faux castle on US 30 lies a compact and very manageable amusement park targeted to the 12-and-under set. Besides 30 kid-friendly rides that include a train, roller coaster, carousel, and paddleboats, it has a fun water park (with lounge chairs for parents) and daily medieval-themed stage shows and princess storytimes. Don't miss the homage to

ALONG ROUTE 340

retired rides in the park's north section. Hershey Park's owners bought the property in 2001, and discounted combo deals are available.

✔ **Strasburg Railroad** (717-687-22; www.strasburgrailroad.com), 301 Gap Rd. (PA 741), Strasburg. Open daily mid-Apr. through mid-Oct. Standard coach fare is $11 adults, $6 ages 3–11. Take a 45-minute ride on a coal-powered 1860s-era steam locomotive though the rural countryside. Guides describe the railroad's history along the way.

✔ ♿ **National Toy Train Museum** (717-687-8976), Paradise Ln., Strasburg. Open daily May through Oct., weekends in Apr., Nov., and Dec.; $3 adults, $1.50 ages 5–12. Owned and operated by the Train Collectors Association, this is a good place to take the kids before or after a ride on the nearby Strasburg Railroad. Young and old train lovers will enjoy checking out the displays of locomotives and cars from the 1800s to the present. It's next to the Red Caboose Motel (see *Inns & Motels*).

✔ **Cherry-Crest Farm Maze** (717-687-6843; www.cherrycrestfarm.com), 150 Cherry Hill Rd., Ronks. Closed Sun.; $14 adults, $11 ages 3–11. This 175-acre farm near Strasburg has hayrides, obstacle courses, and plenty of other kid-friendly activities, but it is best known for its giant cornfield maze, open Fri. and Sat. May through Nov.

Julius Sturgis Pretzels (717-626-4354), 219 E. Main St., Lititz. This downtown attraction claims to be America's first pretzel bakery. Tours cost $3 and end with a hands-on pretzel-twisting demonstration (you get to keep your creation).

SCENIC DRIVES Head south on **PA 896** through the tiny town of Georgetown. The road is dotted with horse farms and small family farm stands selling fresh corn, tomatoes, and other produce that usually let you pay by the honor system.

✳ Outdoor Activities

BICYCLING/RENTALS The Lancaster area offers a labyrinth of winding country roads that are ideal for cycling. For a detailed list of trails and suggested rides, visit www.lancasterbikeclub.org. **Bike Line** (717-394-8998; 117 Rohrerstown Rd.) on Lancaster's west side also has good maps and information on local trails and rents road and mountain bikes starting at $15–35 a day and $25–45 for a weekend.

BUGGY RIDES The competition is fierce for these horse-led backcountry rides, which usually last about 30 minutes and roam the countryside. Most places operate daily, except Sun., from about 9 to 6 with prices starting at about $10 for adults and $5 for kids, plus a tip for the driver (though the ones listed below often have discount coupons available on their Web sites). Trips are usually in an open-air family carriage that seats a dozen or so. Most of the drivers are local Amish or Mennonite men who welcome questions about their culture and lifestyles.

&. **Aaron and Jessica's Buggy Rides** (717-768-8828; www.amishbuggyrides .com), next to the Amish Experience in Bird-in-Hand, offers four different back-country tours led by Amish or Mennonite guides. They usually stop at an Amish farm, where you can buy produce and baked goods. They're also open most Sun. and allow pets on the ride.

Ed's Buggy Rides (717-687-0360; www.edsbuggyrides.com), PA 896, Strasburg. Across the street from the Sight & Sound Theaters, its guides lead you through the cornfields and back roads of southern Lancaster County.

AAA Buggy Rides (717-687-9962, www.aaabuggyrides.com) operates out of the Red Caboose Motel in Strasburg and Kitchen Kettle Village in Intercourse. It's open Sun.

FISHING **Evening Rise Flyfishing Outfitters** (717-509-3636), 1953 Fruitville Pike, Lancaster. A good source for supplies and information on local rivers and streams.

GOLF **Tanglewood Manor Golf Club** (717-786-2500; 866-845-0479), 653 Scotland Rd., Quarryville. An 18-hole par-72 course surrounded by rolling hills with two man-made ponds and putting and chipping practice greens. It's about 5 miles south of Strasburg.

TENNIS **D. F. Buchmiller Park** (717-299-8215; 1050 Rockford Rd., Lancaster) has several public tennis courts.

✳ Green Space

PARKS & REFUGES 🖋 🐾 **Long's Park** (717-735-8883), US 30 at Harrisburg Pike, Lancaster. A 71-acre park with a spring-fed lake, picnic pavilions, tennis courts, a petting zoo, and playground. It hosts many music and crafts festivals throughout the year including the world's largest chicken barbecue every May (see also *Special Events*).

🖉 ✿ **Lititz Springs Park** (717-626-8981), 15 N. Broad St. Owned by the Lititz Moravian Congregation, this charming 7-acre park is anchored by a replica of a 19th-century train depot (home to a visitor center) and has two playgrounds, benches, pedestrian paths, and a pretty stream.

🖉 **Middle Creek Wildlife Refuge** (717-733-1512), 100 Museum Rd., Stevens. This 6,254-acre wildlife management area north of Lititz has three picnic areas, a shallow lake that's open for limited boating and fishing, and 20 miles of year-round hiking trails that traverse the property's varied habitats. Pick up interpretive guides and maps at the visitor center off Hopeland Road (closed Mon.). Around Feb. and Mar., thousands of migrating snow geese can be sighted here.

WALKS The flat and straight **Lancaster Junction Recreation Trail** runs just over 2 miles (one way) passing through acres of scenic farmland and following a shaded creek on its northern half. It's also great for biking and horseback riding. To get to the southern trailhead, take PA 283 west of Lancaster City to Spooky Nook Road and turn right on Champ Road. The trailhead is on the left at road's end.

✳ Lodging

BED & BREAKFASTS Space prevents me from covering all of the excellent B&Bs located in the Lancaster area. For a more comprehensive list, visit www.padutchcountry.com.

Inn at Twin Linden (717-445-7619; www.innattwinlinden.com), 2092 Main St., Churchtown. This graceful 19th-century home is about 20 or 30 minutes from the tourist heart of Amish Country, but some might consider that a blessing. Housed in a historic mansion with gardens that back up to Mennonite farm fields, it has six rooms and two suites, all with feather beds and luxury linens, many with gas fireplaces and jacuzzi tubs. The Polo and Churchtown Rooms and both suites face the back gardens and tend to get less street noise. A three-course breakfast is served in a dining room overlooking the back garden; French toast stuffed with pears and Brie is a specialty. Owners Norman and Susan Kuestner also offer a romantic prix-fixe dinner on Sat. night for their guests and others; cost is $49 per person and you may bring your own wine. $125–265, with a two-night minimum for Sat. stays.

Lovelace Manor (717-399-3275; 866-713-6384), 2236 Marietta Ave., Lancaster. No children under 12. This beautiful 1882 home is about 5 minutes from downtown Lancaster and 15 to 20 minutes from outlying towns like Strasburg and Bird-in-Hand. Named after the 17th-century poet Richard Lovelace (an ancestor of owner Lark McCarley), it has four spacious rooms with private baths, 12-foot-high ceilings, a billiard and games room, and several sitting porches. There's also an outdoor hot tub, wireless access, and 24-hour access to a pantry stocked with soft drinks and snacks. Breakfast is an elegant affair served on china and crystal in the main dining room. Rooms $125–175.

Lititz
🦢 **Alden House** (717-627-3363; www.aldenhouse.com), 62 E. Main St., Lititz. Within walking distance of the

shops and restaurants of downtown Lititz, this 1850s Federal home offers lower rates than many other local B&Bs. It has two rooms and four suites with queen beds, private baths, and televisions; common areas include three porches and a back garden with a fish pond. Breakfast is a large and lavish affair, featuring fruit, a main entree (maybe French Acadian crepes or three-egg omelets), breads and muffins, and desserts such as apple cake or lemon pudding. Rooms $95–115.

Swiss Woods (717-627-3358; 800-594-8018; www.swisswoods.com), 500 Blantz Rd., Lititz. No children under 12. Surrounded by acres of landscaped gardens and countryside, this seven-room Swiss-themed inn is considered one of the best B&Bs in the north Lancaster area. It's about 3 miles from downtown Lititz and has seven large rooms with private baths, goose down comforters, and natural woodwork. A favorite room is Lake of Geneva, which has a private balcony overlooking the gardens and Speedwell Forge Lake. Breakfasts are very good and might include baked berry French toast or peach cobbler. Rooms

$125–190, two-night minimum on weekends.

INNS & MOTELS ✐ ♿ **Amish View Inn** (717-768-1162, www.amishview inn), 3125 Old Philadelphia Pike (PA 340), Bird-in-Hand. I normally would steer visitors away from hotels on traffic heavy routes like 340 and US 30, but this 50-room small hotel is an exception. Opened in 2001, it's adjacent to Plain & Fancy Farm and a good bet for families or anyone who wants to be in the middle of Amish Country bustle. The spacious rooms have mahogany-frame king beds, DVD players, and refrigerators and include a huge breakfast of waffles and made-to-order omelets. The north-facing rooms overlook rolling green pastures. One- and two-bedroom suites have whirlpool tubs and fireplaces. There's also an indoor pool, jacuzzi, and fitness room. Check the hotel's Web site for downloadable $20 discount coupons. Rooms $109–204. Suites $169–374.

✐ **Red Caboose Motel** (717-687-5000; www.redcaboosemotel.com), 312 Paradise Ln., Strasburg. The "rooms" in this motel next to the

RED CABOOSE MOTEL

National Toy Train Museum are actual 25-ton N-5 cabooses, at least on the outside. The insides have been gutted so they resemble a standard-issue motel room, complete with polyester bed covers and small shower stalls. Still, this place is a good value for families looking to stay near Strasburg's train attractions. There's also a playground, petting zoo, lookout tower, and picnic area on the grounds. In summer, movies are screened on the side of the barn. Rooms $69–115.

🍴 ♿ **Harvest Drive Family Inn** (717-768-7186; 800-233-0176; www .harvestdrive.com), 3370 Harvest Dr., Intercourse. Surrounded by corn and alfalfa fields on a quiet road outside Intercourse, this family-owned motel has clean and basic rooms that sleep up to six people. There is a playground and Pennsylvania Dutch–style restaurant on the property. Rates drop considerably Jan. through Mar. Rooms $39–169, including breakfast.

FARM STAYS More than 30 farms in or near Lancaster County offer "farm stays" to guests for rates of about $60 to 125 a night. They are usually a real treat for kids and a heck of a lot more interesting than staying in a chain motel on US 30. Most include a hearty breakfast (except on Sun.), plus activities like hayrides and opportunities to help with chores like milking cows and feeding chickens. The rooms tend to be comfortable but basic, often with shared baths. For a more comprehensive list, go to www .afarmstay.com.

🍴 **Rocky Acres** (717-653-4449; www .rockyacre.com), 1020 Pinkerton Rd., Mount Joy. You might call this the Four Seasons of farm stays, with its romantic Victorian-style rooms, all of which have air-conditioning and private baths. There is also a two-bedroom apartment that sleeps up to seven and a guest house with a full kitchen and private entrance. Located on a 550-acre dairy farm, it offers delicious multicourse breakfasts and plenty of recreational activities, from pony, train, and tractor rides to guided farm tours and a petting zoo. Owners Eileen and Galen Benner have been in the farm stay business for more than 40 years. There is a two-night minimum on weekends. Rooms $115–145, apartments and cottage $135–189.

🍴 **Stone Haus Farm** (717-653-8444; www.stonehausfarmbnb.com), 360 S. Esbenshade Rd., Manheim. Merv and Angie Shenk and their three kids run this two-hundred-year-old stone farmhouse and 100-acre corn, soybean, and celery farm about 5 miles west of Lancaster. The six guest rooms, most of which have shared baths, are nicely decorated with quilts and antique reproductions; some have exposed stone walls and room for extra cots. Kids have access to a game room, playground, picnic area, pedal tractors, and bikes. Rates include a huge breakfast (including Sun.) of eggs, fruit, oatmeal, and baked goods such as shoofly cake and pumpkin muffins. Rooms $65–95.

🍴 **Verdant View Farm** (717-687-7353; 888-321-8119; www.verdant view.com), 439 Strasburg Rd., Paradise. This 118-acre Mennonite dairy farm is a quick drive or walk from most of Strasburg's train attractions. Kids will love watching the Strasburg train pass through the field behind the Ranck family farmhouse; they may also help milk the cows, feed the swans and geese, fish for bass and bluegills in the pond, and pet the many cats, sheep, and rabbits that call the farm home. Basic rooms in the farmhouse are on the second floor, two have private baths and sleep up to 4; additional lodging is available across the street in a small home on the property. A highlight is the optional breakfast (for an extra $5): a feast, usually led by Don or Ginnie Ranck, of yogurt, applesauce, French toast, eggs, toast, fresh milk, coffee, and good conversation. Rooms $65–96; two-room suite $97–127.

CAMPGROUNDS & CABINS Flory's Cottages and Camping (717-687-6670; www.floryscamping.com), 99 N. Ronks Rd. Shaded, level grassy sites with electric, water, sewer, hookups. Tent sites $26–29, with hookups $30–38; cottages $84–234.

Beaver Creek Farm Cabins (717-687-7745), 2 Little Beaver Rd. (PA 896), Strasburg. Eight two-bedroom cabins (and one single bedroom) starting at $90 per night and $585 per week.

✳ Where to Eat

Lancaster County restaurants often specialize in hearty Pennsylvania Dutch foods like chicken pot pie, pepper cabbage, and baked ham. You can also arrange fairly easily to have dinner in an Amish family's home; many inn and B&B owners are happy to help set these up. It typically costs $12 to 15 a person and features a multi-course home-cooked Pennsylvania Dutch meal and genial conversation.

DINING OUT ⅄ Bube's Brewery (717-653-2056; www.bubesbrewery .com), 102 N. Market St., Mount Joy. Open daily for lunch and dinner. Alois Bube, a German immigrant, started

this small brewery in the 1870s, and later opened a hotel next door. Today, the large complex is as much an indoor theme park as a restaurant and bar, with brewery tours, three different dining areas, a summer biergarten, gift shop, and live music from jazz trios to minstrel performances. Dine on a six-course prix-fixe menu at Alois in the hotel portion or in the Catacombs, where costumed guides lead you on a tour of the cellars before your meal. Lunch and dinner are also available at the more casual Bottling Works on the original brewery site. The menu is as vast as the Lancaster County countryside; the baked tomato soup and grilled cheese with crabmeat are a couple of favorites. The house brews change often, but might include oatmeal stout, brown ale, and Heffweizen. Bottling Works dishes: $6–27, Alois: $36 prix-fixe, Catacombs: $20–32.

&. ⅄ **Carr's** (717-299-7090), 50 W. Grant St., Lancaster. Dinner Tues.–Sat., Sunday. This upscale restaurant is a great place to sample creative American dishes before a show at the Fulton Theater. Owner and chef Tim Carr is a Lancaster area native who uses organic and locally made or raised products, from cheese and mustard to free-range chickens, as often as possible. At dinner, try the striped bass on spinach greens with lobster and sweet potato pierogies or the Elysian Fields lamb trio. The downstairs dining room is inviting with a large mural of a Parisian street scene and view of the restaurant's extensive wine collection. Reservations recommended. Lunch $8–13, dinner entrees $23–30.

&. ⅄ **General Sutter Inn** (717-626-2115) 14 E. Main St., Lititz. Open daily; call for hours. The General Sutter has operated continuously since 1764 at the intersection of PA 501 and 772. Its formal restaurant offers a heavy-on-the-sauces menu of steaks, salmon, and lamb. I'm partial to the less expensive tavern menu of crab cake sandwiches, fish and chips, tenderloin steak wraps, and salads. The outdoor patio is a popular place during the summer. Tavern menu: $8–15. Dinner entrees: $17–27.

& ☥ **Lily's American Café** (717-738-2711) 124 E. Main St., Ephrata. Lunch Mon.–Sat., dinner daily, brunch Sun. This modern bistro overlooking Ephrata's downtown is the place to go when you've had enough of smorgasbords and down-home diners. The creative American menu might include raspberry chicken baked in almond bread-crumb crust and topped with melted Brie, lobster macaroni and cheese with roasted tomatoes and asparagus, or sautéed calves liver with sweet red onion preserves. There's also a lighter menu of sandwiches and salads served at both lunch and dinner. It has an extensive wine list with bottles running between $30 and 125. Lunch $7–12; entrees: $16–30.

& ☥ **Olde Greenfield Inn** (717-393-0668), 595 Greenfield Rd., Lancaster. Lunch and dinner Tues.–Sat., Sun. brunch. This restored 1790s stone farmhouse is regularly rated the area's top romantic restaurants by local newspapers and magazines. Try to nab a table in the intimate wine cellar. The American menu includes roasted halibut with hollandaise, grilled pork tenderloin, seafood crepes, and filet mignon. A bar lounge offers live piano on Frid. and Sat. nights. Reservations suggested. Lunch $9–15; dinner entrees $18–28.

EATING OUT & **Café Chocolate** (717-626-0123), 40 Main St., Lititz. Open daily. Besides a large assortment of desserts made from fair-trade chocolate, this cute café serves salads, crepes, quiche, and savory small dishes like hickory-smoked chicken and vegan chili. Dishes $4-10.

& **Central Market** (717-291-4723), 23 N. Market St., Lancaster. Open 6–4:30 Tues. and Fri., 6–2 Sat. Seating is limited, but the delicious food and wide range of choices make this a terrific lunch spot if you're in the downtown area. Housed in a beautiful brick 1880s building, it is home to

CENTRAL MARKET

SMORGASBORDS

These all-you-can-eat buffets are a staple of Lancaster County. Regular patrons debate passionately over which ones are the best and which ones should be left to stew in their canned sweet potatoes. Many of them are big enough to seat hundreds of diners, making them popular with bus tours. Most offer soup and salad bar, carving stations, many Pennsylvania Dutch dishes, and a wide selection of desserts. Selective or light eaters might want to avoid these buffets and stick with smaller á la carte establishments. For others, here are a few favorite standbys.

♿ **Shady Maple** (717-354-8222), 129 Toddy Dr., East Earl. Breakfast, lunch, and dinner Tues.–Sat. This huge complex along PA 23 began as a farm stand and has expanded into a small city with an 1,100-seat restaurant, grocery store, banquet hall, and stadium-like parking. It gets consistent raves from buffet pros for its homemade fruit breads, wide selection of meats, seafood, and vegetables, and hot and cold dessert bar. Lunch buffet $7–10, dinner buffet $14–19.

Dienner's Country Restaurant (717-687-9571), 2855 Lincoln Hwy., Ronks. Open daily 7 AM–6 PM, until 8 PM on Fri. Smaller than other smorgasbords, this homey diner is known for its fall-off-the-bone rotisserie chicken and very low prices (nothing is over $10). It also offers á la carte items like burgers and daily specials of meatloaf and chicken pot pie.

♿ ⍏ **Miller's** (717-687-6621), 2811 Lincoln Hwy. east, Ronks. Breakfast, lunch, and dinner daily. This centrally located restaurant caters to bus tours and out-of-towners; it takes reservations and is one of the few smorgasbords to stay open on Sun. and to serve wine and beer. Its huge serve-yourself buffet features items like top sirloin, baked ham with cider sauce, chicken pot pie, and baked cabbage in cream sauce. The large dining room overlooks the countryside. There are free kitchen tours every Wed. (reservations required). Buffet $10–21.

♿ **Stolfzus Farm Restaurant** (717-768-8156), PA 772, Intercourse. Lunch and dinner Mon.–Sat., Apr. through Oct., weekends in Apr. and Nov. Meals are served family-style (no menu) at long tables and include a typical Pennsylvania Dutch menu of ham loaf, fried chicken, buttered noodles, chow-chow, and pepper cabbage. The sausage and other meats come from the family's adjacent butcher shop. No reservations. Lunch and dinner: $16, $7.50 ages 4–12.

dozens of stalls selling everything from chicken corn chowder and Kunzler hot dogs to Greek salads and Italian *cannoli*. I've never had a bad meal here; the best thing to do is just wander around until your stomach tells you to stop.

✂ ⚒ **Leola Family Restaurant** (717-656-2311), 365 W. Main St., Leola. This 24-hour diner is a good place to stop for a quick meal if you're traveling to or from Lancaster on PA 23. It specializes in home-cooked food like hot turkey sandwiches, pork sauerkraut, and chicken pot pie. Dishes $7–13.

✂ ⚒ **Isaac's Deli** (717-687-7699), Shops at Traintown, Gap Rd. (PA 741), Strasburg. You'll find a reliable selection of salads, soups, flatbread pizzas, and grilled sandwiches at this local kid-friendly chain with a pink flamingo mascot. For a unique twist, try any of the grilled soft-pretzel roll sandwiches. Dishes: $5–8.

BAKERIES & FARM STANDS Farm stands can be found all over Lancaster County on busy highways and rural backcountry roads. They often sell everything from fresh produce and poultry to root beer and homemade potato chips.

Elam and Naomi Fisher sell homemade root beer, whoopie pies, potato chips, and other items from a kiosk on their large farm off PA 340 (3217 Old Philadelphia Pike, Ronks) between Bird-in-Hand and Intercourse. Follow the ROOT BEER FOR SALE signs up the long driveway and ring the bell for service.

⚘ ✂ **Bird-in-Hand Bake Shop** (717-656-7947), 542 Gibbons Rd., Bird-in-Hand. A terrific Mennonite-owned bakery known for its reasonable prices

and whoopie pies, cinnamon raisin bread, and shoofly pies. There's a playground and petting zoo outside for the kids.

✂ ⚒ **Intercourse Pretzel Factory** (717-768-3432), 3614 Old Philadelphia Pike (in Cross Keys Village), Intercourse. Closed Sun. This shop sells soft and hard hand-twisted pretzels; choose from plain, herb, cheddar cheese, and brown butter. Free 12-minute factory tours run at least once an hour, depending on demand.

✂ **Lapp Valley Farm** (717-354-7988), 244 Mentzer Rd., New Holland. A Mennonite dairy farm that produces the best homemade ice cream in the region. Try the vanilla. Seriously.

FARM MARKETS ⚘ **Green Dragon Market and Auction** (717-738-1117; www.greendragonmarket.com), 955 N. State St., Ephrata. Open 9–9 Fri. As the local saying goes: "If you can't buy it at the Green Dragon, it chust ain't fer sale." This venerable old market, about 4 miles north of downtown Ephrata, is a shopper's mecca of four hundred growers and vendors selling fresh flowers, produce, wood furniture, handmade clothing and quilts, and more. Its two auction houses specialize in antiques and livestock, and are fun to watch even if you're not buying. When you get hungry, have a Pennsylvania Dutch meal at the five sit-down restaurants or grab a soft pretzel or sausage sandwich at the many snack stands. Plan to spend at least a couple of hours here, if not an entire afternoon.

Bird-in-Hand Farmers Market (717-393-9674), PA 340 and Maple Ave., Bird-in-Hand. Open 8:30–5:30 Fri. and Sat. year round, Wed.–Sat.

July–Oct., and Wed., Fri., and Sat. April–June and Nov. This small market gets a lot of bus-tour traffic because of its prime location on PA 340. Look for the usual assortment of crafts, produce, baked goods, and hand-rolled soft pretzels. It's owned by Good 'N Plenty Restaurant, which is nearby.

Root's Country Market (717-898-7811), 705 Graystone Rd., Manheim. Open 9–9 Tues. Just off PA 72 between Lebanon and Lancaster, this family-run market has two hundred vendors selling smoked meats, fresh and dried herbs, doll clothes, hand-painted wooden ducks, local produce, and much more.

✳ Entertainment

MUSIC ♿ **Fulton Theatre** (717-397-7425; www.thefulton.org), 12 N. Prince St., Lancaster. A former roadhouse and vaudeville stage that now hosts symphony, opera, and Broadway shows. Tours are available weekdays at 11 AM for $7 a person.

THEATER & MOVIES ♿ **American Music Theater** (717-397-7700), 2425 Old Lincoln Hwy. east (US 30), Lancaster. Live concerts and original Broadway shows.

♿ **Sight & Sound Theatres** (717-687-7800; www.sightandsound.com), PA 896, Strasburg. This Christian theatrical company stages elaborate shows using actors, live animals, special effects, and music on two separate stages, the Millenium Theater and Living Waters. The shows are wildly popular, attracting as many as 900,000 people a year. Evening shows are on weekends at 7 or 7:30. The Christmas shows are especially popular and book up fast.

♿ **Dutch Apple Dinner Theatre** (717-898-1900), 510 Centerville Rd,. Lancaster. Traditional Broadway favorites and comedy shows, accompanied by a buffet dinner.

✳ Selective Shopping

Amish and Mennonites have created their own exquisite baskets, quilts, dolls, furniture, toys, wall hangings, and hex designs for centuries. You will find much of it for sale in stores along Old Philadelphia Pike in Intercourse and Bird-in-Hand, as well as PA 772 between Intercourse and Leola. Most shops are closed on Sun.

CANDLES & CRAFTS **Lapp's Coach Shop** (717-768-8712), 3572 Newport Rd., Intercourse. Wide selection of reasonably priced wooden chests, wagons, and toys made by local craftspeople.

Moravian Mission Gift Shop (717-626-9027), 8 Church Square, Lititz. Open 10–4 Sat. and Sun. Tucked behind the archives building on the square, this is the place to find Moravian crafts, books, etched glass, and beeswax candles.

Old Candle Barn (717-768-3231), 3551A Old Philadelphia Pike, Intercourse. Open daily. Don't be put off by its World War I Quonset hut appearance; this huge shop features an impressive variety of handcrafted candles, potpourri, and crafts. If you're here on a weekday, you can watch the candles being dipped and poured in the downstairs factory.

Weathervane Shop (717-569-9312), 2451 Kissel Hill Rd., Lancaster. The gift shop at the Landis Valley Museum sells pottery, wooden cabinetry, linens, and folk art produced by their own craftspeople.

QUILTS Many back roads have simple signs indicating places where quilts are sold; selection is often more limited than in the shops, but prices are usually lower.

People's Place Old Country Store (717-768-7171), 3513 Old Philadelphia Pike, Intercourse. Open daily. This pleasant shop below the People's Place Quilt Museum has a knowledgeable sales staff and a wide selection of contemporary quilts.

Quilts and Fabric Shack (717-768-0338), 3127 Old Philadelphia Pike, Bird-in-Hand. This recently expanded shop sells quilts and wall hangings handmade by Amish and Mennonite women. They also carry a large selection of fabrics.

Witmer Quilt Shop (717-656-9526), 1070 W. Main St., New Holland. Emma Witmer, who took over the family quilting shop from her mother, sells more than one hundred patterns out of the second floor of her home. Most of the quilts for sale are contemporary, but she also stocks some antique beauties.

FURNITURE **E. Braun Farm Tables**, 3688 Old Philadelphia Pike, Intercourse. This family-owned company makes gorgeous farm tables, chairs, bed frames, and other furniture using wood salvaged from farm buildings from the late 1800s and 1900s. It also has a shop in Bird-in-Hand.

SPECIAL SHOPS **Aaron's Books** (717-627-1990), 43 S. Broad St., Lititz. Named after the owners' son, this pleasant family-owned store sells used books and fair-trade gifts and notecards; there's also a neat children's play area.

& **Doneckers** (717-738-9503), 100 N. State St., Ephrata. This upscale shopping complex began as a designer clothing store in the 1950s and has expanded over the years into three stories of art galleries, high-end furniture showrooms, a restaurant, and a 40-room inn.

& **Intercourse Canning Company** (717-768-0156), 3612 E. Newport Rd., Intercourse. This large shop is known for Pennsylvania Dutch delicacies like chow-chow, apple butter, and pickled red beet eggs, and its generous samples. During the week, you can observe Amish and Mennonite workers canning all kinds of fruits and vegetables.

& **Kitchen Kettle Village** (717-768-8261), PA 340, Intercourse. Yes, it's contrived, but this shopping village is a fun one-stop destination of buggy and tractor rides, kettle corn stands, live music (on weekends), and about 30 shops selling everything from personalized teddy bears to hex signs and soft pretzels. The **Jam & Relish Kitchen** is a favorite stop for chow-chow, jams, jellies, and relishes; they are generous with samples. You can also get **Lapp Valley Farms** ice cream here (see also *Bakeries & Farm Stands*).

Zook's Dry Goods (717-768-8153), 3535 Old Philadelphia Pike, Intercourse. This Amish variety store sells everything from board games to quilting fabrics to knit sweaters.

✳ Special Events

May: **Sertoma Club Chicken Barbecue** (third weekend), Long's Park, Lancaster—the world's largest chicken barbecue (it's even in the Guinness

MUD SALES

Named for the soggy late-winter ground, mud sales are Amish-run auctions that have been a festive rite of spring in Lancaster County for nearly 50 years. Even if you're not in the market for the goods, which range from outdoor sheds to small crafts and handmade quilts, this is an ideal opportunity to mingle with the Amish at their most relaxed and natural, not to mention feast on hot buttered pretzels and roast pork sandwiches. Mud sales are held in small towns throughout the county, with proceeds going to local volunteer fire companies. They are usually on Sat. in late Feb. through early Apr. and start around 8 or 9 AM. Call 1-800-723-8824 or visit www.padutch-country.com for information and a current schedule.

Book of World Records) turns out more than 33,000 chicken dinners for a donation of $7 per person.

August: **Pennsylvania Renaissance Faire** (second weekend, then weekends through Oct.), 2775 Lebanon Rd., Manheim—one of the county's most popular events with lots of jousting knights, costumed wenches, puppet shows, and terrific interactive street performances.

September: **Ephrata Fair** (fourth weekend), downtown Ephrata—a huge country fair featuring carnival rides, live music, livestock competitions, and a street parade; don't miss the toasted cheeseburgers.

October: **Lititz Chocolate Walk** (first weekend), downtown Lititz—two dozen of the area's chocolatiers offer displays and demonstrations of their work around town.

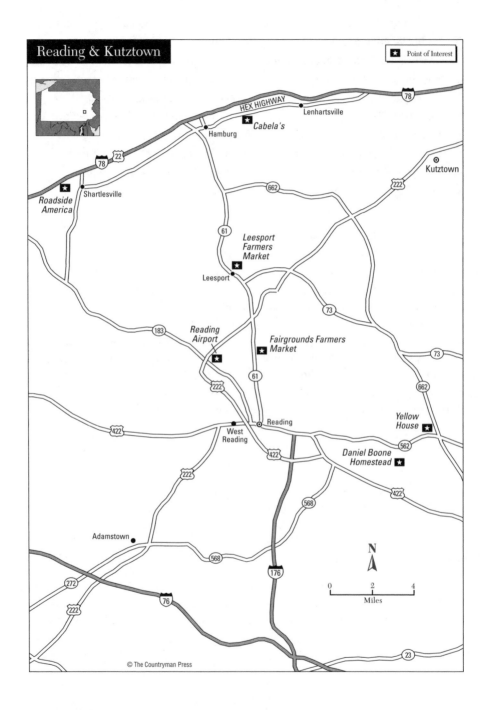

Reading & Kutztown

Point of Interest

HEX HIGHWAY

Lenhartsville

78

Cabela's

Hamburg

22

78

Kutztown

Roadside
America

Shartlesville

662

222

61

Leesport
Farmers
Market

Leesport

73

183

Reading
Airport

Fairgrounds Farmers
Market

73

61

662

222

Yellow
House

422

Reading

West
Reading

Daniel Boone
Homestead

562

422

222

422

568

Adamstown

568

N

272

568

176

0   2   4
Miles

222

76

23

© The Countryman Press

READING & KUTZTOWN

About 60 miles west of Philadelphia, Reading is the state's fifth-largest city with about 81,000 residents. Once a major manufacturing center for hosiery and hardware, it was also the site of one of the nation's oldest and largest railroads, known as the Philadelphia and Reading. In the early 1970s, abandoned textile mills on the outskirts of town were developed to create one of the country's first outlet malls (it still operates under the name VF Outlet Village).

Despite struggles with crime and suburban flight, downtown Reading has seen a revitalization in recent years, with the opening of GoggleWorks, a hip complex of artists' studios, a large performing arts center, and a solid roster of good restaurants and bars. An interesting footnote: Reading was the actual setting (fictionalized as Mount Judge) in the book *Rabbit Run*, written by local boy John Updike.

A few miles to the south of Reading just across the Berks County line, you'll find Adamstown, a shopper's paradise of antiques stores and markets. To the city's north are winding country roads dotted with hex-sign barns, historic hotels, and Pennsylvania Dutch diners.

Kutztown, also featured in this chapter, is about 20 miles to the northeast and more rural, with a rich Pennsylvania Dutch heritage. Founded around 1779 as Cootstown, which was later changed to Kutztown, it is home to a pretty and walkable downtown, Kutztown University, and a comprehensive museum on Pennsylvania Dutch culture and traditions. Every June and July, it hosts the Kutztown Folk Festival, a renowned nine-day celebration of all things Pennsylvania Dutch.

GUIDANCE **Greater Reading Convention & Visitors Bureau** (610-375-4085; 800-443-6610; www.readingberkspa.com) has a large visitor center at 352 Penn St. in downtown Reading. It's open Mon.–Sat. They also have a staffed desk at the GoggleWorks complex (610-374-4600; 201 Washington St.).

GETTING THERE *By air*: Major airports serving Reading and Kutztown are **Lehigh Valley International Airport** in Allentown (888-359-5842) and **Philadelphia International** (215-937-6800). **Reading Regional** (610-372-4666) offers limited service.

By car: From Philadelphia and points east, take I-76 to exit 298 (Morgantown–Reading), then follow US 422 west to downtown Reading. To reach Kutztown from Reading, take US 222 to Old US 22 and head east. From Philadelphia, take the Northeast Extension of I-76 (I-476) to I-78/US 22 west.

GETTING AROUND BARTA (610-921-0601; www.bartabus.com) offers more than 20 bus routes in and around Reading that begin at the Berks Area Reading Transportation Authority (BARTA) Transportation Center downtown and run to FirstEnergy Stadium, Hamburg, and other towns.

MEDICAL EMERGENCY Reading Hospital and Medical Center (610-988-8000), Sixth Ave. and Spruce St., West Reading. Downtown, there's St. Joseph's Medical Center Community Campus on Sixth Street.

WHEN TO GO Most of the antiques and collectors markets that the Reading area is known for are open year-round. The country and hillsides surrounding Reading and Kutztown are ablaze in brown, yellow, and orange in Oct., adding a visual element to visits to the area's flea markets and rural towns. Kutztown is at its best in late June and early July when its Pennsylvania Dutch folk festival is in high gear.

DUTCH HEX SIGN

❊ Villages

Adamstown. As a *Washington Post* writer aptly put it in an article about the area: "If it's old and American, chances are it's in Adamstown." This small town at the northeastern edge of Lancaster County describes itself as the Antiques Capital of the U.S.A. Indeed, it probably has more antiques shops and markets than it does residents. (At last count, the population was 1,200.) Its main street is a shopper's paradise of junk stores, high-end antiques shops, consignment malls, and several massive Sunday-only flea markets. There are a few restaurants to fuel up in between buying and browsing marathons, but little else to amuse those who hate shopping.

Hamburg. Named after the city in Germany and framed by rural countryside and the Blue Mountains to the north, this place epitomizes the American small town. The opening of Cabela's in 2003, and with it several chain hotels and restaurants, changed its look and demographics a bit, but its main street, located on Old US 22 remains frozen in time, with family restaurants that date to the 1800s, a couple of old-fashioned inexpensive hotels, a few antiques shops, and a five-and-dime store.

Shartlesville. Not far from Hamburg, this town boasts on its Web site that in 2004, "our population increased to 410 and growing." Established in the 1800s by German and Swiss tradespeople, it's a good place to stop for an hour or two if you happen to be visiting Cabela's or making your way to or from Harrisburg and Allentown. You'll find here several Pennsylvania Dutch restaurants, homegrown vegetable stands, and Roadside America, an indoor miniature village and beloved landmark of sorts.

GOGGLEWORKS

✳ To See

GoggleWorks (610-374-4600; www.goggleworks.org) 201 Washington St., Reading. Open daily. Housed in a former safety goggle factory (hence the name) near downtown, this hip arts complex and community hub opened in 2005 as a place that lets artists create and display their work in public; you'll find everything from folk art and photography to lithographs and pottery represented, plus a glass-blowing facility, jewelry studio, dance and music studios, movie theater, and cafe. Stop at the front desk for a map before setting off to explore. The best time to visit is the second Sunday of the month, when you'll find many of the artists at work in their studios. Parking is ample and free.

Reading Public Museum (610-371-5850), 500 Museum Rd., Reading. Closed Mon.; $7 adults, $5 ages 5–17. This multifaceted museum has a planetarium (with Fri.-night laser shows), arboretum, and more than a dozen science, art, and history galleries displaying an eclectic mix of dinosaur fossils, Pennsylvania German artifacts, and taxidermy-mounted animals. The art collection includes works by such notables as Winslow Homer, Benjamin West, Milton Avery, John Singer Sargent, N. C. Wyeth, and Edgar Degas.

✳ To Do

Pennsylvania German Cultural Heritage Center (610-683-4000), 22 Luckinbill Rd., on the Kutztown University campus. Open 10–4 weekdays; free. The site of the annual Kutztown Festival, this is also the place to go any time for a crash course in Pennsylvania Dutch history, culture, and traditions. The museum offers thousands of 19th- and 20th-century artifacts, plus ancient farm equipment, a one-room schoolhouse, and reconstructed log homes.

FOR FAMILIES ✐ ⌘ **Crystal Cave** (610-683-6765; www.crystalcavepa.com), 963 Crystal Cave Rd., Kutztown. Open daily Mar. through Nov.; $10.50 adults, $6.50 ages 6–12. Few kids from eastern Pennsylvania completed their childhoods without seeing Crystal Cave. A favorite of individual families and school groups, this natural wonder is named after the shiny calcium crystals that run along its underground walls. Guided tours take about 45 minutes. There's also a short nature trail and geological museum.

✐ **Koziar's Christmas Village** (610-488-1110; www.koziarschristmasvillage .com), 782 Christmas Village Rd., Bernville. Open evenings in Nov. and Dec.; call for days and times. Koziar's began in 1955 as a family's personal holiday display and has turned into one of the state's top Christmastime attractions. Millions of lights decorate an entire farm, plus there's an indoor electric train display, appearances by Santa, and a reasonably priced gift shop selling ornaments and other tis-the-season decorations. The view as you drive in over the hill is amazing.

✐ ⟁ ⌘ **Roadside America** (610-488-6241; www.roadsideamericainc.com), 109 Roadside Dr., Shartlesville. Open daily, except Christmas; $6 adults, $3 ages 6–11. Don't be put off by the giant statue of a smiling Amish couple that greets you at the parking lot entrance. This indoor miniature village 25 miles northwest of Reading draws ooohs and aaahs from its many fans. The brochure might describe it best: "It is . . . the American countryside as it might be seen by a giant so huge he could see from coast to coast." You could easily spend a couple of hours examining the tiny bake shops, churches, theaters, gas stations, and some four hundred other buildings that make up the display. Kids will love the

ROADSIDE AMERICA

DANIEL BOONE'S FARM

buttons that let them ring church bells, operate steamrollers, and participate in other activities.

Daniel Boone Homestead (610-582-4900; www.danielboonevillage.com), 400 Daniel Boone Rd., Birdsboro. Open Tues.–Sat. 9–5, Sun. 12–5; $4 adults, $2 ages 6–17. The famous frontiersman spent his adolescent years on this large farm east of Reading before his father moved the family to North Carolina. Not much data exists on his life back then, but the tour provides a reasonably interesting look at life in the 1700s. Set on more than 570 acres, it includes the original log house where Boone was born, a blacksmith shop, smokehouse, and circa 1810 sawmill. You don't have to take the tour to enjoy the property's two picnic areas, lake, and walking trails.

✳ Outdoor Activities

BICYCLING The 23-mile loop around **Blue Marsh Lake** (610-376-6337; 1268 Palisades Dr., Leesport) was named one of America's top ten bike trails by *Bicycling* magazine in the 1990s. It hasn't changed much since then, with a tight and twisting single track, short uphill climbs, and stellar views.

GOLF **Blackwood Golf Course** (610-385-6200), 510 Red Corner Rd., Douglassville. Attractive and relatively undemanding 18-hole course with three tees to 6,403 yards.

Reading Country Club (610-779-1000), 5311 Perkiomen Ave., Reading. This 18-hole course dates to 1923 and has gently rolling terrain and tree-lined fairways.

HORSEBACK RIDING **French Creek State Park** (see also *Green Space*) has 8 miles of equestrian trails. The clearly marked Horseshoe Trail, which begins in

HEX HIGHWAY

Hex signs are an important part of Pennsylvania Dutch folk art, used to decorate barns and symbolizing good luck and good harvest. This approximately 22-mile drive follows part of the designated Dutch Hex Highway past many old barns and farmhouses decorated with the round and colorful signs, as well as past historic churches, small towns, and rural countryside. Begin in Shartlesville north of Reading and follow Old US 22 east through Shartlesville's frozen-in-time main street. In Hamburg, stop at **Stoudt's Fruit Farm** (610-488-7549) for some apples or nectarines, then continue to Lenhartsville, where you can examine the old hex signs on the **Deitsch Eck Restaurant** (610-562-8520; Old US 22) before dining on pork and sauerkraut or chicken pot pie. From here, head north on PA 143 toward Kempton and turn left at Hawk Mountain Road. Continue another 9 miles through scenic farmland to **Hawk Mountain Sanctuary** (610-756-6961; 1700 Hawk Mountain Rd.), and spend the rest of the afternoon hiking the nature trails or watching raptors fly by at eye level. A complete map of the Dutch Hex Highway is available for download at www.hexsigns.org.

HEX HIGHWAY BARN

Valley Forge, skirts the park's two lakes and continues to the Appalachian Trail near Harrisburg.

✳ Green Space

⊘ ❦ **French Creek State Park** (610-582-9680), 843 Park Rd., Elverson. Set amid picturesque farmland straddling Berks and Chester counties, this 7,340-acre tree-filled park offers two lakes—Hopewell and Scotts Run—plus picnic areas, two disc courses, a campground, and 30 miles of hiking trails. You can fish for trout and bass and ride nonmotorized boats in the lakes. Swimming isn't allowed, but there's a large public pool near Hopewell Lake. This is also a popular spot for orienteering, with a self-guiding course that lets you locate markers in the park with the aid of a map and compass. Maps and other information are available at the park office.

🦅 ✿ ⚓ **Hawk Mountain Sanctuary** (610-756-6961), 1700 Hawk Mountain Rd., Kempton. Open dawn to dusk daily; $5–7 adults, $3 ages 6–12. About 7 miles north of Hamburg, this 2,380-acre preserve is one of the top places in North America to see raptors of all kinds. During fall migration, an average of 20,000 hawks, eagles, and falcons from 18 different species pass by daily, often at eye level, as they travel down the Appalachian corridor. The largest migration takes place between mid-Aug. and Dec., though mid-Sept. and Oct. are considered the peak times and also usually mean spectacular leaf-peeping opportunities. Buy tickets, pick up a Name-that-Raptor guide, and check out the awesome display of hand-carved and painted model raptors at the visitor center, then proceed up a moderately steep trail that links to two viewing platforms (you can also hook up with the 2,000-mile Appalachian Trail from here).

✳ Lodging

BED & BREAKFASTS

Reading

Overlook Mansion (610-371-9173; www.overlookmansionbedandbreakfast.com), 620 Centre Ave. Daphne Miller and Paul Strause are the friendly owners of this Second-Empire mansion across from Centre Park in north Reading. The three large high-ceilinged rooms have queen beds, televisions, wireless access, and refrigerators. Have breakfast delivered to your room or eat outside on the porch overlooking a garden. Miller, a reliable source of information on the area, also hosts theme weekends and events such as chocolate socials and ghostly walking tours through the nearby Charles Evans Cemetery. Rooms $149–179.

⚓ ◐ **Stirling Guest Hotel** (610-373-1522; www.stirlingguesthotel.com), 1120 Centre Ave. This elegant gated mansion across from Charles Evans Cemetery has 15 large suites with fireplaces, whirlpool baths, and terrace balconies. Some are located in a renovated carriage house. There's also a landscaped swimming pool. It is very popular for weddings, so you might want to inquire about that if you're staying over a weekend. Most of the suites sleep two, but one family suite can accommodate four. Suites $125–300.

Nearby

🐾 **Adamstown Inns & Cottages** (800-594-4808, www.adamstown.com), 62 W. Main St., Adamstown. A good place to base an antiquing visit to Adamstown, this complex of two separate inns (Adamstown and Amethyst) is within walking distance of most of the town's shops and flea markets. The rate includes a continental breakfast, served in the dining room of the Amethyst. Two nearby two-story homes (where pets and kids are allowed) are also available for rent. Rooms $79–199. Cottages $195–245.

🐚 ♿ **Land Haven** (610-845-3257; www.landhavenbandb.com), 1194 Huff's Church Rd., Barto. This comfortable B&B was once an 1870s general store, and owners Ed and Donna Land take care to honor its history. The five rooms are named after the original proprietors and have queen or king beds, private baths or showers, and a lovely mix of whimsical and antique decor. It also has an antique store, a large library of old cookbooks (seven-thousand-plus!), and special events like cooking classes and live singer-songwriter concerts. It's about 18 miles from Reading. Rooms $90–125.

🍴 ♿ **Hawk Mountain Bed and Breakfast** (610-756-4224; www.hawk mountainbb.com), 221 Stone Valley Rd., Kempton. This lodge, tucked in the scenic Stoney Run Valley and about 8 miles from the hawk sanctuary, has a large swimming pool and eight attractive rooms with queen beds, TVs, and private entrances and baths. Two deluxe rooms have fireplaces and jacuzzi tubs. A full country breakfast of pancakes or waffles, sausage, and fruit comes with the rate, as do complimentary beverages (including Yuengling lager). Standard rooms $135; deluxe $185, two-night minimum in Sept. and Oct.

CAMPGROUNDS Blue Rocks Family Campground (610-756-6366; www .bluerocksfamilycampground.com), 341 Sousley Rd., Lenhartsville. South of the Appalachian Trail and Hawk Mountain between Allentown and Kutztown. Two swimming pools, lots of kids' activities. Tent sites $25–35; cabins $45–65.

🍴 ♿ 🌳 **French Creek State Park** (610-582-9680), 843 Park Rd., Elver-

son. You'll find 201 wooded tent sites, 50 with electric hookups, near the east entrance of the state park.

✳ Where to Eat

DINING OUT ♿ 🍷 **Judy's on Cherry** (610-374-8511), 332 Cherry St., Reading. Lunch and dinner Tues.– Fri., dinner Tues.–Sat. A Mediter-ranean-style downtown cafe serving simple yet creative dishes like fig and prosciutto pizza, cedar-planked salmon, and tomato basil chicken. Next door is the Speckled Hen Pub (see *Nightlife*). Lunch $10–15; dinner entrees $15–25.

🍷 ⊚ **Gracie's 21st Century Café** (610-323-4004), 1534 Manatawny Rd., Pine Forge. Dinner Wed.–Sat. It's doubtful you will find another restaurant like this in Pennsylvania or quite possibly anywhere. Owner and chef Gracie Skiadas bought a decay-ing early-1800s building in the middle of nowhere more than 20 years ago and turned it into a hip Santa Fe–meets-1776 hangout. The entree prices are high for this area, but the good food and ambiance make it a perfect special-occasion place. The global fusion menu features a huge vegetarian section and might include fried blue corn ravioli, wild black bass stuffed with shrimp, and pan-seared salmon prosciutto; don't miss the leg-endary Jamaican curried crab bisque or the "Ole Hippy" carrot cake for dessert. Extensive wine list. Entrees: $15–38.

♿ 🍷 **Yellow House Hotel** (610-689-9410), 6743 Boyertown Pike, Dou-glassville. Lunch and dinner daily; limited hours Sun. Once a stagecoach stop and general store for travelers between Reading and Philadelphia, this country inn has three attractive dining rooms and a separate bar. The traditional menu offers many steak, chicken, and seafood entrees, as well as lighter fare like burgers, stir fries, and salads. Specialties include crab cakes, barbecued spare ribs, and grilled lamb chops. Entrees $15–23.

Y **American House Hotel** (610-562-4683). 2 N. Fourth St., Hamburg. Dinner Wed.–Sun., breakfast Sat. and Sun. It's no bargain, but this restored old hotel is the best place for fine cuisine in the area. The dining room has tin ceilings, old-style chandeliers, and a full tavern downstairs. Highlights of the diverse menu include Boursin chicken stuffed with crab and asparagus, osso buco, and maple- and ginger-glazed salmon. Entrees $19–28.

EATING OUT

Reading
Y **Jimmie Kramer's Peanut Bar** (610-376-8500), 322 Penn St. Lunch and dinner Mon.–Sat. This downtown Reading institution serves hot and cold sandwiches, salads, fried seafood platters, and a small number of entrees like filet mignon and lemon parmesan flounder. There is also a kids' menu. Join the regulars at the long nonsmoking bar or sit at a table and feel the crushed peanut shells under your feet. Dishes $7≠18.

Y & **Ugly Oyster** (610-373-6791), 21 S. Fifth St. Lunch and dinner Mon.–Sat. This red-walled Irish pub near the downtown convention center has a *Cheers*-like bar, a wide selection of beers and single malt scotch, and very good food. There's a small selection of steak and seafood entrees at dinner, and a lunch and tavern menu (available all day) of crab cake sandwiches, cheesesteaks, salads, a raw bar, and excellent soups. There's live Irish music every Thursday. Dishes $6–25.

Kutztown
Y **Basin Street Hotel** (610-683-7900), 42 E. Main St. Open 11 AM–2 AM daily. A popular college hangout, this circa-1897 tavern and restaurant features hearty sandwiches with names like Professor (sautéed veggies with mozzarella and tomato sauce) and Golden Bear (hot roast beef). There are also salads, fried appetizers, and reasonably priced entrees like

JIMMIE KRAMER'S PEANUT BAR

London broil and crab cakes. Dishes $6–15.

Nearby

♣ ♂ **Deitsch Eck** (610-562-8520), Old US 22, Lenhartsville. Lunch and dinner Wed.–Sun. Hex signs welcome you to this authentic Pennsylvania Dutch restaurant just east of Hamburg on Old US 22. The service couldn't be friendlier and the prices couldn't be more reasonable. Choose from dozens of sandwiches, from burgers to hot roast beef, or a long list of platters such as smoked pork chops, meatloaf, and grilled ham steak. Dishes $2.50–11.

♣ ♿ ♂ **Jukebox Café** (610-369-7272), 535 S. Reading Ave., Boyertown. Breakfast and lunch daily. A 1950s-style diner (with a real jukebox) known for its many vegetarian entrees and liberal use of fresh local produce. Try the vegetarian eggs Benedict (made with portobello mushrooms and sundried tomatoes) or the Boardwalk wrap with Italian sausage, eggs, cheese, and salsa. Cash only. Dishes $2–7.

FARM MARKETS **Fairgrounds Farmers Market** (610-929-3429), N. Fifth St. at US 222, Reading. Open Thurs.–Sat; hours vary. Known for its large and diverse lunchtime market, this indoor market near Fairgrounds Mall also sells fresh local produce, smoked meats, and other items. Iggy's, toward the front of the market, is a great place for breakfast.

Leesport Farmers Market (610-926-1307; www.leesportmarket.com), 312 Gernant's Rd., Leesport. Open 8 AM–9 PM Wed. Eight miles north of Reading, this indoor-outdoor market features a livestock auction plus a large selection of fresh local produce, baked goods, clothes, antiques, and garden items. There's even a barber shop. It also hosts huge crafts fairs and flea markets several times a year.

Zern's Farmers Market & Auction (610-367-2461; www.zerns.com), 1100 E. Philadelphia Ave., Gilbertsville. Open Fri. 2–10 PM, Sat. 11 AM–10 PM. You could easily spend a day at this nearly 90-year-old indoor market, especially if you like shopping for bric-a-brac and people-watching. About four hundred merchants sell everything from vintage clothes and furniture to old books and tube socks. There's also plenty of Pennsylvania Dutch food.

DESSERTS **Haute Chocolate Café** (610-373-4455), 711 Penn Ave., West Reading. Closed Sun. This brown and orange cafe near VF Outlet Village should appeal to everyone from small kids to ladies who lunch. There's a variety of hot and cold drinks (try the "hot chocolate" milkshake), a selection of handmade confections, ice cream, and a chocolate dipping fountain.

✳ Entertainment

MOVIES & THEATER **GoggleWorks Film Theatre** (610-374-4600; www.goggleworks.org), 201 Washington St., Reading. A 131-seat modern venue showing art and independent films in the evenings and Wed. afternoons.

♿ **Reading Civic Theater** (610-898-7200), 136 N. Sixth St., Reading. This large downtown venue hosts everything from Reading Royals hockey games to live musical shows.

Strand Theater (610-683-8775), 32 N. White Oak St., Kutztown. Historic old theater with two screens showing first-run movies.

NIGHTLIFE Ϋ **Speckled Hen Pub** (610-685-8511), Fourth and Cherry sts., Reading. Adjacent to Judy's on Cherry restaurant, this comfortable neighborhood pub has tavern food, happy hour specials, and a nice selection of microbrews and ales on tap. There's live music on Fri. and Sat., when it stays open until 1 AM.

Shorty's Bar (610-683-9600) 272 W. Main St., Kutztown. Closed Sun. Also known as the Kutztown Tavern, this popular bar and nightclub has pool tables, plasma TVs, and a DJ on weekends. Try the house-made lager.

✳ Selective Shopping

ANTIQUES Adamstown, between Reading and Lancaster, might have more antiques shops and flea markets than Lancaster County has cows. Many of them line PA 272 and offer reasonable prices that experts say are tough to beat anywhere else on the East Coast. Pick up a free map and shopping guide to the area at just about any shop. For a more complete listing of shops, visit www.antiques capital.com.

Renninger's Antique and Collectors Market (717-336-2177; www

BASEBALL
READING PHILLIES
Once known as the Reading Pretzels, this Double A farm team began its long affiliation with the Philadelphia Phillies in 1967. Its home games at FirstEnergy Stadium, which lead the Eastern League in attendance, are a mix of carnival-like entertainment, community spirit, and good old-fashioned baseball. There's a swimming pool behind right field, contests and music between innings, hot dogs and funnel cakes, and pre- and post-game concerts. Tickets will set you back no more than $10. Visit www.readingphillies .com for more information.

READING BASEBALL

.renningers.com), 2500 N. Reading Rd. Open 7:30–4 Sun. The granddaddy of antiques marts with more than three hundred indoor and two hundred outdoor vendors selling everything from farm tables to Chippendale desks to comic books and costume jewelry. Expect to see more Windsor chairs than you will ever see again in your lifetime. There are also plenty of food vendors selling everything from cream donuts to soft pretzels. The outdoor section opens at 5 AM, weather permitting; bring a flashlight. Renninger's also operates markets on some weekends in Kutztown (check Web site for a schedule).

Stoudt's Black Angus Antique Mall (717-484-2757), 2800 N. Reading Rd. Open 7:30–4 Sun. Just down the street from Renninger's, this 350-vendor market is known for upscale offerings like 19th-century Normandy farm tables, fine china and porcelain, rare books, gas chandeliers, and more. It is next to Stoudt's Black Angus Steakhouse and Brew Pub and a German-style shopping village that's open seven days.

Adams Antiques (717-355-3166), 2400 N. Reading Rd. Open Mon.–Sat. 10–5, Sun. 8–5. A fun to browse antiques mall featuring 85 booths selling vintage dollhouses, toys, beer steins, lawn ornaments, old postcards, and more. There's an outdoor set-up on weekends as well.

Country French Collection (717-484-0200), 2887 N. Reading Rd. Open 10–4 daily. Housed in an 18th-century stone barn full of exquisite (and expensive) armoires, chairs, farm tables, and copper cookware from France and England. Wine and cheese are served on Sun.

Merritt's Antiques (610-689-9541), 1860 Weavertown Rd., Douglassville. A large warehouse full of hard-to-find antiques and quirky treasures like horsehead hitching posts, mechanical banks, tin signs, weathervanes, and more.

OUTLETS & ⊤ **VF Outlet Village** (800-772-8336), 801 Hill Ave., West Reading. Open daily. Not long ago, this complex was known as Vanity Fair, anchored by the lingerie giant, and it was the place to get discounted pajamas and Lee jeans. It abbreviated its name and underwent a renovation in the 1990s and now includes brands like Bass, Tommy Hilfiger, Coach, and Oneida. It's still a popular shopping destination, especially on weekends. The mom-and-pop shops and cafés that line nearby Penn Avenue are also worth a look.

SPECIAL SHOPS & ⊤ **Cabela's** (610-929-7000), 100 Cabela Dr. (off I-78), Hamburg. Open daily. As much theme park as retail store, this outpost of the Wisconsin-based outdoor adventure catalog has a café, a walk-through aquarium, and a mini-mountain full of taxidermied animals. Prices are comparable to the catalog's; there's also a bargain cave in the back.

✳ Special Events

June/July: **Kutztown Folk Festival** (last weekend/first weekend), Kutztown University—the state's biggest Pennsylvania Dutch—themed party. Nine days of square dancing, agricultural demonstrations, a folk arts and crafts fair, pony rides, hay mazes, home cooking, and much more.

Lower Susquehanna River Valley

HARRISBURG & HERSHEY

GETTYSBURG

YORK COUNTY

HARRISBURG & HERSHEY

Less than 15 miles apart from one another, Hershey and Harrisburg are close in distance but quite different in mood and offerings. Harrisburg is the state capital with grand old buildings, historical museums, expense-account steakhouses, and commanding views of the Susquehanna River. Once an important crossroads for Native Americans traveling to and from the Potomac and upper Susquehanna region, it is named for a later settler, John Harris. During the American Civil War, Harrisburg was a training center for the Union Army and developed into a major rail center and link between the Atlantic coast and the Midwest. Today, it's a city of about 48,000 with a reputation for shutting down on weekends and when the state legislature is out of session. But there is more going on than first meets the eye. The city boasts many beautiful parks, most notably downtown's City Island, good restaurants, and the best nightlife outside of Philadelphia and Baltimore. One could plan a visit based around a visit to the National Civil War Museum alone.

Meanwhile, chocolate, theme-park rides, and a man named Milton permeate

HARRISBURG'S RIVER BRIDGES

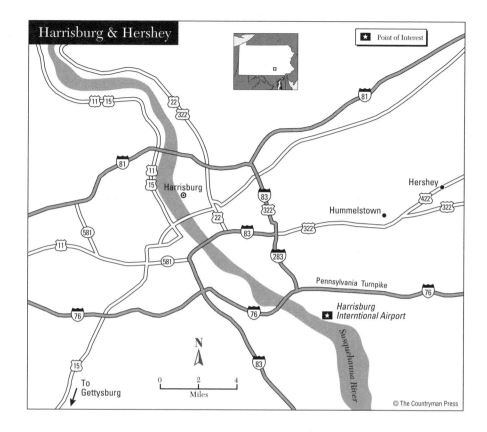

© The Countryman Press

the small town of Hershey. Mr. Hershey died in 1945 after spending decades building his successful candy empire, but his spirit lives on in this Willie Wonka–like realm of resort hotels, gardens, trolley rides, hot-chocolate lattes, and street lamps shaped like Hershey's kisses. You will have a chance to sample chocolate again and again during your visit: upon check-in at many hotels, in the chocolate fondue wraps at the Hotel Hershey's elite spa, and as a gentle scent wafting throughout the town, especially around the main factory on Chocolate Avenue.

AREA CODE Harrisburg and Hershey are within the 717 area code.

GUIDANCE Contact the **Harrisburg-Hershey-Carlisle Tourism and Convention Bureau** (717-231-7788; 800-955-0969; www.visithhc.com), 415 Market St., Harrisburg, for maps and a visitors guide. A **Welcome Center** is open weekdays from 8:30-4:30 in the east wing of the Capitol. In Hershey, Chocolate World and the Hershey Lodge have brochures and maps of the area.

GETTING THERE *By air:* **Harrisburg International Airport** (717-948-3900;

1-888-235-9442) is about 50 miles northeast of Gettysburg. **Philadelphia International** (215-937-6800) is about a two-hour drive.

By car: From Philadelphia, take the Pennsylvania Turnpike to exit 266 (Lebanon–Lancaster), then US 322 west to Hershey. For Harrisburg, Pennsylvania Turnpike to exit 247, then I-83 south to Second Street.

By bus: **Greyhound** (800-231-2222) offers service between Harrisburg and dozens of major cities, operating out of a terminal at 411 Market St., Harrisburg.

GETTING AROUND For Harrisburg, **Capital Area Transit** (717-238-8304; www.cattransit.com) offers bus service throughout the city.

The **Hershey Trolley** (717-533-3000; $11 adults) is a great way for first-time visitors to learn the town's layout and history before heading to the park and other attractions. Guides are witty and generous with the candy distribution. Tours depart regularly in front of Chocolate World.

MEDICAL EMERGENCY Harrisburg Hospital (717-782-3591), 111 S. Front St., Harrisburg.

Milton S. Hershey Medical Center (717-531-8521), 500 University Dr., Hershey.

WHEN TO GO Hershey Park is a seasonal attraction open May through Labor Day and some weekends in the fall. If you're looking for a bargain and don't mind skipping the theme park, plan to go anytime off-season and you will find that many area hotel rates drop significantly. There are still plenty of attractions that stay open year-round, including Hershey Gardens, ZooAmerica, and in Harrisburg the State and Civil War museums. To see Harrisburg at its busiest, plan your visit for a weekday when the legislature is in session.

✷ Villages

Hummelstown. Before the chocolate industry came along, this small town between Harrisburg and Hershey was the driving economic force in the area: supplying brownstone for buildings from Philadelphia to Chicago. Today, you will find charming tree-lined streets anchored by a square with antiques shops, preserved old homes, and restaurants, including the wonderful Warwick Hotel. It is also home to Indian Echo Taverns, limestone caves that once served as a shelter for Native Americans, and the historic Middletown and Hummelstown Railroad. Its historical society operates a museum that has an extensive collection of Indian arrowheads collected between 1914 and 1940 by Philander Ward Hartwell, the town's newspaper editor.

✷ To See
MUSEUMS

Harrisburg
🐾 ♿ 🚻 **State Museum of Pennsylvania** (717-787-4780; www.statemuseumpa.org), 300 North St. Closed Mon.; free. This is arguably the finest no-fee

NATIONAL CIVIL WAR MUSEUM

museum outside of Washington, D.C. Located next to the Capitol building, it has four floors of exhibits and activities on Pennsylvania's history, plus a multimedia planetarium, archaeological artifacts, paintings, decorative arts, animal dioramas, industrial and technological innovations, and military objects.

✦ ↑ **National Civil War Museum** (717-260-1861; www.nationalcivilwar museum.org), 1 Lincoln Circle at Reservoir Park. Open daily April through Aug., Wed.–Sun. Sep. through Mar.; $7 adults. This large museum on the eastern edge of Harrisburg opened in 2001 with the goal of telling the entire story of the American Civil War "without bias to Union or Confederate causes." Its dozen galleries are divided by theme, and include slavery and battle artifacts, electronic battle maps, surgery demonstrations, and interactive displays that are interspersed with artifacts such as Robert E. Lee's pocket Bible and Ulysses S. Grant's sword belt. Plan to spend at least two hours here. Some of the displays might be a bit graphic for younger children.

✦ ↑ **Whitaker Center for Science and the Arts** (717-214-2787; www .whitakercenter.org), 222 Market St. Open daily. Science center: $9 adults; $7.25 children; other prices vary. This 130,000-square-foot complex is home to a science center, an IMAX theater, a musical performance stage, and other attractions that are great for kids of all ages. Call ahead for performance and 3D movie schedules.

✦ ↑ **Hershey Museum** (717-534-3439; www.hersheymuseum.org), 170 W. Hersheypark Dr. Open daily; adults $7, $3.50 ages 3–15. This small museum tells the history of Hershey, including an entire exhibit on the evolution of the foil-wrapped Hershey's Kiss and a collection of Pennsylvania German clocks,

& **Hershey Park and Chocolate World** (717-534-3900; 800-437-7439; www
.hersheypa.com/attractions), 100 W. Hersheypark Dr. Open daily mid-May
through Labor Day, and some weekends through Oct.; hours vary; $46
adults, $27 ages 3–8, $62–90 for two- or three-day flex passes. Built in 1907
by Milton S. Hershey as picnic grounds for the employees of his candy company, this family-friendly amusement park now encompasses more than 100
acres with dozens of rides and attractions. Don't miss the Kissing Tower,
which rises above the nearby stacks of the candy factory and gives way to
a 360-degree view of the town and surrounding valley. The newest attraction is East Coast Waterworks, a mammoth waterplay structure featuring
four slides, a roller coaster, and multistory jungle gym. Modeled after Wildwood, New Jersey, and other Atlantic shore boardwalks, it also offers a pier
for strolling, hermit crab sales, corn-dog carts, water balloon races, and a
sandcastle area for toddlers. You will get wet, so bring a change of clothes
if you plan to hit this area of the park.

A cost-saving tip: Many local businesses offer discount park tickets,
and one of the best places to get them is at Giant Food (717-312-0725; 1250
Cocoa Ave.; open daily), where one-day tickets are $35 and include a free
parking pass (if you buy two adult tickets). Another good value is the pre-
view plan: arrive after 7:30 PM when the park closes at 10 or 11, buy a ticket
for the following day, and your admission for the evening is free.

Within walking distance of the park and open year-round is **Chocolate
World** (717-534-4900). It's a good place to start your chocolate sojourn, with
plenty of seats, sustenance, and a staffed information booth. Take the free

pewter, and glass. At the time of this writing, it was preparing to move to larger
facilities in downtown Hershey in fall 2008.

HISTORIC SITES & GARDENS & **Hershey Gardens** (717-534-3492; www
.hersheygardens.org), 170 Hotel Rd., Hershey. Open daily year-round; $10
adults, $6 ages 3–15, free to guests of any Hershey resort. You'll find Japanese,
rock, and herb gardens, a fun children's garden, and more than seven thousand
roses in bloom June through Aug. on this lovely 23-acre property.

& ⊤ **Pennsylvania State Capitol** (800-868-7672), North and Commonwealth
sts., Harrisburg. No visit to the Harrisburg area is complete without a visit to this
domed downtown building, which was modeled after St. Peter's Basilica in
Rome. Free guided tours include stops at the main rotunda and supreme court
chambers and run every half hour on weekdays between 8:30 and 4. No reservations necessary.

Fort Hunter (717-599-5751; www.forthunter.org), 5300 N. Front St., Harrisburg. Open daily. Built in 1756 at the beginning of the French and Indian War,

ride through a simulated Hershey factory, let the kids wrap their own Hershey's kisses, then browse what is possibly the best and largest chocolate-themed gift shop around. There's also a big and loud 3D show featuring singing and dancing candy bars. The first two hours of parking is free.

HERSHEY PARK

this was one of a string of small forts built by the British along the Susquehanna River. Today, it's a beautiful place to spend an afternoon with picnic pavilions, a playground, a small covered bridge, and several 19th-century buildings that are open for tours. Pick up a walking tour brochure at the mansion gift shop.

✳ To Do

FOR FAMILIES ✍ ♿ **ZooAmerica** (717-534-3860), 100 W. Hersheypark Dr. Open daily except Thanksgiving, Christmas, and Jan. 1; $8.50 adults, $7.50 ages 3–8; free parking. This small yet engaging zoo has more than two hundred species of animals from North America and can be covered in three hours or less. You can enter the zoo via a bridge from Hershey Park (though not vice versa). Watch for special events, like Park in the Dark, which lets visitors bring flashlights to check out the animals after hours.

Hummelstown
✍ ☂ **Indian Echo Caverns** (717-566-8131; www.indianechocaverns.com), 368

Middletown Rd., Hummelstown. Open daily except holidays; $13 adults, $7 ages 3–11. Open for tours since 1929, this small but popular attraction makes a nice side trip for those wanting a break from the chocolate-covered world of Hershey. The *New York Times* calls it "the undisputed king of the state's show caves." The 45-minute guided tours include up-close views of stalactites, stalagmites, cave coral, and more (it requires a long walk up and down steep steps to get there). During the summer, kids can pan for gemstones in a replica sluice near the gift shop.

 **M&H Railroad** (717-944-4435; www.mhrailroad.com), 136 Brown St., Middletown. Open May through Oct.; call ahead for days and times; $11 adults, $6 ages 2–11. Kids will love this 11-mile vintage 1920s coach ride along pretty Swatara Creek; the conductor shares historical anecdotes and leads a singalong on the way back. There's also a boarding platform at Indian Echo Caverns.

City Island. One of Harrisburg's best-known attractions, this 60-acre island in the middle of the Susquehanna River is an easy walk from downtown via Walnut Street Bridge or you can drive onto the island via Market or Front streets and pay to park in designated lots. It offers a long list of seasonal and year-round activities for locals and visitors: boat, train and carriage rides, minor league baseball games, seasonal swimming, mini-golf, shopping, and eating. At **City Island Beach** (717-238-9012) on the north end, you can sunbathe and swim every day but Wed. mid-June through Labor Day. **The Pride of the Susquehanna** (717-234-6500; $6.50 adults, $3.50 children) is an authentic stern paddlewheel riverboat that offers 45-minute rides June through Aug. Kids will love **City Island Railroad** (717-232-2332), a scaled version of a Civil War–era steam train that offers rides around the island for $2. Nearby, an **antique carousel** offers $1

PRIDE OF THE SUSQUEHANNA, CITY ISLAND

rides. Cap the day with a visit to the concession stands and small souvenir shops at **RiverSide Village Park** (open mid-May through Labor Day). For more things to do here, see *Outdoor Activities*.

BREWERY TOURS **Troëg's Hamsburg Brewing Co.** (717-232-1297), 800 Paxton St. This small brewery near the waterfront was launched in 1997 by two brothers from Mechanicsburg and produces seven different handcrafted beers. It offers free brewery tours and tastings every Sat. at 2 PM.

✳ Outdoor Activities

BASEBALL Baseball in Harrisburg goes back as far as 1907 when the local team played in the class D tri-state league. Today, the Harrisburg Senators, a farm team of the Washington Nationals, play at **Riverside Stadium** (717-231-4444; www.senatorsbaseball.com) on City Island. Call for a schedule.

BICYCLING/RENTALS **Susquehanna Outfitters** (717-234-7879) rents bicycles on the west side of City Island's north parking lot. Open daily in summer, weekends in Apr., May, Sept., and Oct.

BOAT EXCURSIONS/RENTALS **Susquehanna River Trail** (www.susquehanna rivertrail.org) is a 51-mile river trail with 25 access points between Harrisburg and Sunbury to the north.

Blue Mountain Outfitters (717-957-2413), US 11 and 15, Marysville, rents canoes and kayaks starting at $45 a day.

GOLF **Iron Valley Golf Club** (717-279-7409), 201 Iron Valley Dr., Lebanon. Built on an abandoned iron mine, this challenging course offers 18 holes with significant elevation changes (11 of them are carved out of a mountain).

Royal Oaks Golf Club (717-274-2212), 3350 W. Oak St., Lebanon. This former cattle ranch has 18 holes featuring 6,730 yards of golf from the longest tees for a par of 71.

SKIING **Ski Roundtop** (717-432-9631, www.skiroundtop.com) 925 Roundtop Rd., Lewisberry. About 20 miles south of Harrisburg, this resort has 16 ski trails (some winding), plus snowboarding, tubing, and year-round paintball.

✳ Green Space

Reservoir Park (717-255-3020) Walnut St. between 18th and 21st sts. Built in 1872, this 85-acre park is home to the National Civil War Museum (see also *Museums*), a restored 1898 mansion that houses several art galleries, a large playground, and a band shell that hosts summer concerts and an annual Shakespeare Fest. The Capital Area Greenbelt passes through here (see also *Walks*).

Italian Lake (717-255-3020) Third and Division sts. This 10-acre city park is a popular local gathering place and features formal Italian Renaissance–style gardens, a Japanese harmony bridge, and two scenic man-made lakes. A paved

SUSQUEHANNA RIVER

walking path winds around the larger of the two lakes. Outdoor concerts are held here Sun. evenings in July and Aug.

Wildwood Lake Sanctuary and Nature Center (717-221-0292; www.wild woodlake.org), 100 Wildwood Way. Grounds open daily dawn to dusk. Nestled in what looks like an industrial section of the city, this lake is home to all sorts of wildlife. Birding is popular along the paved pathway that circles the lake. There are several easy hiking trails and boardwalks that wind through marshes and bogs; bikes are permitted on some trails. Stop by the nature center for a detailed map.

WALKS **Capital Area Greenbelt** (717-921-4733; www.caga.org) This 20-mile trail laces its way around the city like a necklace and can be used for walking, biking, or skating. Start at the zenlike **Five Senses Garden** (717-564-0488) off PA 441 behind the Harrisburg East Mall.

✳ Lodging

HOTELS, LODGES, & MOTELS Keep in mind that rates usually drop considerably in the Hershey area during the off-season of late fall, winter, and early spring.

Hershey
♿ ⌒ **Hotel Hershey** (717-533-2171), 100 Hotel Rd. It was a bold endeavor to build a luxury Mediterranean-style hotel during the Depression, but that's exactly what Milton Hershey did when he returned home from a trip to Europe in the 1930s. It remains one of Pennsylvania's top special-occasion hotels, a grand lodge complete with 232 rooms and 25 suites, palatial gardens, indoor and outdoor pools, and commanding views of the Conewago Valley. Guest rooms have a sophisticated Victorian feel and feature original art work, luxury linens, and chocolate soaps and bath foam. Nearby is Hershey Gardens, to which hotel guests are admitted free. You don't have to be a hotel guest to take a free tour (offered daily at 10 AM) of the premises or indulge in a chocolate

fondue wrap or massage at the Chocolate Spa. Rooms $399–409; suites $624–1,700.

◌ ⬤ ◯ **Hershey Motor Lodge** (717-533-3311; www.hersheypa.com/accommodations) Part of the Hershey Resorts umbrella, this sprawling complex of more than 660 rooms may seem daunting on arrival, but it offers efficient and friendly service, spacious rooms, and a convenient location near Hershey Park and other attractions. It does a huge meetings and convention business. Rooms are decorated in chocolate tones and have refrigerators, TVs, wireless access, and chocolate-scented toiletries; there's also an indoor and outdoor pool and four restaurants. Rates include passes to Hershey Gardens, Hershey Museum, discounted Hershey Park tickets, and shuttle service to the park. Rooms $279; suites $508–787.

◌ ◌ ⬤ **Simmons Motel** (717-533-9177; www.simmonsmotel.com) 355 W. Chocolate Ave. This family-owned motel has 23 rooms and 12 large suites with kitchens and is within walking distance of many attractions, including the park, museum, and Chocolate World. Rooms are clean and basic with desks, TVs, and one or two double beds; try to get one in the back away from busy Chocolate Avenue. Coffee, juice, and local maps are available in the small lobby. Rooms $105, suites $245.

BED & BREAKFASTS ⬤ ⬤ **Inn at Westwynd Farm** (717-533-6764; www.westwyndfarminn.com), 1620 Sand Beach Rd., Hummelstown. This picturesque B&B is located on a 32-acre working horse farm 5 miles west of Hershey. The main house has seven cozy rooms (six with private baths and luxurious linens, some with jacuzzi tubs and fireplaces), two living rooms, and an inviting wraparound porch with a view of the countryside. Owners Frank and Carolyn Troxell started a horse training and boarding operation in the 1980s and added the inn portion in 2002. Breakfast (maybe pumpkin waffles or eggs baked in ham) is served on the sun porch or dining room. Fresh-baked snacks, drinks, and candy

HOTEL HERSHEY

are available day and night. No kids under the age of 5. Rooms $65–159, two-night minimum on weekends.

&. ✐ ▼ **Canna Country Inn** (717-938-6077; www.cannainnbandb.com), 393 Valley Rd., Etters. About 8 miles southeast of Harrisburg, this seven-room B&B is housed in a converted 18th-century barn surrounded by 3 acres of gardens and a picnic grove with hammocks and fire pits. Rooms have king or queen beds, DVD players, and wireless access; some have private entrances and whirlpool tubs. The 600-square-foot common living room invites lounging with a fireplace and window seat overlooking the grounds. Breakfasts are huge and made to order. Skiers from nearby Roundtop fill the inn during winter. Rooms and suites $95–170.

CAMPGROUNDS ✐ **Elizabethtown/Hershey KOA** (717-367-7718), 1980 Turnpike Rd., Elizabethtown. About a 15-minute drive from Hershey off PA 743 with more than two hundred tent and hookup sites, a swimming pool, and lots of activities. Tent sites $30–$39; cabins $60–75.

✐ **Hershey Highmeadow Campground** (717-534-8999), 1200 Matlack Rd., Hummelstown. There are 300 tent sites (few with shade), 22 rustic cabins, swimming pools, and a complimentary shuttle to Hershey Park, about five minutes away. Tent sites $36–45; cabins $67–71; rates drop in spring and fall.

✳ **Where to Eat**

DINING OUT

Hershey
Ⲩ **Circular Dining Room** (717-534-8800), Hotel Hershey. Open for

breakfast, lunch, and dinner Mon.–Sat., Sun. brunch. The area's most elegant (and priciest) restaurant boasts wonderful views of the hotel's immaculate gardens and reflecting pools and a menu that offers a sophisticated twist on the ubiquitous chocolate theme. You might find an appetizer of chocolate-scented pork cheek or cocoa-seared scallops and chipotle chocolate glazed salmon as entrees. There are also more traditional offerings like aged New York strip steak and Niman Ranch pork chops. Chocoholics must leave room for the four-course chocolate tasting menu. Reservations recommended; jackets required for men during dinner. Breakfast and lunch $16–23; dinner entrees $28–39.

&. Ⲩ **Fire Alley** (717-533-3200), 1144 Cocoa Ave., in the Cocoaplex shopping complex. Open for lunch and dinner Tues.–Sun. It's a couple of miles from the park, but good food and pleasant ambiance make it worth the drive. Choose from a long list of appetizers, salads, and sandwiches. Entrees range from creative (chicken wrapped in bacon and drizzled with a root beer glaze) to traditional (filet mignon, crab cakes). Lunch and appetizers $5–14; dinner entrees $14–26.

Harrisburg
Sammy's (717-221-0192), 502 N. Third St. A two-story bistro near the Capitol with a traditional Italian menu; try the shrimp scampi or eggplant rollatini stuffed with ricotta. BYO. Reservations recommended on weekends. Lunch: $7–14; dinner entrees $14–24.

Ⲩ **Scott's Grille** (717-234-7599), 212 Locust St. Open for lunch and dinner Mon.–Fri., dinner Sat. A traditional steak and seafood restaurant and weeknight happy hour spot that fills up with VIPs from the nearby Capitol. There is also a lighter bar menu and outdoor seating in summer. Extensive wine list. Lunch $10–14; dinner entrees $14–32.

EATING OUT **What If Café** (717-238-1155), 3424 N. Sixth St., Harrisburg. Lunch and dinner Mon.–Sat. The rooms at this popular BYO eatery are bright and stylish, and the diverse menu includes pesto-grilled shrimp, Mediterranean chicken, and veal Marsala. Lunch $6–11; dinner $12–25.

Hershey

Ý **Fenicci's** (717-533-7159), 102 W. Chocolate Ave. Open Mon.–Fri. for lunch and dinner, dinner Sat. and Sun. The original home of the H.B. Reese Candy Co. (and the birthplace of Reese's Peanut Butter Cups), this dimly lit tavern has a wide selection of pastas, steaks, and seafood, but it's the pizzas that draw the biggest raves. Toppings include fried eggplant, shrimp scampi, and buffalo chicken. It has live music and stays open late on weekends. Dishes $12–22; pizzas $10–13.

Ý **Warwick Hotel** (717-566-9124), 12 W. Main St., Hummelstown. Open Mon.–Sat. for breakfast, lunch, and dinner; dinner only Sun. The 12-page menu at this local favorite features all kinds of burgers, sandwiches, salads, pastas, steaks, and seafood. Dishes $9–25.

ICE CREAM **Mazzoli Ice Cream** (717-533-2252, www.mazzoliice cream.com), 72 W. Governor Rd., Hershey. Open daily in spring and summer; call for other times. Milton Hershey's personal dairy chef, Fred Mazzoli, started this gourmet ice cream business in 1956. Located in a

residential neighborhood off US 322, it still makes and sells spumoni, gelato, Italian ice, and fruit-based sorbets. Don't miss the tortoni, a French custard made with toasted coconut, almond flavoring, and wine bisque.

✳ Entertainment

MUSIC Many Harrisburg bars feature live music on Thurs., Fri., and Sat. nights. Pick up copies of *Fly* magazine or *PA Musician* available for free around town. They highlight what's going on music-wise each week in the Harrisburg area.

Harrisburg

Ý **Appalachian Brewing Company** (717-221-1080), 50 Cameron St. This large microbrewery hosts top-notch acoustic acts and open-mike nights in the Abbey Bar. There's usually no cover, and there's free pool on Sun. and Tues.

Ý **Winner's Circle Saloon** (717-469-0661), 604 Station Rd. This "eatin, drinkin, and dancin place" features live country bands Wed. through Sat. and line dancing on Sun., Mon., Tues., and Thurs.

THEATER & FILM ♿ **Hershey Theater** (717-534-3405; www.hershey theater.inovat.com),15 E. Caracas Ave., Hershey. This renovated and gorgeous 1933 building hosts everything from Broadway shows to classic films. Tours are given on Fri. and Sun. during the summer for $7 a person. Call for times.

Allen Theatre and Coffeehouse (717-867-4766), 36 Main St., Annville. A wonderful single-screen theater showing first-run films. The owner introduces most of the screenings, and local college students and aspiring musicians provide prescreen enter-tainment. There's an adjacent cafe.

Haars Drive-In (717-432-3011), 185 Logan Rd., Dillsburg. Open Apr. through Sept. This 1950s-style drive-in off US 15 shows first-run movies on weekends.

✳ Selective Shopping

Shopping in downtown Harrisburg centers around the **Shops at Strawberry Square** (717-255-1020), 11 N. Third St., home to more than 40 shops, galleries, and restaurants, and a popular children's theater. Just off I-83 at Paxton St., **Harrisburg East Mall** (717-564-0980) is another main shopping area, anchored by Macy's, Bass Pro Shops, and Boscov's.

Hummelstown
♿ **Olde Factory** (717-566-5685), 139 S. Hanover St. Three floors of antiques, folk art, quilts, and unusual crafts located in a former dress factory.

♿ **Rhoads Pharmacy** (717-566-2525), 17 W. Main St. This old-fashioned multiservice store sells candles, beer steins, Boyds Bears, and other collectibles in addition to the usual drugstore inventory.

✳ Special Events

January: **Pennsylvania Farm Show** (second weekend), 2300 N. Cameron St., Harrisburg—the largest indoor agricultural event in America includes farm equipment displays, cooking demos, and some of the best food the state has to offer. A highlight is the life-size butter sculpture designed in a different likeness each year.

A DAY OF CHOCOLATE

I don't include many spas in this guide, but the **Chocolate Spa** at the Hotel Hershey (717-520-5888; 877-772-9988) stands out for its unique cocoa-themed treatments. Opened in 2001 amid an elegant marble-floored setting overlooking the hotel's formal gardens, it offers such indulgences as chocolate hydrotherapy, chocolate-oil massages, and cocoa butter scrubs. A Cuban theme was later added in a nod to Milton Hershey's ties to the island's sugar industry, featuring *mojito* sugar scrubs and green coffee body wraps. For a truly indulgent day, start with a hot-chocolate latte at the hotel's Cocoa Beanery. Follow this with a whipped cocoa bath ($45 for 25 minutes of soaking) or a chocolate fondue wrap, a gentle body brushing and rinse (for $110) that will leave you smelling sweetly, but not overwhelmingly, of cocoa. (For the more traditional spa-goer, there's also a roster of plain old massage, facial, and manicure treatments.) Spend the rest of the afternoon lounging in the spa's quiet areas (guests who partake of any treatment may stay at long as they like at the spa and nearby fitness center). Cap your day with a chocolate soufflé served with malted milk ball gelato in the hotel's Circular Dining Room.

GETTYSBURG

One of Pennsylvania's top tourist attractions, the small town of Gettysburg sits between Harrisburg and the Maryland border, surrounded by the battlefield that made it famous. It was a tiny isolated farming community before the Union and Confederate armies arrived in 1863 and fought one of the bloodiest battles of the Civil War, with more than 50,000 casualties. Four months later at the dedication of the Soldiers Cemetery, President Abraham Lincoln delivered the Gettysburg Address, considered one of the greatest speeches in American history, rededicating the nation to the war effort and to the ideal that no soldier here had died in vain. The war would continue for two more years.

Today's Gettysburg, without a doubt, remains steeped in its Civil War history. It is difficult to find a prewar building that didn't serve as a shelter for wounded soldiers or isn't full of bullet holes, or an attic that wasn't taken over by sharpshooters. Its main streets are lined with souvenir shops, hotels and B&Bs, all types of restaurants, and sightseeing attractions that range from fading kitsch to garish. Buses, RVs, and motorcycles crawl along the battlefield's one-way roads at any given time of day. Yet despite the crowds and touristy vibe, a visit to Gettysburg remains a soul-stirring experience. The force of the battle and the spirits of the dead soldiers stay with you at just about every turn and long after you've left town.

One of the most enjoyable things about Gettysburg is the people. Whether they grew up here or elected to retire, buy a bullet-pocked B&B, or become a guide after years of playing tourist, their fascination with the town's history is earnest and very contagious. Talk to them; they are often happy to share their stories and knowledge.

Another thing to keep in mind is that the area is a pleasant place to spend a few days even if you or your companions don't care much about cannonades and infantry positions. Adams County is a mecca of apple, peach, and pear orchards that is awash in harvest celebrations and gorgeous foliage in the fall. Nearby villages like New Oxford and East Berlin have antiques shops and quaint inns; to the west, Michaux State Forest offers plenty of biking and hiking opportunities. Five miles to the south, Boyd's Bears operates a kids' wonderland of stuffed animals in all shapes, sizes, and costumes.

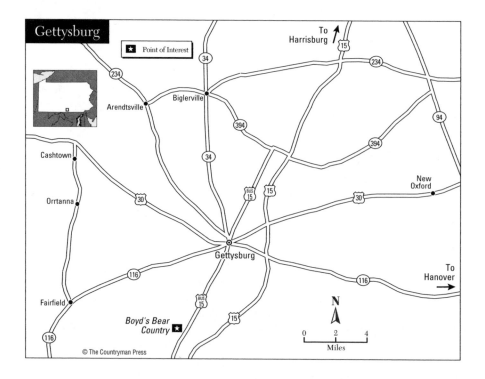

AREA CODE The Gettysburg area lies within the 717 area code.

GUIDANCE Gettysburg Convention and Visitors Bureau (717-334-6274; 800-337-5015; 35 Carlisle St.), located in the town's original railway station near Lincoln Square, has maps, brochures, and a central location. It also operates a staffed desk at the military park's new visitor center.

GETTING THERE *By air:* **Harrisburg International Airport** (717-948-3900) is about 50 miles northeast of Gettysburg. **Baltimore-Washington International** (301-859-7111) is about 80 miles away.

By car: Gettysburg is about four and a half hours from New York City, about an hour and a half from Baltimore, and two hours from Philadelphia. From the Pennsylvania Turnpike, take exit 17 to US 15 south.

GETTING AROUND Lincoln Square, where US 30 and 15 meet, is the center of downtown Gettysburg. Carlisle, Baltimore, Washington, and York streets are main thoroughfares off or near the square.

Gettysburg Town Trolley (717-334-6296) runs through town and stops at many major attractions, including the Gettysburg Hotel and the American Civil War Museum. A one-way token costs $1.25. Pick up a map at the Gettysburg Tour Center, 778 Baltimore St.

Self-guided historic walking tours begin at the **Lincoln Railroad Station**, 35 Carlisle St. Pick up a map at the visitor center in the station.

PARKING Parking in Gettysburg can be a challenge. There is a two-hour limit on most of the metered downtown spaces. A small parking garage is located downtown behind Gallery 30 on Racehorse Alley. A handful of metered parking spaces are located here also.

Limited free parking is available in some of the side streets and alleys behind the shops.

A tip: If you opt for on-street parking, bring a roll of dimes. While it may seem easier to pitch three quarters into the meter for an hour's worth of parking, six dimes for the hour ends up being cheaper at the end of the day.

MEDICAL EMERGENCY Gettysburg Hospital (717- 334-2121), 147 Gettys St., at Washington St., a few blocks north of the park's visitor center.

WHEN TO GO Sept. is a good time to go if you're looking to find fewer people and decent weather—the summer crowds have left and leaf peeping season and Halloween are a few weeks away. Though hotels often fill up, another quiet time to visit the battlefield is the first week of July, when most people are attending the reenactment outside of town.

Spring brings wildflowers and thawed monuments, but it also means busloads of school groups.

LINCOLN SQUARE

Gettysburg National Military Park (717-334-1124; www.nps.gov/gett), 97 Taneytown Rd. Open 6 AM–10 PM daily Apr. through Oct., until 7 PM Nov. through Mar.

The Battle of Gettysburg was a crucial and devastating turning point in the Civil War. It ended General Robert E. Lee's most ambitious invasion of the North and was one of the war's bloodiest battles. Managed by the National Park Service since 1933, the battlefield where it all happened is the town's marquee attraction and should not be missed, no matter how short your stay.

However you choose to see the battlefield, the **Visitor Center** (717-334-1124; 1195 Baltimore Pike) is an excellent place to start your tour. As this book was going to press, the National Park Service was preparing to open a new and bigger museum and visitor center two-thirds of a mile from the old Taneytown Road one. Slated to open in spring of 2008, the new visitor center features 11 galleries of historical exhibits and artifacts, a bookstore, refreshment "saloon," and nine theater "experiences." The fully restored Cyclorama, a giant circular mural by Paul Philippoteaux that explains the story of Pickett's Charge through light and sound, was slated to open here in the fall of 2008.

From the visitor center, many people choose to drive around the battlefield with the help of a self-guided map. Allow two to three hours to cover all the monuments and key cannonade sites. Here are several other ways to view the battlefield:

By guided walking tour. They cover only a fraction of the field, but these free walks by knowledgeable guides are one of the best deals around. Mid-June through mid-Aug., the National Park Service offers more than 15 different themed walks across sections of the battlefield, lasting from 30 minutes to 3 hours. There is no need for reservations; just show up at the visitor center and join one. The walks are also offered occasionally in spring and fall.

By car with a licensed battlefield guide. This is a favorite choice of battlefield veterans. For $45 for 1–6 people, a rigorously trained Civil War buff will drive your car around the battlefield for two hours and vividly recount the battle with facts and anecdotes. Guides are available daily at the park's visitor center on a first come, first served basis. During busy times

✳ Villages

Biglerville. Six miles north of Gettysburg, this rural town along PA 34 is home to a country store, a museum that chronicles and celebrates the history of the apple in Pennsylvania, and a couple of casual restaurants. Best of all, it's surrounded by good produce stands. There's no real downtown, but it's a good place to stock up on apples and other fruit on your way north out of town. Just down of the year, the tours often sell out before noon. Reservations may be made up to 7 days in advance, but it will cost you an extra $15. Call 877-874-2478 for more information.

By car with audiocassette. At a cost of $10–15, you can buy or rent a cassette or CD from the visitor center, the Civil War Museum, and many shops around town (B&Bs also often keep some on hand for guests) and follow along as the voice guides you past important monuments and highlights of the battle.

By bus with a tour guide. These tours operate year round and take two hours. An open-air double-decker bus runs seasonally accompanied by an audio guide complete with sound effects. An enclosed bus runs year-round and is narrated by a live licensed guide. Both tours depart from the Gettysburg Tour Center (717-334-6296), 778 Baltimore St. $22–25 adults, $12–15 ages 4–11.

Other options for touring the battlefield include by guided horse or bicycle, or by hiking several trails that wind through the battlefield (see *Outdoor Activities*).

GETTYSBURG BATTLEFIELD

the road is Arendtsville, home to the popular apple harvest and apple blossom festivals.

Cashtown. Eight miles west of Gettysburg, Cashtown dates back to 1797 and stems from the business practices of the village's first innkeeper, Peter Marck, who insisted on cash payments for the goods he sold and the highway tolls he collected. In June 1863, Confederate leaders met at the Cashtown Inn to discuss their course of action. Still in existence, the inn operates as a restaurant and B&B and is one of the few main commercial establishments in town.

Fairfield. During the Gettysburg Campaign in the American Civil War, the Battle of Fairfield played an important role in securing the Hagerstown Road, enabling Robert E. Lee's army to retreat through Fairfield toward the Potomac River. Lee and his officers stopped to eat at the Fairfield Inn, which still operates as a small hotel.

New Oxford. Anchored by an attractive town square with brick sidewalks and tree-lined streets, this town of neat Victorian and colonial homes north of Gettysburg is home to dozens of quaint shops, as well as a few B&Bs and restaurants. Every June, it's the site of a huge antiques and crafts show.

✳ To See

HISTORIC SITES **Soldiers National Cemetery**, 97 Taneytown Rd. Open daily dawn to dusk. Created after the war and dedicated on November 19, 1863, this solemn graveyard is the site of President Lincoln's Gettysburg Address and a reminder that the Battle of Gettysburg was a horrific and fatal event for many. Today, American veterans of all the major wars are buried here. Take a guided walking tour or wander through on your own. Be sure to pause to read the passages from Theodore O'Hara's stirring poem, *Bivouac for the Dead*, located on stone tablets throughout the grounds.

Eisenhower National Historic Site (717-338-9114; www.nps.gov/eise), 250 Eisenhower Farm Dr. $6 adults, $4.50 ages 13–16, $3.50 ages 6–12. Allow two or three hours for this worthwhile tour of Ike and Mamie Eisenhower's dairy farm and weekend retreat from Washington. Adjacent to the battlefield but a separate entity, it was the only home the Eisenhowers owned and remains much as it was when they retired here in 1967, right down to their TV dinner trays and pink monogrammed towels. After a short introduction by a guide in the formal living room (which has hosted Winston Churchill and other VIPs), visitors are free to stroll the house and grounds. Kids will enjoy the Junior Secret Service Agent program and black angus cows that roam the farm. You must buy tickets at the park's visitor center and take a shuttle bus to the farm. Buy your tickets early during the busy summer months; they sometimes sell out.

General Lee's Headquarters (717-334-3141; www.civilwarheadquarters.com), 401 Buford Ave. Open 9–5 mid-Mar. through Nov.; $3 adults. Located near McPherson Ridge, this tiny stone house was the home of Gettysburg resident Mary Thompson and the impromptu headquarters of Confederate general Robert E. Lee. It has a surprisingly large collection of Union and Confederate artifacts, uniforms, and newspaper clippings.

MUSEUMS ↑ **Shriver House Museum** (717-337-2800), 308 Baltimore St. Open daily Apr. through Nov., weekends only Feb. and Mar.; closed Jan. Adults $6.95; kids 12 and under $4.75. If I had time to hit just one Civil War attraction besides the battlefield, this restored 1860 house would be it. It offers a rare glimpse into civilian life back then, thanks largely to the Shriver family's neigh-

bor, Tillie Pierce, who kept a detailed diary of their experiences. The 30-minute tour, led by a costumed guide, includes a look at the bullet-riddled attic that was taken over by Confederate sharpshooters and the basement saloon of George Washington Shriver, who died before he could open it. The museum hosts a reenactment of Confederate soldiers occupying the home, which occurs annually during the anniversary weekend of the Battle at Gettysburg.

⚑ **Rupp House History Center** (717-334-7292, www.friendsofgettysburg.org/therupphistorycenter.html), 451 Baltimore St. Open daily June through August, weekends only Apr., May, Sept., and Oct. Free. This is another favorite Civil War attraction in the heart of downtown and a good place to stop before heading to the battlefield. It operated as a tannery during the battle, then later as a B&B until the nonprofit Friends of the National Parks of Gettyburg bought it in 2001 and turned the first floor into three rooms of interactive exhibits that use sight, sound, touch, and smell to show what life was like for civilians and soldiers of the time. You can build your own monument, carry the pack of a Civil War soldier, and take part in scavenger hunts and computer games, all designed to make the scope of the Civil War easy for anyone to digest.

⚑ **Jennie Wade House** (717-334-4100; www.jennie-wade-house.com), 548 Baltimore St. Jennie Wade was the only civilian killed during the Battle of Gettysburg, and it happened in this unassuming brick home near the Dobbin House. A stray bullet struck the 20-year-old while she was baking biscuits for Union soldiers. The self-guided tour begins in the kitchen where Wade was struck, and recounts the scene through a talking mannequin dressed like the Confederate soldier. It's a popular stop for ghost lovers.

⚑ **Battle Theater** (717-334-6100; www.gettysburgbattlefieldtours.com), 571 Steinwehr Ave. $6.95 adults. Call ahead to find out when local actor James A. Getty's captivating portrayal of Abraham Lincoln is on the schedule. On other days, the theater runs a 30-minute multimedia show on the Battle of Gettysburg.

⚓ ⛪ **Lincoln Train Museum** (717-334-5678), 571 Steinwehr Ave. Closed Dec., Jan., and Feb.; $7.25 adults, $3.50 ages 4–11. A narrow hallway lined with shadow boxes tells the story of the railroad's importance in Gettysburg, then gives way to a room filled with a jaw-dropping display of more than a thousand miniature trains and real train whistles. Admission includes a 15-minute simulated train ride that reenacts Lincoln's famous 1863 trip from Washington, D.C., to Gettysburg.

⛪ **American Civil War Museum** (717-334-6245; www.gettysburgmuseum.com), 297 Steinwehr Ave. Open daily Mar. through Dec., weekends in Jan. and Feb. $5.50 adults; $2.50 ages 6–12. This kitschy wax museum is a bit shopworn, but its five hallways of life-size dioramas offer an easy-to-follow approach to the war's precursors and strategies behind the three-day battle. The gift shop has one of the best selection of Civil War books around.

✳ To See

FOR FAMILIES ⚓ **Gettysburg Scenic Railway** (717-334-6932; www.gettys burgrail.com), 106 N. Washington St. Open Apr. through Dec.; call for a schedule; $21–65 adults; $9–20 ages 4–12. Hop aboard the train for a scenic trip through the surrounding countryside, an after-dark ghost tour, or a murder mystery dinner theater. Conductors offer an insider's view of the battlefield and the surrounding town. The cars are not air-conditioned, so arrive early on hot summer days to get a seat on the top level of the double-decker rail car, or call in advance to book a seat in the engine car.

⚓ **Land of Little Horses** (717-334-7259; www.landoflittlehorses.com), 125 Glenwood Dr. Open daily April through Aug.; weekends only Sep. and Oct. $12 adults and children 2 and older. This farm park north of town stages several daily performances by trained Falabella miniature horses from Argentina in an enclosed arena. Kids of all ages will love the clever shows, which also star a posse of Jack Russell terriers, plus miniature donkeys, cows, and sheep. Call ahead for show times and a schedule of special events, such as petting time with the animals and hands-on activities like goat milking and horse grooming.

✳ Outdoor Activities

BICYCLING Bikes are permitted on all paved roads within the battlefield; it's a great way to combine exercise with history lessons.

GettysBikes (717-752-7752; www.gettsybike.com) rents bikes for $8 an hour or $40 per day. It also offers three-hour battlefield tours led by licensed guides. Reservations recommended.

Gettysburg Bike and Fitness (717-334-7791; 307 York St.) rents bikes for $7 an hour or $25 a day. Reserve ahead on weekends.

GOLF **The Links at Gettysburg** (717-359-8000; www.thelinksatgettysburg .com), 601 Mason Dixon Rd. Rated one of the top ten public courses in Pennsyl-

vania by **Golfweek,** this 18-hole course plays 6,979 yards from the tips, with a
73.9 rating and 140 slope.

Mulligan MacDuffer Adventure Golf (717-337-1518), 1360 Baltimore St. 36
holes of mini-golf spread over two courses.

HORSEBACK RIDING **Artillery Ridge Campground** (717-334-1288; 610
Taneytown Rd.) offers one- and two-hour guided tours by horseback of the battlefield starting at $38 a person. It's especially nice in spring when the dogwood
and redbud are blooming or during fall foliage season.

SKIING **Liberty Mountain Ski Resort** (717-642-8282; www.skiliberty.com), 78
Country Club Trail, Carroll Valley. Ski trails, terrain parks, and snow tubing during the winter. It's about 10 miles south of Gettysburg.

✳ Green Space

Pine Grove Furnace State Park (717-486-7174), 1100 Pine Grove Rd.
Gardners. Once the site of an iron furnace that made Revolutionary War–era
kettles, stoves, and munitions, this 696-acre state park north of Gettysburg is
now home to two man-made lakes (Laurel and Fuller), primitive camp sites, picnic areas, and several miles of easy hiking trails. Swimming and fishing are
allowed in both lakes; limited boating is allowed on Laurel. You can also access
the Appalachian Trail here. Stop at the visitor center on Pine Grove Road for a
map and info on overnight parking.

Strawberry Hill Nature Center and Preserve (717-642-5840; www.straw
berryhill.org), 1537 Mount Hope Rd., Fairfield. This 609-acre preserve about 8
miles west of town has three ponds, 10 miles of easy to moderate trails, picnic
tables, and a nature center with hands-on wildlife and plant displays. Wildflowers cover the grounds in spring; great blue herons, great horned owls, wild
turkeys, and other birds have been spotted here year-round.

✳ Lodging

HOTELS ♿ **Historic Gettysburg
Hotel** (717-337-2000; www.hotel
gettysburg.com), 1 Lincoln Square.
You can't beat the prime location or
the guest list of this historic 1797
hotel: Carl Sandburg, Ulysses S.
Grant, and Henry Ford are some of
the VIPs who have stayed here. Now
a Best Western, it has the efficient
vibe of a business hotel with family-
friendly amenities like an outdoor
pool and babysitting services. Many of
the rooms and suites have jacuzzis
and fireplaces; the ones that face the

square can be noisy. The Town Trolley
stops out front. Rooms $120–300.

♿ **James Gettys Hotel** (888-900-
5275; www.jamesgettyshotel.com), 27
Chambersburg St. This upscale 11-
room inn is named after the town's
founder and operated as a hotel
before and after the 1863 battle. Centrally located a block west of Lincoln
Square, it was restored to 1920s-style
splendor in the 1990s and is known
for its attention to detail. All rooms
have full or queen beds and private
baths, and feature Egyptian cotton

linens and luxury toiletries. Expect some traffic noise in the front-facing rooms. A breakfast of pastries and orange juice is delivered daily to each room. Ask about special rates and packages if you're staying off-season. Rooms $135–250.

BED & BREAKFASTS Baladerry Inn (717-337-1342, www.baladerryinn .com) 40 Hospital Rd. This elegant inn on 4 acres at the southeast edge of the battlefield will appeal to visitors looking for a peaceful escape at the end of a day of sightseeing. There are 10 attractive rooms, five in the main house and five in a separate carriage house (including a large suite that sleeps four). Elaborate breakfasts are served in a large dining area next to a wood fireplace. Owner Suzanne Lonky will share stories about the inn's history of ghost sightings if you ask. Rooms $135–240.

☙ **Battlefield Bed and Breakfast Inn** (717-334-8804), 2264 Emmitsburg Rd. Civil War buffs love this comfortable old farmhouse at the southern edge of the park. The eight rooms and suites are comfortable and the surrounding 30 acres bucolic, but it's the daily breakfasts that get people raving. They begin at 8 with an animated lecture by a Civil War expert, and are followed by a lavish breakfast of fresh fruit and frittatas, French toast, or crepes. Homemade cookies are served in the afternoon. Kids and dogs are allowed, with some restrictions. Rates $175–235, two-night minimum on Sat.

Brickhouse Inn (717-338-9337; www.brickhouseinn.com), 452 Baltimore St. This beautiful three-story Victorian inn has 13 rooms and suites, a manicured garden with a koi pond,

and a downtown location within walking distance of the military park's visitor center. Five of the rooms are located next door in the Welty House, a restored 1830 home that stood in the battle's firing line and still bears the scars. All rooms have queen beds, original wood floors, and cable TV. The Kentucky Suite, with its private porch, skylight, and clawfoot tub, is a favorite. Rooms $139–179, two-night minimum.

☙ **Doubleday Inn** (717-334-9119; www.doubledayinn.com), 104 Doubleday Ave. This quiet house near Gettysburg College is located in a small neighborhood on the actual battlefield at Oak Ridge. Owners Todd and Christine Thomas were veteran Gettysburg tourists before buying the place in 2006 and are happy to share their insider knowledge of the area with guests. Many of the comfortable rooms have splendid views of the battlefield, and breakfasts are ample and delicious (caramel French toast is a specialty). The Paul Room in the attic, which sleeps up to five, is a great choice for families. A licensed battlefield guide runs a Q&A from the living room on most Wednesday and Saturday evenings. Rooms $95–150.

&. **Farnsworth House Inn** (717-334-8838; www.farnsworthhouseinn.com), 401 Baltimore St. Named after a brigadier general, this Victorian inn revels in its status as one of the most haunted inns in America, hosting regular candlelight walks and other ghost-related events. Confederate sharpshooters took shelter here during the battle; the south wall is riddled with bullet holes, and one of the men is believed to have shot Jennie Wade (see *Museums*). Despite its central location, inside is relatively quiet with common areas that include a trellised back garden and enclosed second-story porch; there's also a restaurant and tavern on premises (see *Dining Out*). Each of the nine rooms has a private bath and antique furnishings; some have TVs and jacuzzis. Rooms in the main house are on the small side and more susceptible to street noise than the ones off the back garden. No kids under 16. Rooms $140–180, including breakfast served by costumed employees, with a two-night minimum on weekends.

Nearby

Fairfield Inn (717-642-5410 or 334-8868, www.thefairfieldinn.com), 15 W. Main St., Fairfield. Veteran Gettysburg B&B owners Sal and Joan Chandon bought this 18th-century inn in 2002 and spent the next few years restoring the six rooms and common areas. A 2007 episode of HGTV's "If Walls Could Talk" chronicled its rich history as a field hospital for Confederate soldiers and a stop on the Underground Railroad. The antiques-filled rooms have private baths with whirlpool or clawfoot tubs; there's also a suite that sleeps four on the third floor with a private balcony. The Squires Miller tavern is one of the coziest places you will ever raise a glass; there's also a full restaurant. Rooms $130–150; suite $225.

MOTELS & COTTAGES ♿ 🐾 **Quality Inn** (717-334-3141, www.gettysburg usa.com), 401 Buford Ave. There are probably more chain motels in and around Gettysburg than there are walls with bullet holes in them, but this one stands out for its family-friendly amenities, reasonable rates, and central location next to General Lee's Headquarters. It has 41 standard

rooms that ring a large swimming pool and seven large suites that sleep four to six. Rates include admission to Lee's Headquarters and continental breakfast. Rooms $64–118, suites $125–200.

🐾 **Cricket House** (717-891-0607; www.crickethouseatgettysburg.com), 162 E. Middle St. Owners John and Debi Pedersen live in the main house and rent out their two-story guesthouse year-round. It includes a master suite, a living room with a double futon, full kitchen, three TVs, and a washer/dryer. There's even a covered jacuzzi on the back patio. $175–195 daily; $975 weekly.

CAMPGROUNDS **Artillery Ridge Camping Resort** (717-334-1288; www.artilleryridge.com), 610 Taneytown Rd. Open daily Apr. through Oct., weekends in November. This campground and equestrian center near the southern edge of the battlefield has more than 40 tent sites and several air-conditioned one-room cabins that sleep up to four. It's also home to the Gettysburg Battlefield Diorama, a popular attraction on its own. Tents $31; cabins $57.

Granite Hill Camping Resort (717-642-8749; www.granitehillcamping resort.com), 3340 Fairfield Rd. Open April through Nov. The site of an annual bluegrass festival, this scenic property about 8 miles south of town has three hundred sites for tents and RVs, plus five two-room cabins. It also has a swimming pool, fishing pond, tennis courts, four playgrounds, and a packed activity schedule. Tent sites $25–40; cabins $61–76.

Round Top Campground (717-334-9565; www.roundtopcamp.com), 180 Knight Rd. One of the few campgrounds that is open year-round, it has 200 sites with full hookups and 60 sites with water and electricity. The campground also rents basic air-conditioned cabins and cottages. It also has a swimming pool, mini-golf course, and tennis court. Tents $21–36; cabins $53–73; cottages $102–125.

✳ Where to Eat

DINING OUT ♿ ☙ **Dobbin House** (717-334-2100; www.dobbinhouse .com), 89 Steinwehr Ave. Dinner daily. The dining rooms can get quite loud, especially when bus tours descend upon the place, but this colonial house is a perfect way to cap a day of historic sightseeing. Waiters dress in period breeches, bonnets, and petticoats, and some authentic 18th-century dishes like Hunter's chicken and broiled pork tenderloin are on the menu. For a more casual and intimate experience, head downstairs to the Springhouse Tavern (also open for lunch). Reservations are recommended for the restaurant. Tavern dishes $6–20; dinner entrees $20–32.

♿ ☙ **Farnsworth House** (717-334-8838; www.farnsworthhouseinn.com), 401 Baltimore St. Dinner daily. You'll be surrounded by Civil War–era paintings, photographs, and antiques when you dine in the candlelit rooms of one of Gettysburg's legendary haunted homes. The house specialty is game pie, a rich casserole of turkey, pheasant, and duck. Other menu highlights: peanut soup, Yankee pot roast, and sweet potato pudding. In the summer, you can eat on the back patio overlooking a stream. Dinner entrees $16–27.

♿ ☙ **Herr Tavern and Publick House** (717-334-4332; www.herr tavern.com), 900 Chambersburg Rd. Open for lunch and dinner Mon.–Sat., dinner only Sun. This historic prewar building has been a tavern, an Underground Railroad stop, and a temporary Confederate hospital; today, it's a small inn and restaurant known for its superb food and service. The lunch menu includes salads, sandwiches, and a few hot entrees like

DOBBIN HOUSE

smoked salmon cheesecake and grilled beef shoulder. A dinner specialty (served weekends only) is prime-rib marinated in herbs and slow roasted in applewood bacon; also good is shrimp and scallops in red-pepper fondue. Its high-ceilinged dining rooms overlook Herrs Ridge, where Union general John Buford's cavalry camped the night before the Battle of Gettysburg. Reservations recommended. Extensive wine list. Lunch $7–12, dinner entrees $24–34.

Nearby

♟ **Cashtown Inn** (717-334-9722; 1-800; www.cashtowninnn.com), 1325 Old Route 30, Cashtown. Open for lunch and dinner Tues.–Sat. This small 18th-century inn west of town provides a nice escape, either overnight or for a couple of hours, from the downtown Gettysburg crowds. It served as headquarters for the Confederate general A. P. Hill and was featured in the film *Gettysburg*. Jack and Maria Paladino took over in 2006 and spruced up the dining rooms, tavern, and parlor; they also operate a B&B upstairs. The extensive American menu includes salmon, ahi tuna, New York strip, pecan chicken, and pasta primavera. Reservations are recommended. Lunch $5–14; dinner entrees $16–26.

EATING OUT ♿ ♟ **Spiritfields** (717-334-9449), 619 Baltimore St. Open daily for lunch and dinner. This charismatic Irish pub near the Jennie Wade House is known for its brisket dishes and sangria. Dishes $7–22.

♿ **Dunlap's Restaurant and Bakery** (717-334-4816), 90 Buford Ave. Open daily for breakfast, lunch, and dinner. This family-owned diner near the north end of the battlefield is a good place for an inexpensive sit-down meal. Reliable menu choices include honey-dipped fried chicken and Maryland crab cakes; they also have daily specials like prime rib and a Fri. night fish fry for $8. Save room for dessert. Breakfast $2–4, lunch and dinner $4–13.

🦐 **Ernie's Texas Lunch** (717-334-1970), 58 Chambersburg St. Breakfast, lunch, and dinner daily. This always-crowded spot serves the best hot dogs in town. Try the lunch special of two chili cheese dogs or two hamburgers and a soda for $5.

Lincoln Diner (717-334-3900), 32 Carlisle St. This 24-hour diner near the center of town is popular for breakfast and has an everything-but-the-kitchen-sink menu and wonderful baked desserts. Cash only. Dishes $2–15.

♿ **General Pickett's Buffets** (717-334-7580), 571 Steinwehr Ave. Lunch and dinner daily. Located next to the field where Confederate general George Pickett led his infamous doomed charge, this all-you-can-eat buffet elicits mixed reactions from those who have tried it. Its central location in the basement of the Battle Theater makes it very popular with bus tours; some say the food suffers as a result. It's tough to beat the price, though—$11 ($7 at lunch) for a huge soup and salad bar, hot entrees such as roast beef, fried catfish, and baked chicken, and desserts.

CAFES & BAKERIES Ragged Edge (717-334-4464), 110 Chambersburg St. This hip art-filled coffeehouse has indoor and outdoor seating, a light breakfast and lunch menu, and a stay-as-long-as-you-like vibe. It's open until 10 PM on Fri. and Sat., until 8

PM the rest of the week. Dishes $2–6.

Cannonball Malt Shop (717-334-9695), 11 York St. The small but comfortable, old-fashioned shop offers superb ice cream, malts, and handmade phosphate sodas, plus a selection of sandwiches. Dishes $2–5.

Hunt's Café (717-334-4787), 61 Steinwehr Ave. This small eatery and souvenir shop is known for its hand-cut Battlefield Fries (a twist on the Jersey Shore's Boardwalk Fries), cheesesteaks, and hand-dipped ice cream. Dishes $2–8.

✳ Entertainment

Much of Gettysburg's entertainment revolves around the battlefield; one of the most popular evening activities is the ghost tour (See *Haunted Gettysburg*). Several convivial watering holes, including the **Pub** (717-334-7100; 20 Lincoln Square) and **Blue Parrot Bistro** (717-337-3739; 35 Chambersburg St.), stay open late on weekends.

THEATER & FILM ⅊ **Majestic Theater Performing Arts and Cultural Center** (717-337-8200, www.gettys burgmajestic.org), 29 Carlisle St. This gorgeous 1925 850-seat theater was restored in 2005 and hosts live performances of everything from musical groups to plays and quiz shows. It also has a two-screen cinema showing art films.

⅊ **Gettysburg Gateway Complex** (717-334-5577; US 30 and US 15) shows first-run films, plus the 30-minute film *Fields of Freedom*, based on the discovered diaries of two sol-diers, one Union and one Confederate. Call for showtimes.

✳ Selective Shopping

All stores are downtown Gettysburg unless otherwise noted. Many of the shops stay open later in the summer. Call ahead to check times.

CIVIL WAR GOODS **Abraham's Lady** (717-338-1798), 25 Steinwehr Ave. Browse for Civil War–era dresses, corsets, and ankle boots. There's also a nice selection of 1860s-style jewelry, hair nets, and men's civilian vests. Dressmakers are usually on hand to do custom fits.

Stoneham's Armory (717-337-2347); 5 Steinwehr Ave. This small shop is known for its collection of reproduction and replica guns.

Horse Soldier (717-334-0347), 777 Baltimore St. Home to one of the largest collections of military antiques around, with items dating from the Revolutionary War through World War II. The emphasis, of course, is on the Civil War, and the shop guarantees that all of its inventory, from firearms to discharge papers, is genuine. It also offers a genealogical research service that will help search for an ancestor's war records.

Regimental Quartermaster and **Jeweler's Daughter** (717-338-1864; 717-338-0770), 49 Steinwehr Ave. These two shops share a roof and, as the name implies, target Civil War buffs of both genders. On one side, there are bayonets and scabbards, carpet bags, first-aid kits, and an impressive selection of civilian and soldier hats; on the other, you'll find a huge

HAUNTED GETTYSBURG

With more than 50,000 casualties, it's no surprise that ghosts and spirits have been sighted and felt all over Gettysburg. From May through Nov., you'll stumble upon more than a dozen nightly ghost tours offered in or around downtown. Most run twice nightly and last between one and two hours; kids under age seven are often free. Keep in mind that the tours that center around Baltimore Street can get traffic and pedestrian noise. **Civil War Hauntings Candlelight Ghost Walks** (717-752-5588; www.cwhauntings .com) offers one-hour tours that begin near the Civil War Museum and hit haunted spots along Steinwahr Avenue. Kids like the electronic ghost finding equipment and glow-in-the-dark bracelets. For storytelling at its most macabre, try the Farnsworth House's **Civil War Mourning Theater** (717-334-8838; www.farnsworthhouseinn.com). **Ghosts of Gettysburg** (717-337-0445; www.ghostsofgettysburg.com) offers several popular walking and bus tours that are based on Mark Nesbitt's best-selling book series *Ghosts of Gettysburg.* The Seminary Ridge and Carlisle Street walking tours are favorites.

collection of reproduction Victorian jewelry, from earrings and necklaces to pocket watches and hair ornaments.

GIFT SHOPS AND GALLERIES

Antiques, Apples, and Art (717-339-0017; www.17onthesquare.com), 17 Lincoln Square. Just as the name implies, this multi-vendor shop captures three of Gettysburg's staples: Civil War–era antiques, apple-related items to celebrate the nearby orchards, and local crafts. There's also an Internet cafe on site.

Gallery 30 (717-334-0335), 30 York St. Current books share space with paintings and sculpture by local and regional artists in this pleasant downtown shop.

Misty Mountain Fiber Workshop (717-339-0088), 23 Chambersburg St. This unique shop sells spinning wheels, looms, and wool and fine

BOYDS BEAR COUNTRY

yarns for knitting, weaving, and crochet.

Nearby

✄ ♈ ♈ **Boyds Bear Country** (717-630-2600; www.boydsbearcountry .com), 75 Cunningham Rd., Gettysburg. Open daily 10–7. Bears of all sorts and sizes—including Confederate and Union bears, bears masquerading as skunks, bears in sundresses, and stuff-your-own bears—fill the top three floors of this big red barn 5 miles south of town. The basement doubles as a restaurant and food court. Special events include scavenger hunts and costumed bear reenactments. From the top floor, the view of the Gettysburg countryside is unrivaled. In Dec., the place is decorated head to toe in Christmas finery.

✳ Special Events

May: **Apple Blossom Festival** (first weekend), South Mountain Fairgrounds, Arendtsville—some locals prefer this lesser-known event to the popular harvest festival in Sept.

July: **Annual Civil War Battle Reenactment** (first weekend), Table Rock Rd., north of town. Costumed volunteers commemorate the famous battle with faux rifles and swords at this three-day ticketed spectator event. For more information, go to www.gettysburgreenactment.com. A week later motorcycles from all over the country roar into town for **Gettysburg Bike Week** (800-374-7540; www.gettysburgbikeweek.com), three days of live music, fireworks, tattoo contests, and a "chrome parade."

August: **Civil War Music Muster** (last weekend), Gettysburg National Military Park—brass bands, fife and drum groups, and individuals bring to life the band and parlor music of the Civil War period.

October: **National Apple Harvest Festival** (first two weekends), Arendtville—a popular country gathering of food, music, crafts, and pony rides that seems to get bigger each year. The food alone (pumpkin funnel cake, caramel apples, sweet potato fries) is worth the trip.

November: **Remembrance Day** (third weekend)—this solemn event begins with a parade of living history and reenactment groups through town to the battlefield, is followed by the placement of candles at each Civil War grave, and ends with a recitation of Lincoln's Gettysburg Address.

YORK COUNTY

Y ork County likes to call itself the snack capital of the world. Spend some time here and you will find this to be a reasonable conclusion. Potato chips, candy, ice cream, and pretzels are all made in the small towns and rural countryside that make up this county of more than 200,000. So are Pfaltzgraff pottery, cast-iron banks, and the bulk of Harley-Davidson's Touring and Softail motorcycles.

Situated between Gettysburg and Amish Country, the region often gets squeezed out by its two more famous neighbors. The pace is a little slower here, the prices a little lower—it feels more like a 9-to-5 kind of place than a tourism destination. This is not to say that the region lacks history or amenities. You will find real farmers markets, homey B&Bs, and free hands-on tours of Harley-Davidson, Utz Potato Chips, and a dozen other factories and farms. You will leave with a strengthened respect for chocolate-covered pretzels and high-butterfat ice cream.

The small city of York, which anchors the county, was founded in 1741 and named for the English city of the same name. It served as the temporary capital of the Continental Congress during the Revolutionary War. The Articles of Confederation were drafted here in 1777. Several original 18th-century buildings are open for tours downtown, which also features many other colonial-era buildings, Gothic Revival churches, and wide sidewalks.

About 20 miles to the west sits Hanover, the county's second-largest city and the site of a small but significant Civil War battle. Though small hotels, big-box stores, and franchise food operations are prevalent along the main drag, its town center remains attractive, anchored by a large square and surrounded by historic well-kept homes and churches.

Surrounding York and Hanover are miles of rolling countryside, several golf courses, and small towns with mom-and-pop antiques shops, farm stands, and ice cream stands.

AREA CODE All towns in York County fall under the 717 area code.

GUIDANCE **York County Convention & Visitors Bureau** (717-852-9675; 1-888-858-9675; www.yorkcountypa.org) has a large welcome center at 149 W. Market St. next to the Plough Tavern. It also operates a small one at the

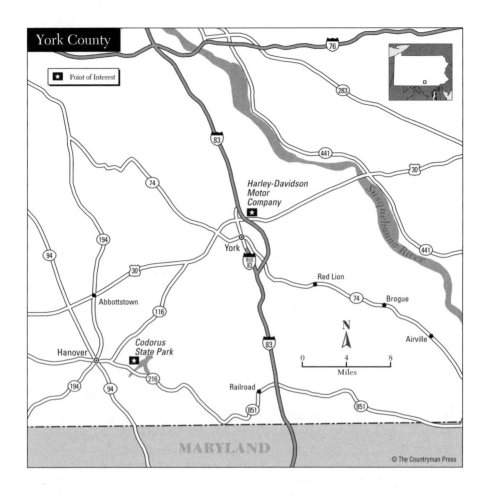

© The Countryman Press

Harley-Davidson plant (717-852-6006; 1425 Eden Rd.) just off US 30. In Hanover, stop by the **Guthrie Memorial Library** (717-632-5183; 301 Carlisle St.) for maps and brochures.

GETTING THERE *By air:* **Harrisburg International Airport** (888-235-9442) is 30 miles north of downtown York.

By car: US 30 south from Lancaster; I-83 from Harrisburg and Maryland.

By bus: **Greyhound** (800-231-2222) and **Rabbit Transit** (717-846-7743) offer regular service between York and Harrisburg. **Capitol Trailways** has service through Lancaster to Philadelphia and New York.

GETTING AROUND Downtown York is walkable, especially the area around Market and George streets, but you will need a car to get to most of the factories, including Harley-Davidson and Hope Acres. **Rabbit Transit** operates bus routes in the city and surrounding area.

WHEN TO GO Fall is particularly scenic in this rural part of the state, but most of the factories and museums here are open for tours year-round. Keep in mind that many of the factories aren't air-conditioned, and some, like Susquehanna Glass, close down when temperatures surpass 90 degrees.

MEDICAL EMERGENCY York Hospital (717-851-3500), 1001 S. George St. About 30 miles to the southwest is **Hanover Hospital** (717-637-3711), 300 Highland Ave., Hanover.

✳ Villages

Railroad. This tiny town of three hundred people near the Maryland border is home to the Jackson House B&B, a popular crab shack, and not much else. It takes its name from the century-old North Central Railroad that passes through town on its way to and from Baltimore and York.

Red Lion. About five miles outside York, Red Lion is a quaint town of antiques shops, a B&B, and a few restaurants and serves as a sort of gateway to the rural countryside east of York. Founded in 1880, it is named after one of its first taverns and was once a major manufacturer of cigars (to this day, the town raises a giant cigar on New Year's Eve, instead of the traditional ball). Also found near Red Lion is Family Heirloom Weavers, a small weaving factory that specializes in Civil War–era clothes, and one of the few robotic dairy farms in the nation.

Wrightsville. Named for one of the area's early settlers, John Wright, this sleepy town on the Susquehanna River is a pleasant place to stop if you're on your way to York from Lancaster or Philadelphia. It was once home to one of the longest covered bridges in the country, which unfortunately was burned during the Civil War to stop the eastern advance of Lee's army. A diorama, housed in a former barber shop, tells the story of the bridge and Wrightsville's role in the Civil War. Today, John Wright cast-iron products are made here and sold in a nearby warehouse. The Susquehanna Glass factory is right across the river in Columbia.

✳ To See

FACTORY TOURS All tours are free unless otherwise noted. Most require advance reservations.

&. ✍ **Hope Acres** (800-293-1054, www.hopeacres.com), 2680 Delta Rd., Brogue. Tours run Tues.–Sat. Reservations required; call for times. This might just be the cleanest and most impressive dairy farm you'll ever visit. One of only a handful of U.S. farms to have a completely automated milking system, it lets its Jersey heifers milk when they want with no human intervention. The 75-minute tours offer a fascinating look at the cows' cushy lifestyle, one that includes climate-controlled barns, mechanical back-scratchers, and waterbeds. At the end, all visitors get a free scoop of sinfully-high-in-butterfat ice cream from the Brown Cow Country Market (see also *Eating Out*).

Family Heirloom-Weavers (717-246-2431, www.familyheirloomweavers.com), 775 Meadowview Dr., Red Lion. Tours Mon.–Fri.; reservations required. This family-run weaving factory specializes in Civil War–era clothing and other historically accurate items; it made all the Confederate uniforms for the film *Cold Mountain* and has supplied historic homes belonging to Abraham Lincoln, Mark Twain, and Walt Whitman with ingrain carpets that were popular at the time. Free weekday tours of the small factory, given by founder David Kline, are available and include an up-close look at 40 power-driven looms dating from 1890 to 1980. Leave time to check out the gift shop next door.

Susquehanna Glass (717-684-2155, www.theglassfactory.com) 731 Ave. H, Columbia. Tours Mon.–Fri. at 11 and 1, May through Sep., and Wed. and Thurs. at 11 and 1 Oct. through Apr. Reservations required. This century-old glassmaker, located just off US 30 between Lancaster and York, performs etching, silkscreening, and other intricate services for Pottery Barn, Williams-Sonoma, and many other large home-decor companies. A tour lasts about 30 minutes. The gift shop features three floors of heavily discounted glassware, crystal, and crafts.

Hanover

✐ ⚑ **Snyder's of Hanover** (1-800-233-7125), 1350 York St. Tours 10, 11, and noon Tues., Wed., and Thurs. Reservations required. You'll see some of the largest pretzel ovens in the world churning out 40 pretzels a second on this hour-long tour that covers the production process of pretzels and potato chips from start to finish. Leave time to shop at the outlet store, where the tours start, which offers great bulk deals on many Snyder's products, plus hard-to-find products like caramel-dipped pretzels.

✐ ⚑ **Utz Potato Chips** (717-637-6644), 900 High St. Tours 8–4 Mon.–Thurs. No reservations. Bill and Salie Utz started their company in 1925 in a small summer house behind their Hanover home. Now run by fourth-generation family members, it's still going strong and continues to offer self-guided tours that use videos and audio presentations to describe the process of making hand-cooked chips, flavored chips, and other products.

PLOUGH TAVERN

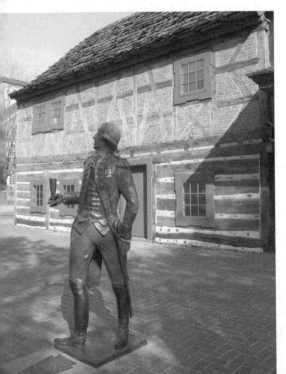

MUSEUMS & HISTORIC SITES Colonial Complex (717-845-2951), 157 W. Market St., York. Open Tues.–Sat. Apr. through mid-Dec.; $6 adults, $5 ages 12 and up. This complex of historic buildings includes a 19th-century log cabin, a tavern, and a replica of the colonial courthouse where the Continental Congress met in 1777 and 1778. Don't miss the half-timbered **Plough Tavern**, where a plan to overthrow General Washington was derailed in 1778 by the visiting Marquis de Lafayette. A statue of

Harley-Davidson Vehicle Operations

(414-343-7850; 877-883-1450, www
.harley-davidson.com), 1425 Eden
Rd., York. Tours are first come, first
served and run 9–2 Mon.–Fri.; Mon.–
Sat. in the summer. Children under 12
aren't allowed on the tour. One of
four Harley-Davidson plants to give
tours (the others are in Wisconsin
and Missouri), this plant just off US
30 is home to the company's largest
manufacturing facility, covering more
than 200 acres and 1.5 million square
feet.

The hour-long tours take you
right onto the factory floor, where
the bikes are being formed, welded,
machined, polished, and painted,
then to the end of the line, where
you can watch them inching along
the line by color code on their way to
Japan, Australia, and other destinations. The bikers who come from all
over to take the tour are just as
interesting as the assembly line; their
passion for chrome is infectious. Not
surprisingly, the gift shop sells plenty of Harley-emblazoned gear, from shot
glasses and T-shirts to helmets and heated hand grips.

HARLEY-DAVIDSON COMPANY

Lafayette, wine glass raised in a toast to Washington, stands in his honor outside
the tavern. Call ahead for tour schedules.

🐾 ♂ **Indian Steps Museum** (717-862-3948; www.indiansteps.org), 205 Indian
Steps Rd., Airville (south of Brogue). Open Thurs.–Sun., mid-Apr. through mid-
Oct.; free. Eccentric local attorney John Vandersloot built this home on the
Susquehanna River for the main purpose of displaying his huge collection of
Indian artifacts. More than 10,000 artifacts are embedded in the masonry walls
to form Indian patterns, birds, animals, and reptiles. A favorite stop is the kiva, a
reproduction of a circular room used by the Hopi Indians for religious assem-
blies. A second-floor gallery traces the evolution of early Indians who lived by or
passed along the nearby Susquehanna River. Outside, there's plenty of open
space for kids to run around.

✴ Outdoor Activities

BICYCLING/RENTALS Serenity Station (717-428-9575; 11 Church St., Seven Valleys), a stop along the 21-mile Heritage Rail Trail (see also *Green Space*), has a bike shop that rents single bikes, child trailers, and tandems starting at $7.50 an hour.

BOAT EXCURSIONS/RENTALS Appalachian Outdoor School (717-632-7484) rents canoes, kayaks, and pontoon and motor boats at the marina at Codorus State Park outside Hanover daily Memorial Day through Labor Day (see also *Green Space*).

In Wrightsville, **Shank's Mare Outfitters** (717-877-554-5080; 2092 Long Level Rd.) gives kayak lessons and rents single, double, and triple kayaks for trips along the Susquehanna River starting at $20 for two hours.

FISHING Lake Marburg in Codorus State Park (see also *Green Space*) is a warm-water fishery stocked with yellow perch, bluegill, northern pike, crappie, large-mouth bass, and catfish. A state fishing license is required; visit www.fish.state .pa.us for more information.

GOLF Heritage Hills Golf Course (717-755-0123), 2700 Mount Rose Ave., York. Nestled in the rural countryside less than a mile from downtown, this 18-hole course has wide fairways, well-maintained large greens, and a par of 71. There's also a driving range and mini-golf course.

✴ Green Space

✐ ✿ **Heritage Rail Trail County Park** (717-840-7440, ycwebserver.york -county.org/parks/railtrail.htm). Established in 1992, this 176-acre park has a 21-mile hiking and biking trail that follows the path of a historic railroad between the Mason Dixon line and downtown York. It's also popular with horseback riders. The trail offers many places to stop and rest or explore, including two history museums (New Freedom and Hanover), and a spa/restaurant (Serenity Station) that offers massages, facials, food, and live entertainment on weekends. Download a map from the website before you go, or pick one up at one of the station stops.

& ✐ ✿ **Codorus State Park** (717-637-2816), 2600 Smith Station Rd., Hanover. The 3,300-acre park is 3 miles southeast of Hanover and about an hour's drive from York. Its top attraction is the 1,275-acre Lake Marburg, which has 26 miles of shoreline and offers boating, sailing, and fishing opportunities. It also has a public swimming pool, disc golf course, and several miles of hiking, biking, and equestrian trails.

✴ Lodging

HOTELS & **Yorktowne Hotel** (717-848-1111, www.yorktowne.com), 48 E. Market St., York. F. Scott and Zelda would be right at home mingling under the brass and crystal chandeliers in the high-ceilinged lobby of this 11-story 1920s-era hotel.

The Fitzgeralds never stayed here, but Bill Clinton, Johnny Cash, and B. B. King did. It's also popular with business travelers and anyone performing at the nearby Strand-Capitol Theatre. All rooms and suites are spacious and handsomely decorated and come with king beds, sitting areas, writing desks, coffeemakers. There are also two restaurants on site, plus a small fitness center and laundry room. Rooms $149, suites $159–199.

BED & BREAKFASTS The Beechmont (717-632-3013, www.thebeech mont.com), 315 Broadway, Hanover. A couple of blocks off Hanover's main square, this stately inn has nine elegant rooms with private baths and a small back garden anchored by a 140-year-old magnolia tree. The yellow-hued Birch Room, which overlooks the garden, is a favorite. I also like the Walnut Room, a small room decorated in blues and greens with an antique rope bed. Breakfast is a lavish affair of fruit smoothies, sticky buns, and a main course that might feature spiced pancakes, buttermilk pie, or an herbed cheese tart. Cookies and other goodies are served in the evening, and there is wireless access throughout the house. Owners Kathryn and Tom White are well-versed in the area and will make dinner reservations or steer you to their favorite shops, eateries, and attractions. Rooms $104–169.

Jackson House (717-227-2022, www.jacksonhousebandb.com), 6 E. Main St., Railroad. George and Jean Becker made this small B&B next to the Heritage Rail Trail hugely popular with bicyclists and motorcyclists. They retired in 2007, but left the place in the very hospitable hands of

Pam Nicholson and Bob Wilhelm. The front of the 1859 red-shingled building abuts a busy Main St. intersection; the back features terraced gardens, a patio, and a hot tub. There are two small rooms with private baths, two large suites with private entrances and sitting areas (the Bordello Suite shows off a collection of vintage nude pinups from the 1930s and 1940s), and a separate one-room cottage. A lavish breakfast of eggs, coffee cake, fresh fruit, and more is served in the elegant stone-walled dining room. Rooms $90–100; suites $129; cottage $159.

&. ▼ **Stone Crest** (717-741-2105), 321 Imperial Dr., York. The outside of

YORKTOWNE HOTEL

this hilltop house has a bit of 70s' feel, but the inside is all about modern luxury and comfort. Owner George Simpson runs small business retreats and weekend workshops on massage and other themes; he also rents to individuals and couples, though kids and pets aren't allowed. The 10 rooms and suites are large with queen beds with luxury linens, wireless access, and private baths; common areas include a handsome billiard room, outdoor jacuzzi, and gardens with a stream and waterfall. Rooms $129–169; suites $229–269.

✳ Where to Eat

DINING OUT

York

& ♈ **Left Bank** (717-843-8010) 120 N. George St. Lunch and dinner Tues.–Fri., dinner only Sat. One of York's finest restaurants, serving creative American cuisine, such as sautéed margarita shrimp, Chilean sea bass, and marinated grilled steaks. Eat in the formal dining room or the smoking-allowed bistro. Desserts are grand; try the frozen s'mores tower. Reservations recommended. Lunch: $16–23; dinner entrees: $26–36.

& ♈ **Roosevelt Tavern** (717-854-7725) 50 N. Penn St., York. Lunch and dinner daily. This downtown establishment has an extensive menu of steaks, seafood, chicken, and salads. Try the sautéed crab cakes or applejack chicken. A choice of tasty sides like corn pudding and sweet potatoes drenched in honey butter comes with every entree. Lunch $7–16. Entrees $20–$32.

Hanover

& ✿ **Bay City Seafood** (717-637-1217), 110 Eisenhower Dr. This local favorite offers a large wide selection of steaks, seafood, and lobster in a casual fisherman-themed environment. Try the crab cakes any way or the crab pretzel, a huge baked soft pretzel smothered with melted cheese and crabmeat. Lunch $5–9; dinner entrees $12–34.

EATING OUT & 🍴 ✿ **The Brown Cow** (717-927-9944) Delta Rd., Brogue. Lunch and dinner Mon.–Sun. Hours can change with the season, so call ahead. This casual restaurant at Hope Acres serves stuffed pork chops, Delmonico steaks, lump crab cakes, and more. The main dining room overlooks the farm and surrounding countryside. All dinners include a large soup and salad bar and dessert. Save room for the creamy house-made ice cream; try the peanut butter with chocolate-covered pretzels and marshmallow swirl. Dishes $5–12.

& ✿ **Captain Bob's Crabs** (717-235-1166), 1 Main St., Railroad. Dinner daily Mar. through Dec. This casual outdoor eatery is known for its steamed Maryland crabs, but it also has crab cakes, crab fries, crab dip, and other fresh seafood dishes. The all-you-can-eat crab fests for $26.95 on Tues. and Wed. draw big crowds. Dishes $8–20.

& 🍴 ✿ **Central Family Restaurant** (717-845-4478), 400 N. George St., York. Breakfast, lunch, and dinner daily. This down-home diner is up with the chickens and makes up in good food what it lacks in decor. Breakfast includes omelets, hot cakes, and creamed chipped beef on toast. For lunch or dinner, there are burgers, crab melts, fried chicken, hand-cut steaks, and homemade meatloaf. Dishes $4–16.

Hanover

🍴 **Famous Hot Weiner** (717-637-1282) 101 Broadway. This small diner serves everything from eggs to hamburgers, but it's best known for its hot dogs with mustard, chili sauce, and chopped onions. There's also a branch in North Hanover. Dishes $2–5.

Reader's Café (717-630-2524), 125 Broadway. Open 9–5 daily, until 10 PM Fri. and Sat. The handwritten menu usually includes soup, coffee drinks, and several tasty sandwiches. Best of all, you get to eat surrounded by neatly arranged books and magazines (all for sale, of course). Dishes: $3–5

ICE CREAM & FARMERS MARKETS
🦽 **Central Market** (717-848-2243)

FAMOUS HOT WEINER

34 W. Philadelphia St., York. Open 6–2 Tues., Thurs., and Sat. Saturday is the best day to visit this historic downtown market for local produce, fresh-cut flowers, and homemade peanut butter donuts. It's also good for a quick lunch. Try the Greek salads at Tina's or the seasoned potato wedges at Bair's Fried Chicken. There are a few tables and a public piano in the center.

Perrydell Farms (717-741-3485), 90 Indian Acres Farm, York. Open daily. This small working farm south of downtown sells delicious chocolate milk and hand-dipped ice cream. Self-guided tours are available.

✳ Entertainment

THEATER 🦽 **Strand-Capitol Performing Arts Center** (717-846-1111, www.strandcapitol.org), 50 N. George St. This restored Italian Renaissance–style theater was once a vaudeville house and now features musicals, dance performances, film festivals, and other events.

✳ Selective Shopping

🦽 **Markets at Shrewsbury** (717-235-6611), 12025 Susquehanna Trail, Glen Rock. Open Thurs.–Sat. Shop for handcrafted Amish furniture, crafts, and quilts, then sample the wide selection of food offerings at this large indoor-outdoor market just off I-83 near the Maryland border. Sticky buns, soft pretzels, roast beef sandwiches, and local produce are just a few of the highlights.

York Emporium (717-846-2866), 343 W. Market St., York. Open Wed.–Sun. An extraordinarily good used-book store near the downtown visitor center with more than 200,000 titles in just about every category you can think of, from Gettyburg to flower arranging. Reasonable prices, too. There's free parking in the back.

& **John Wright Store** (717-252-2519), 120 N. Front St., Wrightsville. Open daily. Perched on the west bank of the Susquehanna River, this century-old warehouse sells high-quality cast-iron banks, kettles, garden products, and more. It is about a 15-minute drive from either York or Lancaster. A restaurant with a patio overlooking the river serves breakfast and lunch.

✳ Special Events

September: **York Fair** (second week), York Fairgrounds, 334 Carlisle Ave.— one of America's oldest town fairs, this 10-day event has the usual rides, games, and country food stands, but is best known for attracting nationally known performers like Willie Nelson, Gretchen Wilson, and Lynyrd Skynyrd. **Harley-Davidson Open House** (last weekend), 425 Eden Rd.—three days of extended plant tours, demo rides, and a Sat. night parade through downtown York.

November: **Made in America** (first weekend), throughout York County—dozens of area factories, including ones that don't usually offer public tours, open their doors during this three-day event. For more information, visit www.factorytours.org.

Northeastern Pennsylvania

THE LEHIGH VALLEY

POCONO MOUNTAINS SOUTH

POCONO MOUNTAINS NORTH

THE LEHIGH VALLEY

The Lehigh Valley is Pennsylvania's third most populous area behind Pittsburgh and Philadelphia and is known historically for its production of steel and anthracite coal. For nearly 150 years, it was dominated by Bethlehem Steel, one of the world's largest steel manufacturers and shipbuilders, which closed in 2003 and is now slated to reopen as a large casino, hotel, and retail complex in late 2008. Though the area has plenty to offer vacationers, including a large theme park and picture-postcard historic districts, it sometimes gets overshadowed by its neighbors, the Pocono Mountains to the north and Bucks County to the south.

Today, Allentown, Bethlehem, and Easton are the valley's largest towns. Allentown, the state's largest city, is home to Dorney Park and Wildwater Kingdom, a large art museum, and a revitalization effort that has helped bring a new minor-league baseball stadium and a high-tech transportation museum to the area.

Before steel came to Bethlehem, it was known as a haven for religious freedom. The area was settled by Moravian brethren, a denomination of German Protestant settlers who arrived here in 1740. The city was named a year later when Moravian patron Count Nicholas Ludwig von Zinzendorf visited the settlement's first house on Christmas Eve and bestowed the name "Bethlehem" on the community. It's also home to Lehigh University, founded by the railroad pioneer Asa Packer.

The town of Easton sits in the far east side of the Lehigh Valley near the New Jersey border. Anchored by a large historic square and the nearby Lehigh Canal, it is home to the Crayola Factory, many good restaurants, and a waterfront park offering canal boat rides and picnic tables.

AREA CODE 610

GUIDANCE **Lehigh Valley Convention and Visitors Bureau** (610-882-9200; www.lehighvalleypa.org), 840 Hamilton St., Allentown. Open 10–6 Mon.–Sat. There's also a small welcome center and gift shop in **Bethlehem's historic district** (610-691-6055, www.bethlehempa.org), 505 Main St. Guides lead walking tours from here every Sat. Apr. through Dec. for $8 a person.

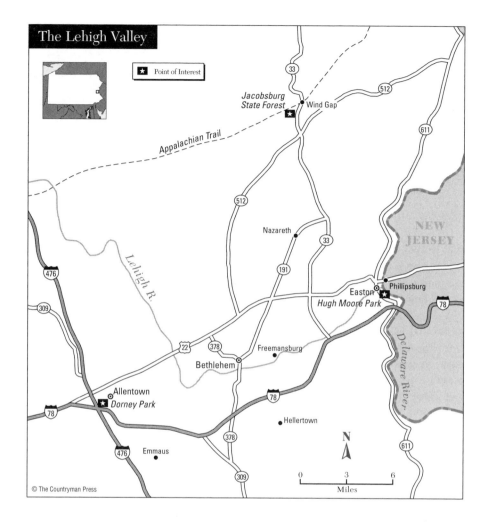

The Lehigh Valley

Point of Interest

Jacobsburg State Forest

Wind Gap

Appalachian Trail

NEW JERSEY

Nazareth

Lehigh R.

Easton

Phillipsburg

Hugh Moore Park

Delaware River

Freemansburg

Bethlehem

Allentown

Dorney Park

Hellertown

Emmaus

N

0   3   6
Miles

© The Countryman Press

GETTING THERE *By air:* Lehigh Valley is about an hour's drive from two major airports: **Philadelphia International** (215-937-6800) and **New Jersey's Newark International** (800-397-4636). **Lehigh Valley International Airport** (888-359-5842), between Allentown and Bethlehem, offers limited service.

By car: The Lehigh Valley can be reached from the north or south via the Pennsylvania Turnpike. I-78 crosses it from east to west, with exits for Easton, Bethlehem, and Allentown.

GETTING AROUND The Lehigh Valley is quite spread out, so you'll need a car. That said, Bethlehem, Emmaus, and Easton all have splendid downtown walking districts with shops, restaurants, and preserved historic buildings and churches.

MEDICAL EMERGENCY **Lehigh Valley Hospital** (610-402-2273), at Cedar Crest

DOWNTOWN BETHLEHEM

Rd. and I-78, Allentown. **St. Luke's Hospital** (610-954-4000), 801 Ostrum St., Bethlehem. **Easton Hospital** (610-250-4000), 250 S. 21st St., Easton.

WHEN TO GO What better time to visit a place called Bethlehem than December? The town truly rises to the occasion with daily concerts, walking tours, carriage rides, and Christkindlmart, a month-long crafts bazaar. Summer is also a good time to be here; top attractions like Dorney Park and Crayola Factory are open daily, the canal boat rides are open for business, and the farm markets are brimming with local produce.

✳ Towns & Villages

Emmaus. Founded as a closed community of the Moravian church in the 1700s, Emmaus couldn't be any quainter or more picturesque. Its downtown area has long been a popular destination for shoppers and strollers, with historic buildings, hip cafés, and mom-and-pop shops. About 6 miles west of Allentown, it was named one of the top 100 Best Places to Live in the U.S. in 2007 by *Money Magazine*. It is the headquarters of Rodale Press, publisher of *Prevention Magazine* and many other health and gardening magazines and books.

Nazareth. This town joins Bethlehem and Emmaus as towns in the Lehigh Valley named after famous Biblical places. Also settled by Moravians, it is about 4 miles north of Bethlehem with a pretty tree-lined main street of shops and cafés anchored by a circular plaza. It is home to the C. F. Martin Guitar Company, known for its quality acoustic guitars, as well as several cement companies that lie on the outskirts of town.

MUSEUMS

Allentown
🐾 ♿ ☂ **Liberty Bell Museum** (610-435-4232; www.libertybellmuseum.org), 622 Hamilton St. Open 12–4 Mon.–Sat. May through Nov.; Wed.–Sat. Feb. through Apr.; free. The Old Zion Reformed Church served as a hiding place for

the Liberty Bell and 11 other church bells while the British occupied Philadelphia in 1777 and 1778 (it was feared the Brits would melt the bells for musket and cannon balls). Today, in the church basement you'll find a full-size replica of the famous bell (which rings, unlike the real one), a multimedia light-and-sound show depicting scenes from the Revolutionary War, and a small exhibit of colonial artifacts and paintings.

& ↑ **Allentown Art Museum** (610-432-4333, www.allentownartmuseum.org), 31 N. Fifth St., Allentown. Closed Mon.; $6 adults, $3 ages 6–12; free on Sun. This small facility houses collections of European Renaissance works and American art by Robert Motherwell, Gilbert Stuart, and local artists. Don't miss the Frank Lloyd Wright–designed library, which was dismantled from his Prairie-style Northome in Minnesota and reassembled here in 1973. Fun and unique special exhibits, too.

& **America on Wheels** (610-432-4200, www.americanwheels.org), 5 N. Front St. This long-in-the-making museum chronicles the history of over-the-road transportation in the United States. At the time of this writing, it was slated to open in spring 2008.

Nearby

✇ & ↑ **Easton Museum of PEZ Dispensers** (610-253-9794; 888-843-7391), 15–19 S. Bank St., Easton. $4 adults, $2 ages 4 and up. Open daily July and Aug.; Tues.–Sat. fall and spring; call for winter hours. Some 1,500 PEZ dispensers fashioned into superheroes, the Beatles, and more, can be found in creative kid-friendly exhibits at this small periwinkle shrine to the hand-held candy holder. It's a fun way to follow a visit to the Crayola Factory next door. Grab an ice cream cone at the nearby Purple Cow and you've got yourself a full day.

✳ To Do

& ↑ **C. F. Martin Guitar Company and Museum** (610-759-2837), 510 Sycamore St., Nazareth. This family-owned guitar maker has been producing

MARTIN GUITAR COMPANY

high-quality acoustic guitars since the early 1800s. Johnny Cash, Paul McCart-ney, Eric Clapton, and Gene Autry are a few artists who have owned them. You don't have to be a serious musician to enjoy the free tours, offered weekdays at 1:15 PM, of its small plant north of Bethlehem. Led by enthusiastic guides, they last about an hour and walk you through the many steps involved in making a guitar. You can stand next to workers as they bend, shape, fit, sandpaper, lacquer, and inspect, as they convert rough fine woods into a brand new instrument. There's also a well-executed display of vintage Martin guitars (including Ricky Nelson's leather-covered one and clips of Elvis Presley playing his Martin in the 1950s) off the lobby and a gift shop that sells new and used Martin guitars, books, T-shirts, and other guitar-related items.

FOR FAMILIES ✍ ♿ ⬆ **Crayola Factory** (610-515-8000), 30 Centre Square, Easton. Open. 9:30–5 Mon.–Sat., 11–5 Sun.; closed Mon. Sept. through May; $9.50 adults and kids over 2. Binney and Smith, the local company that makes Crayola crayons, opened this hands-on discovery center in 1996 after the demand for factory tours became overwhelming. It's more of an activity center aimed at kids 4–12 than a lesson on how crayons are manufactured, but kids will love the coloring stations, drawing on the giant glass walls, and making their own stationery at the printmaking exhibit. Plus, they distribute free crayons and markers here like the town of Hershey hands out chocolate kisses. Weekends can get quite crowded; also keep in mind that school groups flood the place weekdays in late Apr. and May. The price of admission includes entry into the third-floor **National Canal Museum** (610-559-6613), a museum about America's towpath canals that is well worth a stop. It is also geared toward youngsters, with model canals that let them guide their own boats through locks and planes, though adults should find plenty of interesting lore in the railroad and engineering exhibits.

CRAYOLA FACTORY

✍ **Dorney Park and Wildwater Kingdom** (610-395-3724; www.dorneypark.com), 3830 Dorney Park Rd., Allentown. Open daily late May through Aug., Fri.–Sun. Sep. and Oct.; $38 adults, $16 seniors and kids under 48 inches. Discounted tickets are available at local Acme stores. Part of the Cedar Fair chain, Dorney Park has about a dozen thrill rides and roller coasters (including the Steel Force "hypercoaster" and the floorless Hydra: Revenge), plus family-friendly rides like Tilt-a-Whirl, an antique carousel, and Camp Snoopy. Wildwater Kingdom, a water park with 22 slides, tubing rivers, wave pools, and a kids' area, is included in the price of admission. Waits for rides can be long on summer weekends. An interesting factoid: Dorney Park was the amusement park featured in the 1988 John Waters film *Hairspray*.

✒ **Lost River Caverns** (610-838-8767; www.lostcave.com), 726 Durham St., Hellertown. Open daily; $9.50 adults, $5.50 ages 3–12. These limestone caves are at the northern edge of Bucks County about 20 miles south of Allentown. Five cavern chambers, discovered in 1883, have an abundance of stalactites, stalagmites, and other crystal formations; guided tours take 30 to 40 minutes. The adjacent no-admission museum has rare fossils, minerals, and gems as well as a large collection of antique weapons.

✳ Outdoor Activities

BASEBALL In 2008, the Lehigh Valley welcomed its first major league–affiliated baseball team since 1960. The Triple-A team, called the Iron Pigs in a nod to the area's steelmaking days, is affiliated with the Philadelphia Phillies and plays at the brand new 8,100-seat **Coca-Cola Park** on Allentown's east side. For information, visit www.ironpigsbaseball.com.

BOAT EXCURSIONS Canal boat rides, narrated by costumed crew members, run regularly throughout the summer and weekends in Sept. from **Hugh Moore Park** (see also *Green Space*). Cost is $7 adults, $5 ages 3–15.

GOLF **Bethlehem Golf Club** (610-691-9393), 400 Illicks Mill Rd., Bethlehem. Built in 1965, this 18-hole municipal course has a mix of flat and hilly terrain and stretches to nearly 7,000 yards. There's also an executive 9-hole course, a driving range, and mini-golf.

Center Valley Golf Club (610-791-5580), 3300 Center Valley Pkwy., Center Valley. This 18-hole par-72 course near I-78 and PA 309 is in excellent condition with five tees ranging from 4,932 to 6,973 yards.

HUNTING Hunting of squirrels, pheasants, rabbits, and white-tailed deer is permitted on about 900 acres of **Jacobsburg State Park** (see also *Green Space*). Hunters are expected to follow the rules and regulations of the **state game commission** (www.www.pgc.state.pa.us).

SKIING **Bear Creek Ski & Recreation Area** (610-682-7100; www.skibearcreek .com) 101 Doe Mountain Ln., Macungie. Geared toward novice and intermediate skiers, it has 17 slopes and a half-pipe and snow tubing park.

Blue Mountain Ski Area (610-826-7700; www.skibluemt.com), 1660 Blue Mountain Dr., Palmerton. About 17 miles north of Allentown with 110 acres of skiing terrain and 30 slopes. There's also a half-pipe and snow tubing area.

✳ Green Space

✒ **Hugh Moore Historical Park** (610-559-6613), Lehigh Dr., Easton. Named after the founder of the Dixie Cup Company, this city-owned park parallels several miles of the Lehigh River and has picnic areas, flat biking trails, and old-time canal boat rides in the summer. Paddleboats and canoe rentals are also available in season. It's about an 8-minute drive via Fourth Street from the National Canal Museum (see *To See*).

☙ **Jacobsburg Environmental Education Center** (610-746-2801), 835 Jacobsburg Rd., Bushkill Township. This 1,200-acre state park near Nazareth is located on a historic site that once housed two 18th-century rifle factories and an iron furnace and forge. Bounded by Bushkill Creek, it has 18 miles of well-maintained hiking and biking trails. Maps are available at the kiosk in the main parking lot on Belfast Road. The pedestrian-only Henry's Woods Trail, also accessible from here, is a 1.5-mile shaded loop that follows the creek downstream past hemlock and oak forest.

☙ **Sand Island** (610-865-7079), 56 River St., Bethlehem. This 2-mile-long city park on the Lehigh River is near downtown and has tennis and basketball courts, a playground, a boat ramp, and a small cultural center. You'll also find access to the Lehigh Canal and towpath, a popular biking and running trail that follows the canal west to Allentown or east to Freemansburg and then on to Easton. The island can be accessed via car by a small bridge next to an old railroad station just under the Hill to Hill Bridge (I-378).

✳ Lodging

HOTELS & INNS

∞ **Glasbern** (610-285-4723; www.glasbern.com), 2141 Pack House Rd., Fogelsville. Romance meets businesslike efficiency at this family-farm-turned-country inn on 100 acres a few miles outside Allentown. Seven separately renovated buildings, once used to run the farm, now house 35 large rooms or suites, many with fireplaces and whirlpool tubs. There's also a fitness center, spa, and outdoor heated pool. Its fine restaurant is open to the public (see also *Dining Out*). Rates are a bit high for the area, but most folks looking for a luxury getaway find their expectations are met or exceeded here. Rooms $150–375, suites $250–475, includes a country breakfast.

& **Radisson Hotel Bethlehem** (610-625-5000; 800-607-2384), 437 Main St. What this busy urban hotel lacks in warmth it makes up for in rich historical background. Centrally located in the downtown, it was built in 1922 on the site of the area's first house, where a wealthy Moravian patron named Count Nicholas Ludwig von Zinzendorf christened the town Bethlehem. After major renovations, the hotel reopened as a Radisson in 1999 and has 127 rooms and suites with business hotel amenities like a free airport shuttle, fitness center, and wireless Internet access. Even if you don't stay here, be sure to check out the grand old lobby and the seven George Gray murals that have hung in the hotel since 1937 and chronicle the town's history from religious settlement to industrial center. Rooms and suites $179–399.

BED & BREAKFASTS ♫ & ☙

Lafayette Inn (610-253-4500; 800-509-6990; www.lafayetteinn.com), 525

W. Monroe St., Easton. Perched high on a hill overlooking the valley, this inn near Lafayette College is one of your best and friendliest options for lodging in the Easton area. Owners Paolo and Laura Di Liello were electrical engineers before joining the hospitality business; they live on premises with their Siberian husky Lena. All 18 rooms and suites are tastefully furnished with antiques, desks, TVs, and private baths. Deluxe rooms are $175 and can accommodate up to four people; standard rooms are $125 and sleep two. The inn attracts a mix of business travelers, Lafayette College visitors, and general tourists. Breakfast (usually made-to-order omelets and waffles during the week and a feast of homemade granola, fruit, cereals, and stratas or French toast on weekends) is served on individual tables in the sunroom. Kids and pets (in some rooms) are welcome. Rooms $125–175; suites $225.

⊙ **Sayre Mansion** (610-882-2100; www.sayremansion.com), 250 Wyandotte St., Bethlehem. This Gothic Revival home once belonged to Robert Sayre, founder of the Lehigh Railroad. It's in a central location about a 5-minute drive or 25-minute walk across the PA 378/Hill to Hill Bridge to historic Bethlehem. The 18 spacious and attractive rooms have desks, flat-panel TVs, wing chairs, fireplaces, and luxurious feather beds. Four-course breakfasts are served in the elegant dining room, or you may opt to have it delivered to your room. Home-baked cookies are served in the afternoons, and port is available in the evening. Rooms $150–200; suites $225–250.

✳ Where to Eat

DINING OUT ⛾ **Apollo Grill** (610-865-9600), 85 W. Broad St., Bethlehem. Lunch and dinner Tues.–Sat. This busy bistro near the historic district specializes in innovative tapas like shrimp limoncello, chorizo crostini, Thai barbecue scallops, and duck spring rolls. There's also a selection of sandwiches (blackened prime rib, Southwest chicken) and simple pastas. It is always hopping, so reservations are recommended. Tapas and sandwiches $9–14. Entrees $12–21.

♿ ⛾ ▼ **Federal Grill** (610-776-7600), 536 Hamilton St., Allentown. Lunch and dinner Mon.–Fri., dinner Sat. Located near the art museum and Liberty Bell, this convivial bar and restaurant specializes in steaks (choose from Kobe strip steak to center cut Angus prepared a variety of ways) and comfort foods like Yankee pot roast and chicken Alfredo. For lunch, there's she-crab soup, chili, and a variety of specialty sandwiches, burgers, and wraps. There's also a separate cigar lounge on the first floor, with a light fare menu. Lunch: $5–13; entrees: $15–35.

Glasbern (610-285-4723; www.glasbern.com), 2141 Pack House Rd., Fogelsville. Dinner daily; two seatings at 5:30 and 8:30. This romantic restaurant showcases meats and produce raised and grown on its adjacent farm. Dinners Sun. through Fri. are á la carte and might include wild mushroom risotto, tomato soup, roasted gulf shrimp with apples, bacon, and melted onions, and seared sirloin steak with creamed peppers, onions, and asparagus. The dining room is exquisite and welcoming, with stone walls, vaulted rafters, and a fireplace. A prix-fixe four-course dinner for $55 per person is served on Sat.. Reservations required. Entrees $26–30.

Easton

&. ☿ **Pearly Baker's Ale House** (610-253-9949), 11 Centre Sq. Lunch, dinner, and late-night menu daily, closed Mon. Sep.–May. Locals love to steer newcomers to this popular eatery and tavern on the square. Menu highlights include pear and Brie salad, a long list of burgers, and entrees like blackened stuffed chicken breast, halibut primavera, and Eastern Shore crab cakes. Dine outside overlooking the square in the summer or under the dining room's grand chandelier any other time. There's live music on weekends. Lunch and sandwiches: $7–12; entrees: $14–29.

Sette Luna (610-253-8888), 219 Ferry St. Lunch and dinner daily. Small and bustling bistro near Easton's main square serving wood-burning-oven pizzas, homemade pastas, and excellent salads. Don't expect fast service. Wine and beer. Pizzas: $7–14; entrees $10–20.

EATING OUT Billy's Downtown Diner (610-867-0105), 10 E. Broad St., Bethlehem. Open 7–6 Mon.–Fri., 7-2 Sat. and Sun. Local celebrity chef Billy Kounoupis and his wife Yanna took over this former newsstand in 2000 and transformed it into a friendly and upscale noshing place. Breakfast menu includes specialty omelets like smoked salmon or crispy bacon, stuffed French toast, and creamed chipped beef. For lunch, there's a long list of sandwiches, melts, and other diner items like gravy boat fries, pierogies, and mozzarella sticks. Dishes $3–10.

Josie's New York Deli (610-252-5081), 14 Centre Sq., Easton. This is the place to come if you're looking to avoid the McDonald's inside the nearby Crayola Factory. The sandwiches are fresh, large, and cheap. The line to order can be long, but it moves fast. Sandwiches $3–5.

Yocco's Hot Dogs (610-433-1950, 625 W. Liberty St., Allentown. Don't be put off by the gritty white facade and sometimes indifferent service. Founded by the uncle of native son Lee Iacocca, Yocco's makes hot dogs that people drive miles for; the pierogies are tasty, too. There are also branches in Emmaus, Fogelsville, and at 2128 Hamilton St. in Allentown.

ICE CREAM/DESSERT Emmaus Bakery (610-965-2170), 415 Chestnut St. You'll find handmade cinnamon swirl donuts, apple fritters, and more at this family bakery.

Purple Cow Creamery (610-252-5544), 14 S. Bank St., Easton. Tucked in an alley around the corner from Crayola, this ice cream parlor serves Italian ice, milkshakes, real hot fudge sundaes, and delicious ice cream. Choose from tiramisu, toasted coconut Black Forest cake, cotton candy, and other fun flavors.

Wired Gallery and Café (610-317-8010), 520 Main St., Bethlehem. Closed Mon. Unlike many cafés that also call themselves art galleries, this one is the real thing, with an entire adjacent room dedicated to original works in painting, sculpture, photography, and glass. The cafe serves soups and sandwiches, but it's the cakes, scones, and coffee drinks that seem to get the most attention.

✳ Entertainment

&. **Symphony Hall** (610-351-7990), 23 N. Sixth St., Allentown. Home to the Allentown Symphony, the 1,200-seat concert hall also stages non-orchestral music and theatrical performances for adults and kids throughout the year.

& **State Theater** (610-252-3132; www.statetheatre.org), 453 Northampton St., Easton. Renovated in the 1990s, this historic theater hosts concerts by nationally known performers, circuses, and off-Broadway hits like *Late Night Catechism.*

& **Boyd Theatre** (610-866-1521; www.theboyd.com), 30 W. Broad St., Bethlehem. This great old theater opened in 1921 and has been owned by the same local family since 1970. Its single screen shows first-run films.

✳ Selective Shopping

For a pleasant mix of shops and restaurants, head to **downtown Emmaus**. Its pedestrian-friendly streets are lined with antiques and home-decor shops, several upscale consignment stores, historic churches, and a variety of dining options, from vegetarian cafés to family diners. For a complete list of stores and a map, visit www.emmausmainstreet.com.

Nearby

Moravian Book Shop (610-866-5481), 428 Main St., Bethlehem. Open daily except some holidays. Established in 1745 by the Moravian church, this charming retail complex near the Hotel Bethlehem claims to be the world's oldest bookseller. Besides a wide selection of books on the Moravian church and Lehigh Valley history, it also offers bestsellers and children's books, candles, pottery, and exquisite ornaments and gifts featuring the symbolic Moravian star. There's even a deli in back, meaning

you could lose yourself for an entire afternoon in here.

Fairgrounds Farmers Market (610-435-7469), 17th and Chew sts., Allentown. Open 8–6 Thurs.–Sat. More than 60 vendors offering a wide selection of Pennsylvania Dutch prepared foods, imported cheeses, and local produce, plus retail shops selling everything from martial arts uniforms and collectibles to magnetic jewelry and Avon products.

✳ Special Events

August: **MusikFest** (first week), around Bethlehem—more than three hundred musical acts, from polka

MORAVIAN BOOK SHOP

bands to rock legends, perform at this popular 10-day event that brings more than a million people to indoor and outdoor venues around Bethlehem. Tickets for individual concerts are in the $20–50 range. For details, go to www.musikfest.org.

November/December **Christkindl-mart Bethlehem** (late Nov. through Dec.)—modeled after Germany's open-air Christmas markets, this fabulous holiday bazaar features handmade crafts, live holiday music, ice sculpting, and more. Related events include trolley and carriage rides, walking tours, and holiday concerts. For details, go to www.christmas city.org.

INTRODUCTION TO THE POCONO MOUNTAINS

A couple of decades ago, the Pocono Mountains region was widely regarded as an over-the-top honeymoon destination for couples who liked ceilings painted with cherubs and bathtubs shaped like champagne flutes. A few affordable rustic family lodges attracted vacationing city folk from New York and Philadelphia for a week or two in the summer. Candle shops were plentiful.

A handful of couples-only resorts still exist today, but the area has come a long, long way since then and turned itself into a major vacation destination for families and couples of all tastes. Golfers can take their pick of three dozen courses. Outdoor adventure types flock to the Lehigh Gorge area, where stellar whitewater rafting and mountain-biking opportunities abound. Families favor the water parks and affordable camping and cabin rental options. And couples can choose from a long list of upscale B&Bs and country inns that are more-likely to have antique brass beds than the mirrored headboards of yore.

Though they are geologically a southwestern extension of the Catskill Mountains, the Pocono Mountains aren't really a mountain chain at all. They are a combination of deep forests, rolling hills, sparkling lakes, and limitless outdoor pastimes. The entire Pocono Mountains region encompasses more than 2,400

POCONOS RESORT SIGN

square miles and four counties: Carbon, Monroe, Pike, and Wayne. It is home to 8 state and 2 national parks, 170 miles of rivers, 35 golf courses, 63 ski trails, summer camps, and more resorts than anywhere else in the state. The towns of Jim Thorpe, Blakeslee, Marshalls Creek, Stroudsburg, Milford, Hawley, and Honesdale are a part of the Poconos region; the towns of Wilkes-Barre or Scranton are not, though they are within easy driving distance.

To make it more easily digestible, I have divided the region into two chapters: the south region, which includes the Delaware Water Gap, Jim Thorpe, and the region's largest number of resorts, and the north region of Pike and Wayne counties, which is less than 90 miles from New York City and known for its quaint towns, unique museums, and *Green Acres*-meets-Manhattan vibe.

Perhaps because it harks back to the region's heart-shaped-tub days, tourism officials and current business owners tend to frown upon referring to the region by its nickname, the Poconos. I try to adhere to that in this guide, but I apologize in advance if I fall off the wagon occasionally and call it the Poconos. I spent many adolescent summers here, and the area's unpretentious beauty holds a special place in my heart.

POCONO MOUNTAINS SOUTH

AREA CODE The entire southern Pocono Mountain region lies within 570.

GUIDANCE The **Pennsylvania Welcome Center** (570-234-1180) just off I-80 near Delaware Water Gap, is a full-service rest facility with picnic tables, vending machines, maps, and information about attractions throughout the state, as well as the latest road and weather conditions. It's staffed daily 7 AM–7 PM. In Stroudsburg, the **Pocono Mountains Vacation Bureau** (570-421-5791; www.800poconos.com), 1004 Main St., Stroudsburg, is a good spot for area maps and attractions; they will also send you materials by mail upon request. If you're in Jim Thorpe, stop by the visitor center in the old railway station for maps and information on current activities.

GETTING THERE *By air:* **Philadelphia International** (215-937-6800) and Newark are the closest major airports, each more than two hours away. **Lehigh Valley International** (888-359-5842) is about a 45-minute drive from Stroudsburg.

By car: From Philadelphia, I-476 to Lehighton or Blakeslee for the western region. For Stroudsburg and Delaware Water Gap, pick up US 22 in Allentown, then follow PA 33 north. From New York or New Jersey, take I-80 west to Stroudsburg and points beyond.

By bus: **Martz Trailways** (570-421-3040; www.martztrailways.com) runs buses from New York City and Scranton to stations in Delaware Water Gap, Mount Pocono, and Marshalls Creek. **Greyhound** also has service to Scranton and Philadelphia from Delaware Water Gap.

GETTING AROUND Unless you have the Olympian stamina of Jim Thorpe, you'll need a car to get around the region. It can take as long as an hour to drive from Lehigh Gorge to Delaware Water Gap. The main streets of Stroudsburg and Jim Thorpe are pleasant for walking, with plenty of shops, restaurants, and old architecture. Be sure to bring a good map and request very clear directions to your destinations, especially places without numbered addresses.

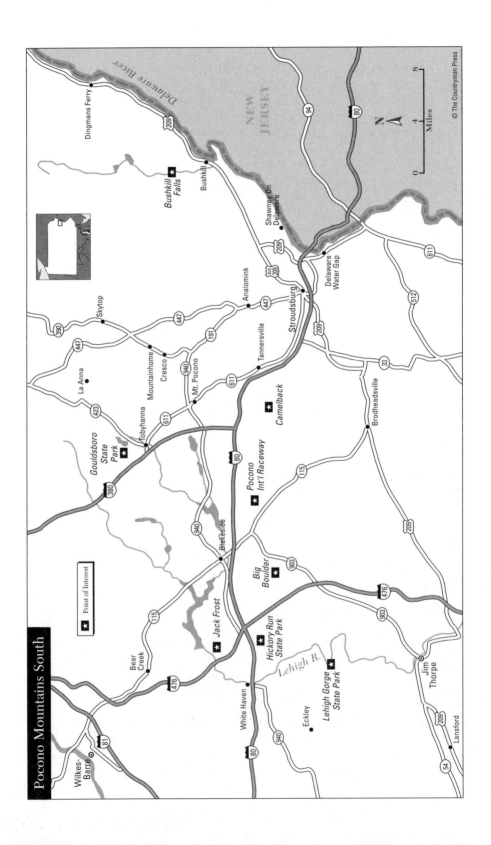

Pocono Mountains South

Delaware River

NEW JERSEY

© The Countryman Press

N

Miles
0   4   8

Dingmans Ferry

Bushkill
Falls

Bushkill

Shawnee On
Delaware

Delaware
Water Gap

Skytop

Analomink

Stroudsburg

La Anna

Mountainhome

Cresco

Mt. Pocono

Tannersville

Brodheadsville

Tobyhanna

Gouldsboro
State
Park

Camelback

Pocono
Int'l Raceway

Blakeslee

Big
Boulder

Point of Interest

Bear
Creek

Jack Frost

Hickory Run
State Park

Lehigh R.

Lehigh Gorge
State Park

Eckley

Jim
Thorpe

Lansford

White Haven

Wilkes-
Barre

MEDICAL EMERGENCY **Pocono Medical Center** (570-421-4000), 206 E. Brown St., East Stroudsburg.

225

POCONO MOUNTAINS SOUTH

WHEN TO GO Summer is the most popular time to visit the Pocono Mountains, and the time when the lakes and rivers are warmest and most attractions are open and in full swing. The fall, however, is my favorite time to visit. The leaves are turning brilliant shades of gold and orange, the air is crisp, and you can't drive a mile without bumping into a pumpkin or harvest fest. Late Mar. through June (and to a lesser extent in Sept. and Oct.) is the best period for white water rafting here because of scheduled dam releases along the Lehigh River.

✳ Villages

Delaware Water Gap. Not to be confused with the natural wonder of the same name, this sleepy town of eight hundred residents was once a thriving resort serving the many people visiting the nearby gorge, including Teddy Roosevelt. Some of its once-grand buildings and hotels are fading and in need of repair, but it still has several worthwhile attractions, like the jazz performances at the Deer Head Inn, a few art galleries, and a terrific BYO restaurant. The Appalachian Trail crosses right through its main street (PA 611).

Mount Pocono. Home to many of the all-inclusive resorts and souvenir candle shops that first put the Pocono Mountains on the map, this central borough probably best epitomizes the Poconos as a honeymoon capitol. It has been heavily developed in recent years and has a Wal-Mart, freestanding casino, and several grocery stores and strip malls. Busy PA 940 cuts through its center, but there are still numerous forested country roads to its north that lead past old general stores, rustic inns, and bait and tackle shops. It's also home to the old-fashioned Casino Theater and Memorytown, a kitschy destination complex comprised of a tavern, picnic area, game room, and lake with faux covered bridge and paddleboats.

Mountainhome. You could call this aptly named town the gateway to the central Poconos. You'll pass through it on your way to destinations like Canadensis, Skytop, La Anna, and Buck Hill Falls. It's not a walkable kind of place, but it has several cafés, shops, and attractions like the Pocono Playhouse and Callie's Candy Factory.

Shawnee. Golf. Ski. Swim. Kayak. Those are your main options in this small community next to the Delaware River. Its dominant resident is the Shawnee ski resort, but you will also find a well-regarded theater, several good B&Bs, and the lovely and regal Shawnee Inn and

SHAWNEE GENERAL STORE

JIM THORPE

Located along the Lehigh River at the southwestern edge of the Pocono Mountains region, **Jim Thorpe** is a former railroad and coal-shipping town that was known as Mauch Chunk until 1955. That's when the famous Native American athlete died and his struggling widow struck a deal to have his remains buried there and the town renamed for the famous Olympian. Though Thorpe never set foot here, a large monument stands in his honor near a sign declaring the town THE SWITZERLAND OF AMERICA. Today, Jim Thorpe is one of those destinations that more than lives up to the expectations based on postcards or word of mouth. Anchored by a thriving little downtown, it is surrounded by miles of pristine forest, rivers, and a free and easy spirit. Just about every outdoor adventure and cycling

JIM THORPE MONUMENT

ASA PACKER MANSION

magazine has ranked it as one of the top biking destinations in the state, if not the country; it is also a popular spot for paintball, hiking, and whitewater rafting.

The nonathlete will also find things to do here. The opulent **Asa Packer Mansion** (home of the founder of the Lehigh Valley Railroad) sits on a hilltop overlooking the town and is open for tours daily from June through Oct. (570-325-3229; www.asapackermansion.com). The **Old Jail Museum** (570-325-5259) on West Broadway was built in 1871 and offers fascinating tours of original cells and tales about the Molly Maguires, a secret society of anthracite miners who used terrorism to force mine owners to improve working conditions (seven were accused and hanged here). Call ahead for hours.

A JIM THORPE DOORWAY

One can also easily spend a couple of hours poking around the frozen-in-time downtown, gawking at the varied styles of architecture and visiting the hip cafés, art galleries, and mom-and-pop shops. The **Mauch Chunk Opera House** (570-325-4439; 41 W. Broadway), built in 1881, still hosts theatrical and music performances, films, and art exhibits. For kids, there's a model train display in the Hooven Building next to the train depot and rides on the **Lehigh Gorge Scenic Railway** (570-325-8485; www.lgsry.com). Sleeping options include the venerable Inn at Jim Thorpe and a handful of B&Bs and nearby campgrounds (see also *Lodging*). I can't say enough good things about this town. Go.

Golf Resort, once owned by Fred Waring and patronized by Arnold Palmer, Jackie Gleason, and other celebrities.

✳ To See

MUSEUMS Frank Frazetta Museum (570-424-5833; www.frankfrazetta.com/ ff/museum), US 209, East Stroudsburg. Open 11–4 Sat.–Sun., mid-Apr. through Christmas. This unique museum features original paintings and sketches by Frank Frazetta, the renowned science fiction and fantasy artist known for his comic-book drawings (*Conan the Barbarian*) and movie posters (*What's New, Pussycat?*, *Mad Max*). A gift shop sells posters, books, and limited-edition prints. The museum is strict about its hours and located on a private road north of Stroudsburg; don't attempt to visit when it's closed. The Web site provides detailed directions with photos.

♿ **Pocono Indian Museum** (570-588-9338, www.poconoindianmuseum.com), US 209, Bushkill. Open daily; $5 adults, $2.50 ages 6–16. Located in a white-

---

DELAWARE WATER GAP

You don't need to be a geologist to appreciate this natural wonder. Millions of years ago, this area was a level plain; it is believed that over time moving water wore down and pushed through a weak spot in the mountain ridge to form a breathtaking gorge that separates two mountains, Minsi and Tammany. For a generation after the Civil War, the Delaware Water Gap was one of the top tourist destinations in existence (before the emergence of names like Catskill, Disney, and Niagara). Today, it's a popular day trip for

DELAWARE WATER GAP

columned mansion, this unsung, if dated, six-room museum is obviously a labor of love for its employees. Instead of just pinning up their collection of ancient artifacts, many of which were found in the Delaware River area, they present them in context with mannequins and other ways that let you see how they worked within the Lenape lifestyle. You will also find a 1843 Cree Indian scalp from the Dakotas and a full-size wigwam among the displays. The gift shop is huge and fun to browse.

SCENIC DRIVES Buck Hill Falls, north of Mountainhome, is home to the region's first golf course and some of the prettiest stone houses you'll ever see. Escape the tourist scene around Mount Pocono and head north on PA 191 for a peaceful 30-minute drive. On the way, you'll pass forested lands and meadows and a handful of antiques and gift shops and old general stores. Bear left onto Bush Mountain Road in Mountainhome, then drive several miles to Buck Hill Road and make a right. Once you get here, there's not much to do except gawk at the stately mansions and natural stone bridges or have a lemonade at the

Pennsylvania and New Jersey residents, as well as outdoors types who come to kayak and canoe the river or hike the Appalachian Trail. The gorge is located at the southern edge of the **Delaware Water Gap National Recreation Area** (570-588-2451; www.nps.gov/dema), a national park that stretches along either side of the Delaware River from Delaware Water Gap north to Milford.

The gap itself can be viewed from several parking overlooks around the town of Delaware Water Gap, including Point of Gap, off PA 611, where there's plenty of parking and nice views of the carved stone side of Mount Tammany (some say it looks like the profile of the Lenape Indian chief for whom the mountain is named). Another good place to stop is **Kittatinny Point Visitor Center** just off I-80 across the state border in New Jersey, where you can pick up maps and speak to helpful park rangers. If you have the time and are in decent shape, consider hiking up Mount Tammany to gorgeous views of the entire gap and surrounding towns. From the New Jersey side, at the Dunnfield Creek parking area in Worthington State Forest, you can access a section of the Appalachian Trail that runs right over the top of Kittatinny Ridge to Sunfish Pond, a beautiful glacial lake surrounded by woods.

If you're short on time or aren't into hiking up a mountain, another good way to learn about the history of the area is via narrated trolley ride. **Water Gap Trolley** (570-476-9766; PA 611; $9.50 adults, $4 ages 3–11) runs tours daily four or five times a day from Mar. through Nov. Guides are informative and funny, and the hour-long trip includes stops at several overlooks and historic buildings and tales about local celebrities like Fred Waring, Jackie Gleason, and Mr. Greenjeans (of *Captain Kangaroo* fame).

semiprivate Buck Hills Tennis Club. Before heading back, you can continue north a few miles on PA 191 to **Holley Ross Pottery** in the tiny village of LaAnna.

✳ To Do

FOR FAMILIES ✐ ☃ **Bushkill Falls** (570-588-6682; www.visitbushkillfalls.com), US 209 and Bushkill Falls Rd., Bushkill. Open daily Apr. through Oct.; $9 adults, $4 ages 4–10. This series of eight scenic waterfalls has long been a popular destination for families. Charles E. Peters started charging visitors a dime to see the falls in 1904. His descendants still run the place. Over the years, they have added a gift shop, Native American museum, small lake with paddleboats, and playground, but it all remains relatively rustic. The "hiking trails" that lead to the falls are actually well-maintained walkways flanked by locust-wood guard rails. You can take an easy path to reach the main falls, or spend as long as two hours hiking to the upper canyons and glens. Families with young kids might want to bring a back carrier. The place gets packed on summer weekends. Don't miss the Bushkill Story cabin, a small house displaying early marketing materials, photographs, souvenirs (like a Bushkill Falls handheld pinball game), and brochures.

VIEW OF MOUNT TAMMANY

↑ **Callie's Candy Kitchen** (570-595-2280), PA 390, Mountainhome. A visit to this multiroom candy shop is a rite of passage for every school-age kid in the area. Harry Callie, who started the business in 1952, still does regular candymaking demonstrations combined with merry lectures on how he got into the candy business. As you browse the store, you'll find that Callie's isn't afraid to dip anything in chocolate, including whole s'mores, crackers, whipped marshmallows, oreos, and even cream cheese.

↑ **Callie's Pretzel Factory** (570-595-3257) PA 191/390, Cresco. Also owned by the Callies and about 3 miles south of the candy store, this place is a must-stop for pretzel lovers. Show up right around opening hour of 10 AM and you can watch the day's batches being made by a huge machine in the back. Choose from garlic pretzels, pretzels stuffed with apples or cheddar cheese, hot dogs wrapped in pretzels, and even funnel-cake pretzels. For some reason, there's also a gift shop for lefthanders in the back.

⚓ **Camel Beach Water Park** (570-629-1661; camelbeach.com), Tannersville. Open late May through Labor Day; $30 adults, $25 ages 3–11. Every summer, Camelback Ski Area transforms into a wild and wacky water park with a giant wave pool, a tubing "river," and 22 slides with names like Vortex and Triple Venom. It's popular with teenagers, but there are a few sedate activities like chairlift rides, mini-golf, and a shallow pool for tots.

✳ Outdoor Activities

AUTO RACING **Pocono Raceway** (570-646-2300; 800-722-3929), Long Pond. Many NASCAR racers consider this 2.5-mile tri-oval speedway to be one of the toughest tracks in the country. Located on a former spinach farm, it draws more than 100,000 fans twice a year to its annual cup races. (See also *Special Events*.) It also has stock car racing and driving school programs.

BICYCLING Once described by *Bicycling* magazine as "Durango East," Jim Thorpe is for riders of all abilities. You'll find several good places to rent bikes in town, including **Blue Mountain Sports** (570-325-4421; www.bikejimthorpe .com) across from the train depot; they also rent kayaks, rowboats, and canoes. (See also *Whitewater Rafting*.)

CANOEING & KAYAKING **Kittatinny Canoes** (800-356-2852), 102 Kittatinny Ct., Dingmans Ferry. Guided canoe and kayak trips at five different points of the Delaware River. Rates start at about $40 per person for two and a half hours. They also do tubing trips.

FISHING **Paradise Trout Preserve** (570-629-0422), PA 191, Paradise, near Cresco. Home to the state's first fish hatchery, the property also has a pond stocked with brown, brook, and rainbow trout. No fishing license is required, though registration costs $2 a person.

Good fishing spots that require a license include **Tobyhanna Lake** in Tobyhanna State Park, a favorite for bass, brook trout, catfish, and perch. **Hickory Run State Park** has two stocked trout streams and you'll find bass and trout in the nearby Lehigh River. In Jim Thorpe, you can fish for bass, pickerel, and trout in **Mauch Chunk Lake**.

GAMBLING The state's first freestanding slots parlor, **Mount Airy Casino Resort** (877-682-4791; www.mountairycasino.com), opened in late fall 2007 on the grounds of a former honeymooners' lodge. It features more than 2,500 slot machines, plus an adjacent hotel, spa, and nightclub.

GOLF **Split Rock Golf Club** (570-722-9901), Lake Harmony. This public 27-hole course at Split Rock Lodge has midsized greens, nice views, and a par of 72.

Taminent Golf Club (570-588-6652), Bushkill Falls Rd., Taminent. Designed by Robert Trent Jones, this 18-hole mountaintop course has tree-lined fairways, undulating greens, and majestic views.

HIKING A popular portion of the **Joseph McDade Recreational Trail** in the Delaware Water Gap National Recreation Area begins at the Hialeah Picnic Area north of Shawnee and follows the river for 5 scenic and flat miles north to Turn Farm. Along the way, you'll pass Smithfield Beach, which offers roped-off swimming in the summer, and stellar vistas of the river and mountain ridges. Biking and cross-country skiing is also allowed on this flat well-maintained trail.

HORSEBACK RIDING **Carson's Riding Stables** (570-839-9841), PA 611, Cresco. This 60-acre facility near Mount Pocono offers hourly trail rides for all levels of riders.

SKIING **Camelback** (570-629-1661; www.skicamelback.com), Camelback Rd., Tannersville. This is the largest ski area in the region, with 33 trails, most of them easy and intermediate, two terrain parks, and a half-pipe area. Three lodges serve food at the base of the mountain; there's also a restaurant at the top.

Jack Frost (570-443-8425; www.jackfrostbigboulder.com) PA 940, Blakeslee. Known for its challenging terrain, this has 27 trails, 9 lifts, a cross-country ski trail, and a popular snow tubing area. It shares some facilities with nearby **Big Boulder**, known for its beginner trails and programs, allowing you to ski both areas on the same day on one ticket.

Shawnee Mountain (570-421-7231; www.shawneemt.com), Hollow Rd., Shawnee. This family-friendly resort is at the southernmost point of the Poconos region, with 23 trails, a terrain park, and half-pipe area. A cozy lodge overlooks the bunny slope.

WHITEWATER RAFTING The Lehigh River offers Class III white-water rafting and many outfitters in the area run regular trips during the summer and during spring and fall dam release weekends. (See also *Lehigh Gorge State Park*.) Many also offer kayaking packages and bike rentals and shuttles.

Pocono Whitewater Rafting (800-944-8392; 570-325-3655), 1519 PA 903, also known as Lehigh Gorge Outpost, runs rafting trips for all levels, plus offers kayaking, paintball, bike rentals, and shuttles to Lehigh Gorge. **Jim Thorpe River Adventures** (800-424-7238; www.jtraft.com) 1 Adventure Ln., off PA 903, offers guided rafting trips and bike rentals.

✳ Green Space

Big Pocono State Park (570-894-8336), Camelback Rd., Tannersville. You can see much of northeastern Pennsylvania and stretches of New Jersey and New York from the summit of this 1,300-acre park, which is also home to Camelback Mountain. It has 7 miles of hiking trails, three picnic areas, and limited hunting grounds. The summit can be reached by foot or car up a steep and winding paved road.

Gouldsboro and Tobyhanna State Parks (570-894-8336). These two family-friendly parks are adjacent and anchored by two large lakes with swimming and boating opportunities and 19 miles of hiking trails for all levels. A park office at Tobyhanna just off PA 423 has maps and other information. The entrance to Gouldsboro is off PA 507.

Lehigh Gorge State Park (570-443-0400), White Haven. This 4,500-acre park follows the Lehigh River from Francis E. Walter Dam in White Haven down to Jim Thorpe in the south. It is dominated by its eponymous gorge, sheer rock walls, rock outcroppings, and dozens of waterfalls. It offers hunting, fishing, and plenty of scenic vistas, but its biggest draw is its white-water rafting and mountain-biking opportunities (see also *Outdoor Activities*). The Lehigh Gorge Trail, which follows 26 miles of abandoned railroad grade along the river, is beloved by mountain bikers for its scenery, tree canopies, and slight downhill north-to-south grade; horseback riders and hikers may also use it. You can access this trail and the river from Jim Thorpe via the Glen Onoko access area, where there's a parking area and rest rooms. Many bike shops offer a shuttle ride that drops you at White Haven in the north and lets you take the trail downhill all the way back to Jim Thorpe. The upper portion of Lehigh Gorge links with **Hickory Run State Park** (570-443-0400), a 15,500-acre park with plenty of recreational features such as a lake, swimming pool, playground, snack bar, visitor center, and dozens of hiking and snowmobile trails.

✳ Lodging

RESORTS ✐ ♿ **Great Wolf Lodge** (800-768-9653;) 1 Great Wolf Dr., Scotrun. If you're a parent or grandparent of a child under age 12, chances are you've heard of this massive resort and water park. One of 10 Great Wolf Lodges around the country, it has 401 large suites, 2 restaurants, and lots and lots of kid-friendly activities, the highlight being a Costco-sized waterpark with 11 slides, 6 pools, and a 4-story treehouse. They also considerately operate a spa for parents who need a break from the splashing action. Prices drop considerably on weekdays after Labor Day. They also have package deals that include passes to nearby attractions like Camelbeach. Rooms: $189–354.

✐ ♿ ∞ **Skytop Lodge** (570-595-7401; 800-617-2389; www.skytop .com), PA 390, Skytop, 3 miles north of Canadensis. Built in the 1920s as a members-only hunting lodge, this secluded mountaintop resort ranks among the best all-inclusive destinations in the area. Sprawled on 5,500 acres of woods, streams, meadows, lakes, and waterfalls, it has an air of country elegance and more activities than you can possibly imagine: tennis, swimming, nighttime deer watching, stargazing, downhill skiing, fly-fishing, golf, massages, lawn bowling, and even high tea, to name a few. You can stay in the original stone lodge, in a nearby modern 20-room inn, or in spacious cottages overlooking the stream, lodge, or golf course; meals are served in the lodge's grandiose dining room, a separate lake-view restaurant, or an English pub. Rates (including three meals): $395–720; there is usually a two-night minimum on weekends.

INNS & GUESTHOUSES ❦ **Deer Head Inn** (570-424-2000; www.deer

headinn.com), 5 Main St., Delaware Water Gap. Most people associate this place with terrific live jazz and don't realize there are eight comfortable rooms and suites for rent upstairs. All the rooms were overhauled in 2007 and have private baths, crown molding, high ceilings, and top-of-line mattresses and linens; the suites have sitting areas as well. Ask about packages that include jazz and dinner for two (see also *Entertainment*). They start at $189 a night and are a very good value if you like jazz. Rooms $110–130; suites $180–190.

🍴 & Inn at Jim Thorpe (570-325-2599; www.innjt.com), 24 Broadway, Jim Thorpe. This historic hotel is in the heart of downtown, and has beautiful wrought-iron balconies from which to take in all the action. The 34 rooms and 9 suites are decorated in understated Victorian style and have private baths and wireless Internet access; some have fireplaces and jacuzzi tubs. Rates include a breakfast

buffet in the adjacent restaurant. They also offer biking and rafting packages that include all equipment and bike shuttles to Lehigh Gorge. Rooms $93–183.

Mountaintop Lodge (570-646-6636; www.mountaintoplodge.com), PA 940, Pocono Pines. Innkeeper Merrily MacKay grew up on the second floor of this rambling inn, located a few miles east of Jack Frost Ski Resort. She and husband Colin remodeled the comfortable 1928 home in 2001 and turned it into a B&B with 14 rooms and suites. The traditional rooms are on the small side with queen beds and private baths (loft rooms have fireplaces and soaking tubs), while two-bedroom suites (located behind the main house) have king beds, separate living rooms, and six-foot soaking tubs. A full breakfast is included in the rate. No kids under 12. Rooms $100–135. Suites $150–219.

& ⊗ Stroudsmoor Country Inn (570-421-6431, www.stroudsmoor

DEER HEAD INN

.com) Stroudsmoor Rd., Stroudsburg. This would be my pick for the best place to stay near Stroudsburg. Just five minutes from town, it's surrounded by woodlands and feels like a quiet country getaway. The main house has 15 small and attractive rooms and junior suites; newer suites with balconies overlooking the forest are just across the way; there are also small cottages with front porches overlooking an outdoor pool. The rates include a full breakfast at the inn's restaurant. This is a popular spot for destination weddings and sometimes hosts several over a single weekend. Rooms and junior suites: $119–165; suites $270–800.

BED & BREAKFASTS Bischwind (570-472-3820; www.bischwind.com) 1 Coach Rd., Bear Creek. Located just outside Wilkes-Barre and about a 20-minute drive from many western Pocono Mountains attractions, this eight-room hunting-lodge-turned-B&B is a must for history buffs. A giant carved wooden bear greets you near the entrance in honor of one-time guest Theodore Roosevelt. Handsome and ornate is the best way to describe the living and dining areas, which are decorated with stuffed deer heads, rich red leather chairs, large fireplaces, and wood floors. The rooms have the same grand feel as the common areas, but come with modern upgrades like TVs, whirlpool tubs, and wireless Internet access; the two-room Teddy Roosevelt Suite is a favorite. Bear Creek is a stone's throw from the inn and there is an achingly beautiful hour-long hiking trail that loops around the lake. Other nice touches include an outdoor swimming pool and a lavish breakfast of poached salmon or filet mignon, sautéed potatoes, eggs, and

cheesecake (though guests may opt for a lighter continental breakfast). Rooms $135–245.

Gatehouse Country Inn (570-420-4553; www.gatehousecountryinn .com), P.O. Box 264, River Rd., Shawnee. Originally built circa 1900 as a stable and carriage house, the Gatehouse was turned into a summer home by bandleader and Pennsylvania native Fred Waring in the 1950s. Gordon and Cindy Way opened it as a B&B in 2001 with three second-floor rooms with private baths and sitting areas. The upstairs game room, where Waring is believed to have entertained friends such as Jackie Gleason and Dwight Eisenhower, features comfy chairs, games, and the original pool table. Guests also have access to a back courtyard flanked by an old-fashioned ice house, which the Ways have turned into a small antiques store. No children under 12. Rooms $125–150.

The Parsonage (570-325-4462; 800-799-0244; www.theparsonagebandb .com), 61 W. Broadway, Jim Thorpe. Built by the town's Presbyterian pastor in the 1800s, this four-story home offers four comfortable rooms with private baths, a pretty yard with a screened gazebo, and close proximity to downtown. Owner Maureen Grant makes the scrumptious breakfasts herself. Rooms $85–110.

Stony Brook Inn (570-424-1100, 888-424-5240; www.stonybrookinn .com), PO Box 240, River Rd., Shawnee. Pete and Roseann Ferguson are the gregarious owners of this cozy 1850s inn next to the Shawnee Playhouse. The four themed rooms (Country Bear, Rose, Oak, and the Bridal Suite) have private baths, TVs, and nice individual touches like clawfoot tubs or Victorian chaise longues. There's also a swimming pool and large patio out back. The Delaware River and access to the McDade Trail are two blocks away. Rooms $105–160.

CAMPGROUNDS & COTTAGES 🐾 🐾

Delaware Water Gap KOA (570-223-8000; 800-562-0375; www.delawarewatergapkoa.com), 233 Hollow Rd., East Stroudsburg. Located just north of Shawnee a few miles off River Road, this year-round campground has over 140 tent sites, primitive and with hookups, plus 5 cabins and dozens of RV sites. Activities include miniature train rides, minigolf, volleyball, horseshoes, and hayrides. Tent sites $36–45; cabins $72–90.

Mauch Chunk Lake County Park (570-325-3669), Jim Thorpe. Open mid-Apr.–Oct. About 4 miles from downtown, this county park has more than 100 primitive tent sites and 12 two-room cabins with electricity. Many people love it for its access to 4-acre Mauch Chunk Lake and the Switchback Railroad Rail Trail, which crosses through the park. Tent sites: $25–32, cabins $68.

🐾 🐾 **Martinville Streamside Cottages** (570-595-2489) PA 390 north, Canadensis. This cluster of cottages has been in the Martin family since the early 1930s. It's ideal for families with children; there's a swimming pool, a pond with a slide and watercraft, and a lovely stream that runs right through the property. The eight separate cottages sleep four to eight and have wraparound decks, full kitchens, and modern living rooms with fireplaces and TVs. Two suites above the main lodge have king beds,

futons, gas fireplaces, and small refrigerators. Cottages $195–450. Suites $125. Weekday and off-season rates are usually lower.

🐾 **Dingmans Campground** (570-828-1551), 1006 US 209, Dingmans Ferry. Its primo riverfront location is what most campers love best about this rustic property about 10 miles north of Delaware Water Gap. Choose from 133 sites; the ones on the river go fast. Primitive tent sites: $25–28, with a two-night minimum weekends.

✳ Where to Eat

DINING OUT 🐾 **Antelao Restaurant** (570-426-7226), 84 Main St., Delaware Water Gap. Dinner Thurs.–Sun. There are no bad tables in this welcoming bistro owned by Elvi and Michael De Lotto, who ran a popular bakery before opening their own restaurant in a Victorian home near the Delaware Water Gap. Named after a mountain in the Dolomite mountain range in Italy, the restaurant emphasizes seasonal produce: in summer, there might be roasted garlic flan with grilled eggplant, scaloppini of pork tenderloin, and shrimp and basil sauté. Leave room for tiramisu. Reservations strongly recommended; no parties oversix. BYO. Entrees $16–25.

Black Bread Café (570-325-8957), 45 Race St., Jim Thorpe. Closed Tues. One of the region's few upscale bistros features a creative Italian-influenced menu. The dinner menu might include corn-fried brook trout with crawfish etouffee, venison osso bucco and cassoulet, or shrimp in black pepper lacquer. An inviting upstairs lounge (with live music on weekends) serves a less expensive menu of burgers, crab cake sandwiches, and appetizers like house-cured smoked salmon. Lounge menu $6–16; dinner entrees $20–29.

&. ☿ **Blakeslee Inn** (570-646-1100), PA 940, Blakeslee. Dinner Wed.–Sat.; brunch Sun. Renovated in 2002, this upscale restaurant is a local favorite. Chef Jim Evans served as the executive chef for two Pennsylvania governors (Robert Casey and Tom Ridge) before taking over the dining room, which is attached to a small motel. His menu changes seasonally, but signature dishes include stacked filets of sea bass layered with crabmeat, grilled beef tenderloin medallions in a bordelaise sauce, and crab-stuffed beef Wellington. For dessert, you might find Grand Marnier chocolate mousse filled with strawberries rolled in toasted coconut. Reservations are strongly recommended. Extensive wine list. Entrees $22–32.

&. ☿ **Tokyo Tea House** (570-839-8880), PA 940, Pocono Summit. Lunch and dinner daily, except Tues. This small strip-mall restaurant is arguably the best place for quality sushi in the Poconos. The teriyaki and tempura dishes are good, too. Lunch $8–12; dinner entrees $10–25.

EATING OUT &. **Barley Creek Brewing Company** (570-839-9678), Sullivan Trail and Camelback Rd., Tannersville. Lunch and dinner daily. Part Ye Olde Pub and part timbered ski lodge, this microbrewery near Camelback Ski Area is known for its handmade ales and tasty pub grub. Try the fish and chips or special reuben of the day. If you happen to be here for lunch, you can join the free brewery tours that begin at 12:30

every day. Sandwiches and appetizers $7–11; entrees $10–20.

&. ☿ **Sam Snead's Tavern** (570-424-0990), River Rd., Shawnee. It's a chain with branches in Florida, Georgia, and Hawaii, but don't let that keep you from trying this above-par eatery near the entrance of the Shawnee Resort. For lunch, there's an interesting assortment of sandwiches such as baked broccoli chicken, oak-grilled grouper, and filet mignon with griddled onions. Dinner entrees include baby back ribs, shrimp Carolina, and a variety of steaks. In summer, you can dine on a deck overlooking a pretty stream. Lunch $8–15; dinner $18–40.

&. ☿ **Van Gilder's Jubilee Restaurant** (570-646-2377), PA 940, Pocono Pines. Breakfast, lunch, and dinner daily. A local favorite known for its large portions, juicy burgers, and friendly service. Breakfasts are legendary; try the chef's free-for-all Pocono Sampler or any of the omelets. After your meal, you can join in games of billiards, darts, and TV sports-watching in the adjacent pub. Breakfast and lunch: $5–8; dinner: $14–18.

Village Farmer and Bakery (570-476-9440), River Rd., Delaware Water Gap. Open daily at 8 AM. This bakery doesn't have an address on its business card; it just describes its location as between the town's two traffic lights. It's tough to miss—just look for the giant red-lettered sign that says APPLE PIE AND A HOT DOG FOR JUST $1.49. If that sweet deal doesn't interest you, try any of the donuts, cookies, brownies, or other desserts that were made that day. They also sell whole pies—apple is the specialty, but they usually have at least a dozen other kinds.

BYO **Where to buy wine in the southern Pocono Mountains region:**

You'll find **Wine & Spirits stores** in the Pocono Village Mall (570-839-9586), 87 PA 940, Mount Pocono; in the Blakeslee Corners Shopping Plaza (570-646-8069), PA 115/940; and in downtown Stroudsburg (570-424-3943), 761 Main St.

✻ Entertainment

MUSIC ♈ **Deer Head Inn** (570-424-2000; www.deerheadinn.com), 5 Main St., Delaware Water Gap. Dinner and live performances Wed.–Sun. Enjoy terrific live jazz and blues in one of the oldest jazz bars in the country. Covers vary from none to $15 a person.

♈ **Sarah Street Grill** (570-424-9120), 550 Quaker Alley, Stroudsburg. One of the best places around to hear live original music. Wed. open-mike nights are popular. For sports fans, there are 17 TVs, plus a pool table and surprisingly good sushi bar that's open daily 4–10 PM.

♈ **Penn's Peak** (610-826-9000; 866-605-7325; www.pennspeak.com), 325 Maury Rd., Jim Thorpe. This large venue attracts a mix of country and western bands, tribute bands, and veteran acts like Donny Osmond and Sha Na Na. There's a dance floor, restaurant, two bars, and a deck with views that stretch for 50 miles.

MOVIES **Grand Cinema** (570-420-9885), 88 S. Courtland St., East Stroudsburg. This century-year old theater was restored in the late 1990s and features four screens showing art and independent films. An adjacent cafe serves specialty coffees and snacks.

Casino Theatre and Village Malt Shoppe (570-839-7831), 611, Mount Pocono. This landmark two-screen theater shows first-run films and also has mini-golf, an arcade, and an ice cream parlor.

THEATER ♿ **Pocono Playhouse** (570-595-7456; www.poconoplayhouse.com), PA 390, Mountainhome. This five-hundred-seat venue opened in 1947 as the area's first summer theater and hosts as many as nine Broadway-scale musicals between June and Oct.

♿ **Shawnee Playhouse** (570-421-5093; www.shawneeplayhouse.com), River Rd., Shawnee. This small two-hundred-seat theater stages two musicals in the summer, plus a Christmas show and *Messiah* singalong in Dec.

✻ Selective Shopping

Crossing Premium Outlets (570-629-4650), PA 611 (at I-80) Tannersville. This eight-building complex features more than a hundred factory outlet stores (from Woolrich and Reebok to Ann Taylor and Banana Republic) and draws huge weekend crowds.

Carroll & Carroll Booksellers (570-420-1516), 740 Main St., Stroudsburg. Well-stocked and friendly used book store with many first and rare editions.

Holley Ross Pottery (570-676-3248), PA 191, LaAnna. Open daily May through mid-Dec. Surrounded by a pretty nature park above Cresco, this factory outlet sells Fiesta dinnerware, Robinson Ransbottom pottery, and other home-decor items at steep discounts. They also make their own ceramic vases, centerpieces, and candle holders, and tours of the operation are given weekdays at 11. Picnic tables and nature trails are on the property, making it very easy to pass an afternoon here.

Pocono Bazaar Flea Market (570-223-8640), US 209, Marshalls Creek. Open 9–5 Sat. and Sun. A people-watcher's paradise with vendors selling antiques, produce and baked goods, miracle gadgets, housewares, and more.

Shawnee Falls Studio (570-421-0952), River Rd., Shawnee. Open Wed.–Sat. Gwendolyn Evans Caldwell paints local watercolor landscapes, people, and abstracts out of her studio in one of the oldest homes in the area.

Water Gap Gallery (570-424-5002), Main St., Delaware Water Gap. This small gallery across from the Deer Head Inn sells handcrafted pottery, wind chimes, silver jewelry, hand-painted glass, and a great selection of jazz CDs by local artists.

✳ Special Events

June: **Pocono 500 Nextel Cup Race** (first weekend), Pocono Raceway—a hugely popular event that draws NASCAR superstars to compete, plus 100,000 fans who come to watch them. There's a similar race in late July.

June is also a good time to visit Jim Thorpe, where weekend releases from the Francis E. Walter Dam make conditions on the Lehigh River perfect for white-water rafting.

September: **Pocono Garlic Festival** (Labor Day weekend), Shawnee Mountain Ski Area—this creative and fun event celebrates the region's love affair with the pungent bulb. Expect plenty of garlic-laced food, crafts, and entertainment by the Garlic-Eating Tuba Troubadours. Also in September is the **Celebration of the Arts Jazz Festival** (weekend after Labor Day), a nationally recognized four-day event that unites jazz musicians, chefs, and artists on outdoor stages throughout Delaware Water Gap.

October: **Stroudsburg Halloween Parade** (last weekend), Stroudsburg—Costumed kids, adults, and even dogs take over Main Street beginning at noon and march to Courthouse Square for more fun and games.

POCONO MOUNTAINS NORTH

GUIDANCE For a town map and other information on Milford and its outlying areas, visit the **Pike County Tourism Bureau** (570-296-8700), 209 E. Harford St., Milford. In Honesdale, the **Wayne County Visitor Center** (570-253-1960; 32 Commercial St.) has local maps and information; it's also the place to buy tickets for the adjacent Stourbridge Railway Excursions. For information on Lake Wallenpaupack, stop by the **Hawley–Lake Wallenpaupack Visitor Center** (570-226-3191) just below the dam overlook on US 6/PA 507, or visit www .hawleywallenpaupackcc.com.

GETTING THERE *By air:* **Newark International** (800-397-4636) is about an hour's drive from Milford. Alternatives include **Scranton/Wilkes Barre Airport** in Avoca (877-235-9287) and **Lehigh Valley International** in Allentown (888-359-5842).

By car: From the Pennsylvania Turnpike: I-81 to I-84 east. From New York: I-80 west to exit 34B (Sparta); then follow PA 15/US 206 north to Milford. Follow US 6 west to Hawley and Honesdale.

By train: Metro-North line from Manhattan to Port Jervis, New Jersey, across the river from Milford.

By bus: **Short Line** (800-631-8405) runs daily bus service between New York's Port Authority and Milford, Hawley, and Honesdale.

GETTING AROUND While Hawley, Honesdale, and Milford are all pleasant walking towns, you'll need a car to get around up here.

MEDICAL EMERGENCY Wayne County Memorial Hospital (570-253-8100), US 6, Honesdale. **Community Medical Center** (570-969-8000), 1800 Mulberry St., Scranton.

WHEN TO GO For nonskiers, summer and fall are the best times to visit the northern Pocono Mountains. Many outdoor (and some indoor) attractions don't even open their doors until Memorial Day and stay open through Oct.

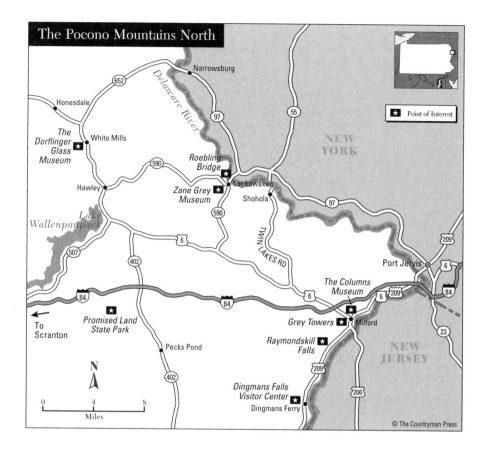

The Pocono Mountains North

✳ Villages

Hawley. Named for the first president of the Pennsylvania Coal Company, this town of 1,300 was a thriving center for anthracite coal distribution in the mid-1800s. The coal and lumber industries were replaced by fine cut-glass and silk and textile mills in the 1920s.

Also changing Hawley's identity in the 1920s was the Pennsylvania Power and Light Company's decision to dam a nearby creek to create hydroelectric power. This created Lake Wallenpaupack, the state's third largest man-made lake. The town became known as a recreational destination for families from Pennsylvania, New Jersey, and New York, a reputation it still has today. Hawley is home to one of the state's top family resorts, Woodloch Pines, as well as many well-regarded antiques shops, and several upscale inns and mom-and-pop lakefront motels.

Honesdale. Like Hawley, its neighbor to the north, Honesdale was named for a railroad VIP: Philip Hone, president of the Delaware and Hudson Canal Company and former mayor of New York. It is the largest municipality in Wayne

County and home to the Stourbridge Lion, the first steam locomotive to run on rails in the U.S.; rides on a full-scale replica run on a regular basis from the original station. Honesdale doesn't have many hotels or inns, but it makes a pleasant day trip from Hawley or Scranton. Its bustling main street is a treasure trove of Victorian architecture and antiques shops. Detour to Church Street and you'll find many lovely historic churches that date to 1860. On its outskirts is a commercial district, as well as the Dorflinger Glass Museum and Wildlife Sanctuary.

Lackawaxen. This quiet village is named after the river that flows through it. It was once a major center for bluestone quarrying and is home to Roebling Bridge, the oldest existing wire suspension bridge in the country. Zane Grey lived here between 1905 and 1918 and wrote several novels from his home overlooking the river, now a museum run by the National Park Service. It's also a great place to spot eagles in Jan. and Feb.; there is an observation platform next to Roebling Bridge.

Milford. This pretty little town has a prime location along the Delaware River where Pennsylvania, New York, and New Jersey intersect. A few years ago, *New York Magazine* dubbed it the "New Hamptons," stemming from the influx of New Yorkers who have bought second homes here or use its upscale hotels and country inns for frequent getaways. Settled in 1796 and used as a setting in some of the earliest silent movies starring Mary Pickford and Lillian Gish, Milford has art galleries, antique shops, preserved Victorian-era homes, upscale restaurants and cafés, and a bucolic getaway-from-it-all setting. You will also find Grey Towers, a French chateau–style estate that belonged to a leader of the U.S. conservation movement, and a fascinating little museum, the Columns, which houses a piece of American history: the flag that cushioned Abraham Lincoln's head after he was shot at the Ford Theatre. Go now before Starbucks discovers it.

GREY TOWERS

✳ To See

🅰 **Grey Towers National Historic Site** (570-296-9630; www.fs.fed .us/na/gt), 151 Grey Towers Dr., Milford. Grounds open daily; tours daily 11–4 Memorial Day through Oct.; $5 adults, $2 ages 12–17. Gifford Pinchot, a former governor of Pennsylvania and the founder and first chief of the U.S. Forest Service, used this stunning French chateau–style home

THE COLUMNS

a mile outside of town as a summer retreat. If you have the time, join one of the hour-long tours of this fascinating home, which showcases Pinchot's quirky and conservation-conscious ways. Fun items on display include artifacts collected in his travels, like a pair of terra-cotta camels from China's Tang Dynasty, and the family's infamous Finger Bowl dining-room table, which had a pool in the center and required guests to pass the salt by floating it downstream by wooden bowl. The tour isn't for small children, but they will enjoy the broad sloping grounds, which include paved paths and a moat full of koi fish.

The Columns (570-296-8126), 608 Broad St., Milford. Open Apr. through November; call for hours; $5 adults. The marquee exhibit in this grand old building is the Lincoln flag, a bloodstained American flag that was used to cradle the president's head after he was shot at Ford's Theatre. It found its way to Milford via the daughter of the stage manager who took the flag home that tragic night. She inherited it before moving to the area in 1888, then passed it on to her son, who donated it the county historical society. The Pike County Historical Society have built an interesting little museum around the bloody flag, with exhibits on local history, a vintage clothing collection that includes two fedoras owned by William Jennings Bryan, and a Hiawatha stagecoach from the 1950s.

Zane Grey Museum (570-685-4871), 135 Scenic Dr., Lackawaxen. Open Fri.–Sun. in summer and weekends through mid-Oct.; free. The prolific Western author wrote his first novel, *The Heritage of the Desert,* as well as *Riders of the Purple Sage* in this decidedly Eastern riverfront retreat near Roebling Bridge. It was turned into a museum in the 1970s and purchased by the National Park Service in 1989; Grey and his wife Dollie are buried nearby. Rangers lead 20-minute tours through Grey's old study, which includes original manuscripts and the Morris chair where he did much of his writing. There's also a gift shop that sells a wide selection of his writings. Every July, the museum holds a Zane Grey festival that celebrates the writer's link to the area.

☙ Dorflinger Glass Museum (570-253-1185; www.dorflinger.org), Long Ridge Rd., White Mills. Open Wed.–Sun. mid-May through early Nov.; $3 adults, $1.50

ZANE GREY MUSEUM

ages 6–18. In the late 1800s and early 1900s, the factory that operated here produced some of the finest glass in the world and counted two presidents (Lincoln and Wilson) among its clientele. All sorts of cut, enameled, etched, and gilded glass are displayed among period antiques and artifacts from the glass factory. The gift shop sells phenomenal Christmas ornaments, as well as paperweights, jewelry, and a wide assortment of glassware. The museum is surrounded by the Dorflinger-Suydam Wildlife Sanctuary (see also *Green Space*).

✳ To Do

Roebling's Delaware Aqueduct (570-729-7134) in Lackawaxen is the oldest existing wire suspension bridge in the country; it runs 535 feet from Minisink Ford, New York, to Lackawaxen and is known locally as Roebling Bridge. Begun in 1847 as one of four suspension aqueducts on the Delaware and Hudson Canal, it was designed by John A. Roebling, the future engineer of New York's Brooklyn Bridge. Its suspension design allowed more room for ice floes and river traffic than conventional bridges and its was considered a huge time-saving success during its 50 years of operation. There is a small parking lot and information kiosks on the Pennsylvania side, and a pedestrian walkway across that affords terrific views of the river.

FOR FAMILIES ♪ **Claws 'N' Paws Wild Animal Park** (570-698-6154), PA 590, Hamlin. Open daily May through Oct.; $13, $9 ages 2–11. This private zoo is home to more than 120 species of animals, including a white tiger, snow leopard, and the usual allotment of monkeys, reptiles, and meerkats. There are lots of hands-on activities that let kids feed parrots and giraffes, mingle with turtles, and participate in a fossil dig.

♪ **Stourbridge Railway** (570-253-1960; 800-433-9008; www.waynecountycc .com), 303 Commercial St., Honesdale. On August 8, 1829, the Delaware & Hudson Railroad launched the first commercial locomotive on rails in the western hemisphere. Diesel passenger trains still leave from this spot on themed excursions late spring through early Dec. Check the Web site for a schedule. The cost usually ranges from $15-18 per ride. They also run weekday rides for groups in summer and fall, and there is usually extra seating for individuals. The rides last about an hour and a half and cost between $5 and 8.

SCENIC DRIVES For breathtaking scenery, head to NY 97, at the intersection of US 6 and US 209 in Port Jervis, and follow it north a few miles to the hamlet of Sparrow Bush. Continue on 97 to a dramatic section of the road known as Hawk's Nest, a stunning and winding road perched high above the Delaware on rocky cliffs that has been featured in many car commercials. Continue on to Barryville, New York, where you can cross back over the river to Pennsylvania and follow Twin Lakes Road to US 6 back to Milford.

✳ Outdoor Activities

BICYCLING Bicycling along the Lackawaxen River affords level terrain and a pretty river view on the lightly traveled road known as the Towpath. **Northeast Sports** (570-253-1145; 107 Eighth St.; Honesdale) rents mountain bikes starting at $30 a day; they also rent kayaks in season.

BOAT EXCURSIONS/RENTALS In Promised Land State Park (see also *Green Space*), a boat concession off PA 390 (570-676-4117) offers rowboat, canoe, and kayak rentals. Electric motors are also available. On Lake Wallenpaupack, **Pocono Action Sports Marina** (570-226-4556) at Tanglewood Lodge rents power boats, sailboats, canoes, and jet skis. **Wallenpaupack Scenic Boat Tour** (717-226-6211) offers 30-minute cruises by patio boat twice a day from the end of June through Sept.

FISHING Between Dingmans Ferry and Promised Land State Park lies a hidden anglers' paradise known as **Pecks Pond**. There's not much here, just a rustic inn and tavern and a natural shallow pond filled with bass, pickerel, perch, and other panfish. **Pecks Pond Backwater Adventures**, a small outfitter (570-775-7237; www.peckspond.com), rents rods and reels and all kinds of boats.

Also: the Lackawaxen River is stocked with rainbow, brook, and brown trout in the spring and fall. For condition

STREAM NEAR DINGMANS FERRY

COAL MINING

Northeast Pennsylvania was once a huge coal mining center that supplied nearly 80 percent of the country. The towns of Hawley and Honesdale were major distribution centers that funneled the coal to New York via boat or railroad. The areas around Scranton and Wilkes-Barre were among the few places in the world that harbored anthracite, or hard, coal beneath their surfaces. There are no remaining active deep mines left, but a few attractions allow you to get an up-close understanding of this once-mighty industry. For more information, visit www.pacoalhistory.com.

Lackawanna County Coal Mine Tour (570-963-6463; www.themine game.com), McDade Park, Scranton. Open daily Apr. through Nov., except Easter and Thanksgiving; $7 adults; $5 kids. Informative hour-long tours are led by former mine workers and take you via a yellow transport car 300 feet down into an underground city of offices, stables, and hundreds of rooms; be prepared to walk about a quarter of a mile. Before or after your tour, stop by the adjacent **Pennsylvania Anthracite Heritage Museum** (570-963-4804) to round out your visit, well worth the $4 admission.

No. 9 Coal Mine and Museum, (570-645-7074), 9 Dock St., Lansford. Open Wed.–Sun.; museum and mine tour $7; museum only $3. About 10 miles southwest of Jim Thorpe, this deep mine produced coal for more than a century before closing in 1972. It reopened as a tourist attraction in the 1990s, and offers hour-long underground tours. The museum displays include an armored coal car and the mine's original elevator shaft.

Eckley Miners' Village (570-636-2070), Freeland. Open daily, except some holidays; $5.50 adults, $2.50 ages 6–12. About 30 minutes from either Jim Thorpe or Wilkes-Barre, Eckley is an authentic anthracite coal mining "patch town" and is worth the effort it takes to get here. The coal operation

updates and supplies, visit or call **Angler's Roost** (570-685-2010), 106 Scenic Dr., Lackawaxen. They also run canoe and rafting trips for small and large groups.

Rivers Outdoor Adventures (570-943-3151; www.riversflyfishing.com) runs trips to the Upper Delaware River, where smallmouth bass, trout, shad, and walleye are popular catches. Fishing this region requires either a New York or Pennsylvania license.

GOLF **Country Club at Woodloch Springs** (570-685-8075), 1 Woodloch Dr., Hawley. Serious golfers love this challenging 18-hole par-72 course, though it's accessible only to guests of nearby Woodloch Pines and a few other resorts in the area.

closed in 1971, but the town was saved from demolition by the 1970 Sean Connery film *The Molly Maguires,* which filmed many scenes here and in Jim Thorpe; several movie props like a general store and a mini-coal breaker remain. Exhibits in the visitor center demonstrate the dangers, misery, and class divisions endured by miners and their families; check these out and then stroll down the main street and see how the workers' homes were ranked by skill level and religion; about 50 descendants of the miners, mostly widows and offspring, still live in many of the homes. Guided tours are offered daily and included in the admission fee. Bring a map and detailed directions; this is definitely off the beaten path.

ECKLEY MINERS' VILLAGE

Cricket Hill Golf Club (570-226-4366), US 6, Hawley. More than 10 ponds dot this 18-hole public course with tees to 5,790 yards.

HIKING **Promised Land State Park** has some of the region's best hiking trails, from easy to strenuous (see *Green Space*). In Milford, folks like to hike up to the Knob, an overlook with views of the entire town and surrounding valley. Access it via the Mott Street Bridge off Harford Street.

HORSEBACK RIDING **Black Walnut Stables** (570-296-9336) in Milford offers one- to three-hour trail rides starting at $30 an hour.

Malibu Dude Ranch (570-296-7281) in Milford offers hourly rides starting at $25, as well as pony rides and guided day trips through the countryside.

SWIMMING **Lake Wallenpaupack** has a public beach where swimming is allowed; it's just south of the visitor center off US 6/PA 507; you can also swim at designated spots by the lakes in Promised Land State Park. In Milford, a favorite spot is **Milford Beach** (570-729-7134), a former farm overlooking the Delaware River that was spruced up by the National Park Service. There's no sand, but you will find lifeguards (in summer), comfort stations, and picnic areas. There's a small fee to park.

SKIING For a comprehensive list of ski resorts in the region, contact the Pocono Mountains Visitors Bureau (800-762-6667; www.800poconos.com).

Elk Mountain Ski Resort (570-679-4400), Union Dale, north of Scranton. One of the largest ski areas in northeast Pennsylvania with 27 trails and a terrain park on the east side of the mountain.

Ski Big Bear at Masthope (570-685-1400; www.ski-bigbear.com), 196 Karl Hope Rd., Lackawaxen. This small facility near the New York border caters to families and groups. It has 18 trails, 3 lifts, snow tubing, and a terrain park. There's also a ski school for first-timers and kids.

✳ Green Space

Promised Land State Park (570-676-3428), PA 390, Promised Land Village. The early settlers who named the area mistakenly thought it would be great for farming; yet once you see the place you'll realize the name isn't entirely off base. Located a few miles south of Lake Wallenpaupack, it has two large swimming and boating lakes with sand beaches, several camping areas, and some of the best hiking and cross-country ski trails in the region. Also within the park is Bruce Lake Natural Area, a 2,700-acre natural site including two lakes. The loop around Conservation Island is a popular easy trail; serious hikers can take the Bruce Lake Loop through hemlock and oak forest to a glacial lake, about 9.5 miles round-trip.

Dorflinger-Suydam Wildlife Sanctuary (570-253-1185), White Mills. Acres of scenic forest and meadows surround the Dorflinger Glass Museum (see also *Museums*). No picnicking or pets are allowed, but visitors may wander along any of the easy nature trails (pick up a map at the kiosk on the way in). The Wild-flower amphitheatre is the site of regular summer concerts and an annual wild-flower festival.

WATERFALLS The Pocono Mountains region has more than two dozen named waterfalls. Here are a few favorites. There is no charge to see them. Swimming is prohibited.

Dingmans Falls (570-828-7802), Johnny Bee Rd., near the junction of US 209 and PA 739. Take the flat boardwalk trail past a slender but pretty cascade of water, then continue another half-mile through a hemlock ravine to the base of the steep and stunning Dingmans Falls. The fit-minded can walk to the top of the falls via a steep trail to the left of the base.

Childs Falls, George W. Childs Recreational Site, Silver Lake Rd. A few miles upstream from Dingmans Falls, this three-tiered waterfall in a secluded gorge can be reached via a steep 1.8-mile loop trail framed by sheer rock walls and hemlock forest. Bring a picnic and settle in at one of the tables near the falls.

Raymondskill Falls, Raymondskill Falls Rd., off US 209. These exquisite cascades are only 3 miles south of Milford, and some feel that they are the state's most splendid (at 165 feet, they are definitely the highest). It's a very short hike to the Upper Falls, but the best views can be found at the Middle Falls, which require a steep half-mile hike down uneven stairs.

Shohola Falls, off US 6 between Milford and Hawley. Located on state game lands in the Shohola Recreation Area, these pretty falls can be reached via an easy path that leads past a scenic dammed lake.

✳ Lodging

BED & BREAKFASTS 🗡 ⏀ 🐾 **Black Walnut Country Inn** (570-296-6322; www.theblackwalnutinn.com), 179 Fire Tower Rd., Milford. This English Tudor–style estate is five minutes from downtown and on 160 acres of grounds that include woods, hiking and equestrian trails, and a pond for swimming and fishing. There are 12 antiques-filled rooms with full or queen beds, some with shared baths, plus a three-bedroom cabin with a full kitchen and deck that rents for $150–175 a night per couple, and an efficiency apartment that sleeps four. Kids are welcome and will love the paddleboats and petting zoo; they also have horse stables and offer trail rides around the property. A multi-course breakfast is served in a glass-walled dining room overlooking the lake. The

DINGMANS FALLS

inn closes in Jan. and Feb., but the cabin and efficiency remain open for guests. Rooms $105–140, two-night minimum on weekends.

Roebling Inn (570-685-7900; www .roeblinginn.com), 155 Scenic Dr., Lackawaxen. This stately home two doors down from the Zane Grey Museum is nestled in an extraordinary setting overlooking the Lackawaxen River. Each of the five rooms has a private bath, TV, and queen bed; the corner rooms facing the river are especially nice and have fireplaces. A cute one-bedroom cottage nearby sleeps three and allows children under 12. Owners JoAnn and Donald Jahn know the area well and are happy to proffer sightseeing advice. Rooms $95–175. Cottage: $149–185, with a two-night minimum.

INNS & RESORTS

Milford

⊙ **Cliff Park Inn** (570-296-6491; 800-225-6535; www.cliffparkinn.com), 155 Cliff Park Rd. This is the only B&B in the 70,000-acre Delaware Water Gap National Recreation Area, and its views alone are worth the price of a night or two. Yet the rooms and ambiance are outstanding, too. All 14 rooms have private baths, TVs, luxury linens, and wireless Internet access; some have sun porches, claw-foot tubs, and king beds. The restaurant on the premises serves lunch, dinner, and Sun. brunch and has been (along with the inn) awarded three stars by the *Mobil Travel Guide*. There's also a 9-hole golf course (for an extra fee), a wide front porch with rocking chairs, and 7 miles of hiking trails. No children under 12. Rooms $129–249, with a two-night minimum on weekends May through Oct.

&. ▼ **Hotel Fauchere** (570-409-1212; www.hotelfauchere.com), 401 Broad St., Milford. Step through the doors of this sophisticated 19th-century inn and you might think you've been transported to a boutique hotel in SoHo. The place is popular with New Yorkers, perhaps because of its connection to the famous Delmonico's Restaurant (see *Dining Out*) or because owner and former Manhattanite Sean Strub is a tireless promoter of Milford's beauty and amenities. Luxuries abound: Kiehl's bath products, luxury Frette linens, heated bathroom floors and towel racks, and complimentary wine. The two second-floor rooms with large balconies are especially nice. Rooms $275–350, including breakfast.

Hawley

♪ & **Woodloch Pines** (570-685-8000; 800-572-6658; www.woodloch .com), PA 590 east. This popular lakefront resort outside Hawley bills itself as being "like a cruise on land." Indeed, you'll never have to leave the complex if you don't want; there are indoor and outdoor pools, a 9-hole golf course, and plenty of morning-till-night organized activities, from movies and boat rides to bocce and scavenger hunts. It also helps that the lake-and-forest setting is gorgeous and shouts "getaway" from the tips of its blue spruce trees. Standard rooms in the main lodge sleep up to four with small sitting areas and fold-out couches. Deluxe lakeview rooms are spacious with two queen beds, a pullout couch, and small balcony. There are also large homes available for rent a few minutes' drive away in the Woodloch Springs golfing community. Rates typically start at $405 a night and include three meals and most activities.

▼ **Settler's Inn** (570-226-2993; 800-833-8527; www.thesettlersinn.com), 4 Main Ave. This 20-room inn near downtown is first-class all the way, from the stylish guest rooms to the attentive service and excellent on-site restaurant. Standard rooms are $140–160, while deluxe rooms, many of which have jacuzzi tubs and fireplaces, run $190–250. They also offer room and dinner packages.

MOTELS ✿ **Myer Country Motel** (570-296-7223; 800-764-MYER; www.myermotel.com), 600 US 6 and 209, Milford. If you're looking for a good value in Milford, this is it. Located just outside of town near the

New Jersey border, it has been in the same family for generations and features 19 separate cottage units. The decor is more appealing than the usual standard motel offering, and all rooms have TVs, refrigerators, and front porches. There are smoking and non-smoking rooms, and coffee and juice are available in the office each morning. The place fronts a busy road, but is surrounded by several acres of blue spruce and pine trees. Reserve early; these rooms go fast; prices drop in the off-season. Rooms $62–97.

East Shore Lodging (570-226-3293; www.eastshorelodging.com), US 6, Hawley. It doesn't look like much from the outside, but this friendly motel right on Lake Wallenpaupack is a terrific value. Rooms are bright and attractive with one or two queen beds, private baths, and TVs. The rate includes breakfast. Rooms $90–127; suites $115–165.

CAMPGROUNDS Promised Land State Park (570-888-7275) (see also *Green Space*) offers nearly five hundred camp sites on its property. Centrally located Pickerel Point and Deerfield areas have more than two hundred primitive tent sites; many walk-in sites overlook Promised Land Lake. Sites at Lower Lake Campground at the lake's western edge have hot showers and electricity hookups. Pickerel Point is open year-round. Tent sites: $9–25.

✳ Where to Eat
DINING OUT

Milford
&. ᵞ **Delmonico Room** (570-409-1212) 401 Broad St. It's easy to picture Theodore Roosevelt or Mary Pickford enjoying frog legs in aioli or Alsatian country pate in the grand formal dining room of the Hotel Fauchere. They were among the famous who patronized the hotel when it was owned by Louis Fauchere, a well-known chef at Delmonico's in New York. Today, the dining room stays true to its *haute cuisine* roots, offering a prix-fixe menu featuring items such as crown roast of lamb and roasted red snapper pot-au-feu. For a more casual meal, try the downstairs **Bar Louis**, which serves a delectable sushi pizza. Prix-fixe menu: $40–65.

ᵞ **Dimmick Inn** (570-296-4021), 101 E. Harford St. Lunch and dinner daily. The wide front porch of this 19th-century establishment is among the most coveted people-watching spots in town. Menu specialties include St. Louis–style barbecue ribs and charcoal-grill sirloin filets; the large menu also includes ostrich steak, Maryland-style fried chicken, sandwiches, and several seafood and pasta options. Leave room for dessert; the peanut-butter pie is divine. Sandwiches: $8–11; entrees: $11–29.

🌸 ᵞ **WaterWheel Café** (570-296-2383), 150 Water St. Breakfast and lunch daily; dinner and bar menu Thurs.–Sat. Located in a beautiful creekside location near Grey Towers, this multifaceted eatery features a cafe, restaurant, bakery, and a bar with live music Thurs. through Sun. It's a great spot for lunch; sit on the deck overlooking the creek and choose from a long list of specialty sandwiches including fresh roasted turkey and duck liver mousse with port. Inside, you can watch the three-story-high water wheel in action behind a glass wall. Dinner specialties include crispy hazelnut porkchops

SCRANTON AND WILKES-BARRE

About 30 minutes apart, these are the two of the largest cities around, though they are not considered part of the Pocono Mountains. Both towns served as industrial centers for Pennsylvania's anthracite coal mining industry and offer live theater, art galleries, shopping, and nightlife options.

Scranton, with a population of 77,000, is the bigger of the two and about a 45-minute drive from Hawley in the northern Pocono Mountains. Its baseball team, the Scranton/Wilkes-Barre Yankees, is a Triple-A affiliate of the New York team; you can catch a game at **Lackawanna County Stadium** (570-969-2255), 235 Montage Mountain Rd., Moosic. In recent years, Scranton has become famous as the main setting of *The Office,* the high-rated TV show starring Steve Carrell. Steamtown Mall, Lake Scranton, and Farley's restaurant are a few of the existing sites that have been mentioned on the NBC comedy. Two of the city's marquee attractions are the **Lackawanna County Coal Mine Tour** (see the *Coal Mining* sidebar) and **Steamtown National Historic Site** (570-340-5200; 150 S. Washington Ave.), a huge and fascinating complex of authentic standard-gauge steam locomotives, freight and passenger cars, and historic exhibits located on an old railway yard; ask about their regular train excursions. Across the parking lot from Steamtown is the **Electric City Trolley Museum** (570-963-6590), home to a kid-friendly collection of authentic streetcars, hands-on displays that let you steer model trolleys and ring up fares, and exhibits that chronicle the history of the early electric trolley industry. Both Steamtown and the Trolley Museum are an easy walk to Steamtown Mall's shops and restaurants. For information on the Scranton area, contact the **Lackawanna County Convention and Visitors Bureau** (800-229-3526; www.visitnepa.org).

Between Scranton and Wilkes-Barre is the quaint town of Old Forge,

and several tasty Vietnamese dishes. Reservations are recommended at dinner. Dishes $4–10; dinner entrees: $16–25.

Hawley

♼ **Torte Knox** (570-226-8200; www .torteknox.com), 301 Main Ave., Hawley. Lunch and dinner Thurs.–Sat.; brunch Sun.; weekends only in winter. Located in a former bank (hence the name), this upscale restaurant also serves as a recreational cooking school for aspiring Mario Batalis. A bistro menu of gourmet salads and sandwiches is served at lunch; the small dinner menu changes often and might include quail stuffed with duck sausage and wild cherries, Alaskan king crab legs, or filet mignon with espresso coulis and white-chocolate drizzle. Owner Sheelah Kaye-Stepkin often holds cooking classes, martini which rightly bills itself as the Pizza Capital of the World. Old-fashioned Italian gravy joints line the sleepy main street. A favorite is **Arcaro and Genell** (570-457-5555; 433 S. Main St.), whose rectangular pizza has been featured in *USA Today*. It really is that good.

Thirty minutes south of Scranton, Wilkes-Barre is home to five colleges, a population of 43,000, and more than two hundred historic buildings, including a 1909 Beaux Arts courthouse that is the city's pride and joy. You'll also find here **Mohegan Sun at Pocono Downs** (570-831-2100; 1280 PA 315), one of a handful of racino complexes that have opened in the state featuring slots machines and harness racing, the **Frederick Stegmaier Mansion** (570-823-9372; www.stegmaier mansion.com), an ornate must-see-it-to-believe-it 1870 mansion that rents rooms and suites for $145–325 a night; and **The Tubs Nature Area,** a peaceful Walden-like nature park centered around a stream and seven tub-shaped glacial potholes. For more information about the area, contact the **Luzerne County Convention and Visitors Bureau** (888-905-2872; www.tournepa.com).

WILKES-BARRE COURTHOUSE

theme nights, and other special events. Reservations recommended. Lunch $8–16; dinner $30–55.

EATING OUT ❧ Trackside Grill (570-253-2462), Honesdale. Breakfast and lunch Mon.–Sat. This small diner near the Stourbridge Railway station serves reasonably priced sandwiches like hot turkey and French dip, plus salads, homemade soups, and a kids'

menu. Breakfasts start at $2 for two eggs with toast and go up to $5 for creamed chip beef. Nothing on the lunch menu costs more than $8.

Hawley
❧ ♿ ♈ **The Boat House** (570-226-5027), PA 507, Hawley. Lunch and dinner daily. This casual nautical-themed restaurant overlooks Lake Wallenpaupack and has a huge menu featuring appetizers, salads, sand-

wiches, and burgers, and a lots of seafood and steak platters. Reservations are recommended in summer. Dishes: $7–19.

& ♆ **Cora's 1850 Bistro** (570-226-8878), 525 Welwood Ave. Lunch and dinner daily. Housed in a former hotel and run by two Culinary Institute of America graduates, this attractive yellow-walled eatery seems to have something for everyone on its menu, from burgers and salads to a long list of appetizers and a $5 kids' menu. Entrees include chicken Oscar, Cajun cowboy rib steak, grilled portabella puttanesca, and sesame-seared tuna. If you happen to be here on a Mon., don't miss the all-you-can-eat wings special. Sandwiches and appetizers $5-8; entrees $14-26.

& **Hawley Diner** (570-226-0523), 302 Main Ave. Breakfast, lunch, and dinner Mon.–Sat., breakfast and lunch Sun. If you don't mind the smoke, this downtown diner serves good jumbo Belgian waffles and other typical diner fare. Breakfast and lunch $2–5; dinner dishes $8–13.

✒ **Ledgedale BBQ Pit** (570-689-2200), Ledgedale Rd. and Goosepond Rd., Hamlin. Reasonably priced sandwiches and platters of pork ribs, half chickens, and crab cakes, and clam strips. Try the pulled pork sandwich for $5. Sit in the small dining room or outside at a picnic table. Dishes $5–14.

& **Dawny's Soup Creations** (570-296-1776), 311 W. Harford St., Milford. Closed Sun. Choose from five or six different kinds of delicious soups each day, from cream of asparagus to buffalo chicken; there are also turkey and roast beef sandwiches, veggie wraps, and burgers. Dishes $3–8.

BYO Where to buy wine in the northern Pocono Mountains region:

There are **Wine & Spirits stores** in Milford at 106 W. Harford St. (570-296-7021) and in Hawley at the Village shopping center on PA 739 (570-775-5010).

✳ Entertainment

MUSIC If you're not staying at an all-inclusive resort like Woodloch Pines, your best bets for late-night action in this area are the bars and lounges of popular restaurants and hotels. **Alley Oops Pub** in the Apple Valley Restaurant (570-296-6831; US 6, Milford) hosts karaoke or live bands most weekends. The **WaterWheel Café** in Milford and the **Boat House** in Hawley also feature live music on weekends.

MOVIES & THEATER Cinema 6 (570-251-3456), Route 6 Plaza, US 6, Honesdale. First-run films in a modern setting.

Ritz Company Playhouse, Hawley. A 1930s movie house, now a nonprofit community theater, stages five shows each summer.

✳ Selective Shopping

Antiques are the main inventory of stores around here. Hawley, Honesdale, and Milford all have a robust selection of shops selling antiques, crafts, and other items. The granddaddy of the area's antiques shops is **Castle Antiques & Reproductions** (570-226-8550), 230 Welwood Ave., Hawley, a former lingerie factory on the edge of town that is now home to a massive selection of ceramic vases, cast-iron toys, old tools, cut glass, and every type of furniture imaginable. **Timely Treasures** (570-226-2838) off US 6, between Hawley and Lake Wallenpaupack, also has a good selection of furniture, garden items, and unusual gifts. In Milford, **Forest Hall Antiques** (570-296-4299), 214 Broad St. occupies the upper floors of a French Normandy–style building that once housed Yale's School of Forestry, with wares like Victorian chairs, pewter pitchers, porcelain china, and film posters. Nearby is a great book shop, **Books & Prints at Pear Alley** (570-296-4777), 220 Broad St., with an excellent collection of used and out-of-print books, many of them gleaned from private collections.

✳ Special Events

January: **Eagle Fest** (second or third weekend), Narrowsburg, N.Y, across from Beach Lake, Pa.—Winter is the best time to spot eagles here, and the area welcomes them with a festival featuring live birds of prey demonstrations, lectures, films, and staffed observation areas. Contact the **Eagle Institute** for more information: 570-685-5960.

June: **Milford Music Festival** (second weekend), Ann Street Park, Milford—a mix of jazz, blues, rock, and classical performers take the stage over three days during this popular celebration of live music.

August: **Festival of Wood** (second weekend), Grey Towers National Historic Site, Milford—wood carving demonstrations, forestry walks, and live music.

October: **Black Bear Film Festival** (second weekend), Milford—independent films, lectures, plus displays of life-size bear sculptures. Visit www.blackbearfilmfestival.com.

INDEX

B